P9-CLC-462

Using SANs and NAS

Using SANs and NAS

W. Curtis Preston

O'REILLY®

Beijing · Cambridge · Farnham · Köln · Paris · Sebastopol · Taipei · Tokyo

Using SANs and NAS
by W. Curtis Preston

Copyright © 2002 O'Reilly & Associates, Inc. All rights reserved.
Printed in the United States of America.

Published by O'Reilly & Associates, Inc., 1005 Gravenstein Highway North, Sebastopol, CA 95472.

O'Reilly & Associates books may be purchased for educational, business, or sales promotional use. Online editions are also available for most titles (*safari.oreilly.com*). For more information, contact our corporate/institutional sales department: (800) 998-9938 or *corporate@oreilly.com*.

Editor:	Mike Loukides
Production Editor:	Mary Anne Weeks Mayo
Cover Designer:	Ellie Volckhausen
Interior Designer:	Melanie Wang

Printing History:

February 2002:	First Edition.

Nutshell Handbook, the Nutshell Handbook logo, and the O'Reilly logo are registered trademarks of O'Reilly & Associates, Inc. Many of the designations used by manufacturers and sellers to distinguish their products are claimed as trademarks. Where those designations appear in this book, and O'Reilly & Associates, Inc. was aware of a trademark claim, the designations have been printed in caps or initial caps. The association between the image of a hyrax and a pika and the topic of SANs and NAS is a trademark of O'Reilly & Associates, Inc.

While every precaution has been taken in the preparation of this book, the publisher and author assume no responsibility for errors or omissions, or for damages resulting from the use of the information contained herein.

ISBN: 0-596-00153-3

[M]   [11/02]

With great sadness, this book is dedicated to:

92 lives lost on American Airlines Flight 11
64 lives lost on American Airlines Flight 77
56 lives lost on United Airlines Flight 175
45 lives lost on United Airlines Flight 93
125 lives lost in the Pentagon
Thousands of lives missing or lost in the
World Trade Center

. . . and to the thousands of heroes who have risen from this disaster,
including firefighters, paramedics, police officers, construction workers,
and everyone supporting these fine people who must perform
the saddest job in U.S. history.

"You can tear down our buildings, but you can't tear down our spirit."
—George W. Bush

Table of Contents

Preface

The alphabet soup that is the computing industry has finally made its way to the storage industry. It wasn't enough that we had NFS, SMB, CIFS, and SCSI. Now there are SANs (storage area networks) and NAS (network attached storage). As exciting as these two industries are, and as happy as I am for the solutions they bring, did they have to use terms that are palindromes? I think if those involved could have just changed the name of one of them, some of the confusion I deal with regularly would be avoided.

But, we don't have that luxury. What we've got are two industries based on the same premise: you've got a lot of data to store, and you need somewhere to put it. Both industries are trying to solve the current challenges there are with traditional storage:

Manageability
> Let's face it. Traditional, parallel SCSI systems are difficult to manage when you start talking hundreds of gigabytes or terabytes. Each disk is married to a computer physically, electrically, and logically. When a disk goes bad, replacing it live is almost never possible with parallel SCSI. And if a particular disk or set of disks is no longer needed by one system, it's difficult to reallocate them to a new system. These concerns are just a start.

Scalability
> Sixteen devices per bus? Are you kidding? With systems getting smaller and smaller, and becoming more rack-mount friendly, the backplane real estate required for all those SCSI cards just goes away. A system is needed in which you can store data that grows when needed—without a lot of hassle.

Availability
> Traditional, parallel SCSI systems aren't known for their availability. Does the term *SCSI bus reset* mean anything to you? And, since a disk can be seen only by one SCSI bus, how can you perform maintenance on the SCSI cards when they fail?

Recoverability

Ah, my favorite subject. What about the backups? How on earth are you supposed to get all this data to tape or to some sort of offsite storage device using traditional backup and recovery methodologies designed for slower networks and much less data? We need new answers here.

Many of these problems can be solved by installing a SAN or NAS. But which one should you buy? What's the difference between these two technologies? Their names look almost the same. Are they really that different? Is what your NAS salesperson saying about SANs really true? Is what your SAN salesperson saying about NAS really true? Maybe it is; maybe it isn't.

Boy, Was This Fun!

I got a lot of cooperation from a number of storage vendors while writing this book. In fact, the technical edit of this book was done by a number of people that work for storage vendors. They were very helpful, and the process was also very interesting. (It kind of reminded me of when I wrote *Unix Backup and Recovery* [O'Reilly] and was trying to get the Informix, Oracle, and Sybase guys to agree on terms.) Here are some of the comments I heard while working with both vendors and users of this technology. (These comments are in no particular order.)

- "NFS and CIFS are inefficient protocols. How can they support databases on NAS?"
- "The volume managers and filesystems of today are inefficient. The only efficient filesystem is a NAS filer."
- "Only Fibre Channel is able to run at line speed. Gigabit Ethernet is too slow."
- "The new hardware-accelerated Gigabit Ethernet NICs are way faster than Fibre Channel."
- "Fibre Channel can be routed across WANs now."
- "So can Gigabit Ethernet, and we don't need any special switches to do it."
- "You have to use NDMP to back up NAS filers."
- "NDMP doesn't have any of the usual maintenance associated with traditional client-based push agents."
- "Server-free backups are the wave of the future."
- "Server-free backups are all hype."
- "You can automatically sync this NAS filer with that NAS filer."
- "You can do the same thing with this SAN array,"
- "iSCSI will make all this SAN stuff a thing of the past."
- "iSCSI will probably take off, but Fibre Channel is here to stay."

- "I work for a SAN company. This book just sounds like NAS propaganda."
- "I work for a NAS company. This book just sounds like SAN propaganda."

Like I said, lots of fun! Frankly, I'm really glad that there is fierce competition among storage vendors. It means that you, the customer, get better products.

I worked hard to present a balanced view of these two storage options. I hope you find it useful.

What Is This Book For?

I wrote this book for a few reasons. The first is that I found a good bit of confusion in the industry as to what SANs and NAS are. The second reason is that I've done a lot of really interesting backup and recovery projects with both of them and wanted to share that experience with everyone. Having said this, I believe that this book answers seven main questions:

What in the world are SANs or NAS, anyway?
> Where did they come from? How are they different (and better) than the technologies they are replacing? What are the basics of how they work? Chapter 1, *What Are SANs and NAS?*, Chapter 2, *Fibre Channel Architecture*, and Chapter 5, *NAS Architecture* answer these questions.

What is the difference between SANs and NAS?
> This is a really important question. If you can't understand the fundamental difference between these two technologies, you will never be able to answer the next question. See the end of Chapter 1.

Which is right for me?
> Obviously, I can't answer this question for you, but I can give you enough information to help make the decision. Hopefully after reading the book, you'll have a pretty good idea of how the two technologies can be implemented where you work and which is right for you. See the end of Chapter 1.

What kind of neat things can I do with a SAN that I can't do without one?
> You've heard about LAN-free and server-free backups, but you're not really sure what they are. In Chapter 4, *SAN Backup and Recovery*, they are explained in detail, including command-line information about how to do some of them yourself.

What kind of neat things can I do with NAS that I can't do without it?
> You've heard of dozens of ways to back up filers, but you're not sure what the differences are. Should you use NDMP, dump, snapshots, or some other technology? This is what Chapter 7, *NAS Backup and Recovery*, is about.

What kind of tasks will I find myself doing if I install a SAN?
> Now that you've put all of your storage onto a network—now what? What happens when the network goes down? How do you design it so that this doesn't

impact you? How do you even know that it went down? These answers are in Chapter 3, *Managing a SAN*.

What kind of tasks will I find myself doing if I install a NAS?

How do you manage the volumes, snapshots, quotas, etc? What's it like to get users onto a NAS filer? What other tasks are you performing on a regular basis? See Chapter 6, *Managing NAS*, for the answers to these questions.

Conventions Used in This Book

The following conventions are used in this book:

Italic
> Used for program names, URLs, and for the first use of a term

Constant width
> Used in code examples and to show the output of commands

Constant width italic
> Used to indicate variables within commands

> This icon designates a note, which is an important aside to the nearby text.

> This icon designates a warning relating to the nearby text.

Comments and Questions

Please address comments and questions concerning this book to the publisher:

> O'Reilly & Associates, Inc.
> 1005 Gravenstein Highway North
> Sebastopol, CA 95472
> (800) 998-9938 (in the United States or Canada)
> (707) 829-0515 (international/local)
> (707) 829-0104 (fax)

There is a web page for this book, which lists errata, examples, or any additional information. You can access this page at:

> *http://www.oreilly.com/catalog/sansnas*

To comment or ask technical questions about this book, send email to:

> *bookquestions@oreilly.com*

For more information about books, conferences, Resource Centers, and the O'Reilly Network, see the O'Reilly web site at:

http://www.oreilly.com

Acknowledgments

I got a lot of help on this book from old friends and new friends, and I wish to thank them publicly for their assistance. Without them, this book would not have come into being.

To God: Any abilities I have came from You.

To my wife, Celynn: Now you've got another book to help you sleep at night. Thank you again for all the love and support, and for taking care of our two girls while I tried to get this thing done.

To my older daughter, Nina: Thank you for continuing to ask me when I would be done with this book so that you could show it off in Mrs. Plunkett's class. Tell Alex A., Alex T., Andrew, Christina, Eduardo, Eric, Genesea, Ian, Jacqueline, K.C., Kyle G., Kyle K., Mason, Megan, Olivia, Rachel, Scott, Stephanie, and Tanner that I said hello. I love you, honey.

To my younger daughter, Marissa: Thank you for the constant breaks while writing the book, as you would come in to tell me you love me one more time. Hugs. I love you, too!

To my parents: Without your encouragement and support, I would have never had the *chutzpah* to attempt writing a book in the first place. Thanks!

To my wife's family: Thank you again for raising such a wonderful daughter and treating me as a member of your family.

To all those who made me who am I today (whatever that is): There are too many of you to list. This includes my friends and family growing up, my teachers and professors, and all of my coworkers over the years. Thank you for your contribution to my life.

To JF, JT, and ET: Thank you for pushing me out of the nest and letting me fly on my own.

To Todd Toles and Julie Stewart at Veritas; Grant Melvin, Greg Linn, and Eyal Traitel at Network Appliance; Roberto Basilio at Hitachi Data Systems; Charles Curtis at Compaq; Julie Stewart at Veritas; and David Eeoff at Legato: Without all your help, this book would be sadly lacking in data. Your answers to my constant questions and support while writing this book was invaluable. You are a credit to your respective companies, and I wish you and your companies continued success.

To Eyal Traitel: Thank you for writing the *Managing NAS* chapter. It's not easy writing a chapter to fit into somebody else's book, but you managed to pull it off. Thanks a bunch.

To Chely, from Eyal: "You are my one and only girlfriend and wife. Thanks to you, and to my always supporting family."

To Derek Brawdy: Thank you for helping me get the *Managing SANs* chapter started. Too bad you had to leave to go you know where and help them find you know whom. I hope you find him. Make us proud.

To the technical editors: This includes Stephen Potter, Todd Toles, Mark Perino, Melvin Grant, Greg Linn, Eyal Traitel, John Norman, Scott Aschenbach, Daniel Pigg, William Welty, Richard Hirtler, Chris O'Regan, Megan Restuccia, and Brian Kirouac. Thanks for keeping me in check. As always, the book is better because of you.

To O'Reilly & Associates: Thank you for the opportunity to bring another much-needed book to market.

To Michael Loukides: Thank you for sticking with me through this trying time. Thank you for your guidance and patience as I continually molded this book into what it is now.

To the reader: Thank you for purchasing this book. I hope it helps you to understand this confusing industry.

To everyone else: Buy the book, already! :)

What Are SANs and NAS?

Throughout the history of computing, people have wanted to share computing resources. The Burroughs Corporation had this in mind in 1961 when they developed multiprogramming and virtual memory. Shugart Associates felt that people would be interested in a way to easily use and share disk devices. That's why they defined the Shugart Associates System Interface (SASI) in 1979. This, of course, was the predecessor to SCSI—the Small Computer System Interface. In the early 1980s, a team of engineers at Sun Microsystems felt that people needed a better way to share files, so they developed NFS. Sun released it to the public in 1984, and it became the Unix community's prevalent method of sharing filesystems. Also in 1984, Sytec developed NetBIOS for IBM; NetBIOS would become the foundation for the SMB protocol that would ultimately become CIFS, the predominant method of sharing files in a Windows environment.

Neither storage area networks (SANs) nor network attached storage (NAS) are new concepts. SANs are simply the next evolution of SCSI, and NAS is the next evolution of NFS and CIFS. Perhaps a brief history lesson will illustrate this (see Figure 1-1).

From SCSI to SANs

As mentioned earlier, SCSI has its origins in SASI—the Shugart Associates System Interface, defined by Shugart Associates in 1979. In 1981, Shugart and NCR joined forces to better document SASI and to add features from another interface developed by NCR. In 1982, the ANSI task group X3T9.3 drafted a formal proposal for the Small Computer System Interface (SCSI), which was to be based on SASI. After work by many companies and many people, SCSI became a formal ANSI standard in 1986. Shortly thereafter, work began on SCSI-2, which incorporated the Common Command Set into SCSI, as well as other enhancements. It was approved in July

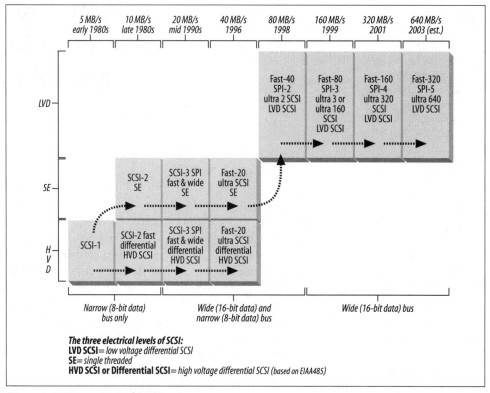

5 MB/s early 1980s	10 MB/s late 1980s	20 MB/s mid 1990s	40 MB/s 1996	80 MB/s 1998	160 MB/s 1999	320 MB/s 2001	640 MB/s 2003 (est.)
				Fast-40 SPI-2 ultra 2 SCSI LVD SCSI	Fast-80 SPI-3 ultra 3 or ultra 160 SCSI LVD SCSI	Fast-160 SPI-4 ultra 320 SCSI LVD SCSI	Fast-320 SPI-5 ultra 640 LVD SCSI

Figure 1-1. Generations of SCSI

1990.* Although SCSI-2 became the de facto interface between storage devices and small to midrange computing devices, not everyone felt that traditional SCSI was a good idea. This was due to the physical and electrical characteristics of copper-based parallel SCSI cables. (SCSI systems based on such cables are now referred to as parallel SCSI, because the SCSI signals are carried across dozens of pairs of conductors in parallel.) Although SCSI has come a long way since 1990, the following limitations still apply to parallel SCSI:

- Parallel SCSI is limited to 16 devices on a bus.
- It's possible, but not usually practical, to connect two computing devices to the same storage device with parallel SCSI.
- Due to cross-talk between the individual conductors in a multiconductor parallel SCSI cable, as well as electrical interference from external sources, parallel SCSI has cable-length limitations. Although this limitation has been somewhat

* This brief history of SCSI is courtesy of John Lohmeyer, the chairman of the X10 committee.

overcome by SCSI-to-fiber-to-SCSI conversion boxes, these boxes aren't supported by many software and hardware vendors.

- It's also important to note that each device added to a SCSI chain shortens its total possible length.

Some felt that in order to solve these problems, we needed to change the physical layer. The most obvious answer at the time was fiber optics. Unlike parallel SCSI, fiber cables can go hundreds of meters without significantly changing their transmission characteristics, solving all the problems related to the electrical characteristics of parallel SCSI. It even solved the problem of the number of connections, since each device in the loop had its own transmitting laser. Therefore, additional devices actually increase the total bus length, rather than shorten it.

The problem was, how do you take a protocol that was designed to be carried on many conductors in parallel and have it transmitted over only one conductor? The first thing that needed to be done was to separate the SCSI specification into multiple levels—a lesson learned from network protocol development. Each level could behave any way it wanted, as long as it performed the task assigned to it and spoke to the levels above it and below it according the appropriate command set. This was the beginning of the SCSI-3 specification. This separation of the various levels is why the SCSI-2 specification is contained in one document, and the SCSI-3 specification spans more than 20 documents. (Each block in Figure 1-2 represents a separate document of the SCSI-3 specification.)

Once this was done, it became possible to separate the physical layer of SCSI from the higher levels of SCSI. Once the physical layer was given this freedom, limitations caused by the physical layer could be addressed. You can see this separation in the SCSI-3 Architecture Roadmap in Figure 1-2, which was graciously provided by the T10 committee, the group responsible for defining the SCSI-3 architecture. It shows five alternatives to SPI (the SCSI Parallel Interface), including serial SCSI, Fibre Channel, SSA, SCSI over ST, and SCSI over VI. A relatively recent addition to this list that has been gaining acceptance is the iSCSI protocol. iSCSI uses IP as the transport layer to carry serial SCSI traffic.

 As of this writing, iSCSI is gaining ground and market share but is still very new. Once it's in full swing, I'll prepare a second edition to this book that includes iSCSI coverage. More information about iSCSI is available in Appendix A.

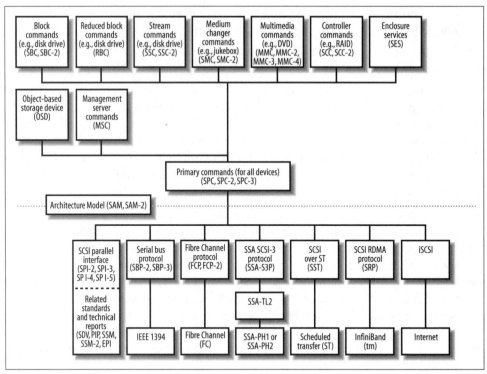

Figure 1-2. SCSI-3 Architecture Roadmap

The most popular alternative to SPI is the *Fibre Channel Protocol*. Fibre Channel, in contrast to SPI, is a serial protocol that uses only one path to transmit signals and another to receive signals. Fibre Channel offers a number of advantages over parallel SCSI:

Distance

The distance between devices is no longer important. You can place individual devices up to 10 kilometers apart using single-mode fiber and theoretically go unlimited distances with bridging technologies such as ATM. (It's impractical at this time to use this for online storage due to the latencies involved in the long distance between the host and storage. However, most people using ATM bridging use it to make remote copies, not for live data access.)

Speed

Although the bus speed of a single gigabit Fibre Channel connection is now slower than the fastest parallel SCSI implementations, you can trunk multiple Fibre Channel connections together for more bandwidth. (Also, Fibre Channel is much faster than the majority of installed SCSI today, which is usually 20 or 40 MB/s. Additionally, 2-Gb Fibre Channel is now available.)

Millions of devices connected to one computer

You can connect one million times more devices to a serial SCSI card (i.e., a Fibre Channel host bus adapter [HBA]) than you can to a parallel SCSI card. Parallel SCSI can accept 16 devices, and a Fibre Channel fabric can accept up to 16 million.

Millions of computers connected to one device

You can easily connect a single storage device to 16 million computers. This allows computers to share resources, such as disk or tape. The only problem is teaching them how to share!

 Most current implementations place limitations on the number of devices that can be connected to a single fabric. It's unclear at this time how close to 16 million devices we will ever get.

I should probably mention that Fibre Channel doesn't necessarily mean fiber optic cable. Fibre Channel can also run on special copper cabling. I cover this in more detail in Chapter 2.

What Is a SAN?

At this point, my definition of a SAN is as follows:

A SAN is two or more devices communicating via a serial SCSI protocol, such as Fibre Channel or iSCSI.

This definition means that a SAN *isn't* a lot of things. By this definition, a LAN that carries nothing but storage traffic isn't a SAN. What differentiates a SAN from a LAN (or from NAS) is the protocol that is used. If a LAN carries storage traffic using the iSCSI protocol, then I'd consider it a SAN. But simply sending traditional, LAN-based backups across a dedicated LAN doesn't make that LAN a SAN. Although some people refer to such a network as a storage area network, I do not, and I find doing so very confusing. Such a network is nothing other than a LAN dedicated to a special purpose. I usually refer to this sort of LAN as a "storage LAN" or a "backup network." A storage LAN is a useful tool that removes storage traffic from the production LAN. A SAN is a network that uses a serial SCSI protocol (e.g., Fibre Channel or iSCSI) to transfer data.

A SAN isn't network attached storage (NAS). As mentioned previously, SANs use the SCSI protocol, and NAS uses the NFS and SMB/CIFS protocols. (There will be a more detailed comparison between SANs and NAS at the conclusion of this chapter.) The Direct Access File System, or DAFS, pledges to bring SANs and NAS closer together by supporting file sharing via an NFS-like protocol that will also support Fibre Channel as a transport. (DAFS is covered in Appendix A.)

It's common for a NAS filer to be comprised of a filer head with SAN-attached storage behind it.

In summary, a SAN is two or more devices communicating via a serial SCSI protocol (e.g., Fibre Channel or SCSI), and they offer a number of advantages over traditional, parallel SCSI:

- Fibre Channel (and iSCSI) can be trunked, where several connections are seen as one, allowing them to communicate much faster than parallel SCSI. Even a single Fibre Channel connection now runs at 2 Gb/s in each direction, for a total aggregate of 4 Gb/s.
- You can put up to 16 million devices in a single Fibre Channel SAN (in theory).
- You can easily access any device connected to a SAN from any computer also connected to the SAN.

Now that we have covered the evolution of SASI into SCSI, and eventually into SCSI-3 over Fibre Channel and iSCSI, we'll discuss the area where SANs have seen the most use—and the most success. SANs have significantly changed the way backup and recovery can be done. I will show that storage evolved right along with SCSI, and backup methods that used to work don't work anymore. This should provide some perspective about why SANs have become so popular.

Backup and Recovery: Before SANs

A long time ago in a data center far away, there were servers that were small enough to fit on a tape. This type of data center led to a backup system design like the one in Figure 1-3. Many or most systems came with their own tape drive, and that tape drive was big enough to back up that system—possibly big enough to back up other systems. All that was needed to perform a fully automated backup was to write a few shell scripts and swap out a few tapes in the morning.

For several reasons, bandwidth was not a problem in those days. The first reason was there just wasn't that much data to back up. Even if the environment consisted of a single 10-Mb hub that was chock full of collisions, there just wasn't that much data to send across the wire. The second reason that bandwidth wasn't a problem was that many of the systems could afford to have their own tape drives, so there wasn't a need to send any data across the LAN.

Gradually, many companies or individuals began to outgrow these systems. Either they got tired of swapping that many tapes, or they had systems that wouldn't fit on a tape any more. The industry needed to come up with something better.

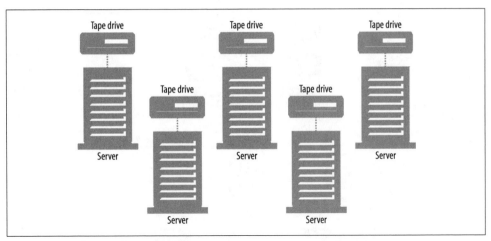

Figure 1-3. Backups in the good old days

Things Got Better; Then They Got Worse

A few early innovators came up with the concept of a centralized backup server. Combining this with a tape stacker made life manageable again. Now all you had to do was spend $5,000 to $10,000 on backup software and $5,000 to $10,000 on hardware, and your problems were solved. Every one of your systems would be backed up across the network to the central backup server, and all you needed to do was install the appropriate piece of software on each backup "client." These software packages even ported their client software to many different platforms, which meant that all the systems shown in Figure 1-4 could be backed up to the backup server, regardless of what operating system they were running.

Then a different problem appeared. People began to assume that all you had to do was buy a piece of client software, and all your backup problems would be taken care of. As the systems grew larger and the number of systems on a given network increased, it became more and more difficult to back up all the systems across the network in one night. Of course, upgrading from shared networks to switched networks and private VLANs helped a lot, as did Fast Ethernet (100 Mb), followed by Etherchannel and similar technologies (400 Mb), and Gigabit Ethernet. But some had systems that were too large to back up across the network, especially when they started installing very large database servers that contained 100 GB to 1 TB of records and files.

A few backup software companies tried to solve this problem by introducing the *media server*. In Figure 1-5, the central backup server still controlled all the backups, and still backed up many clients via the 100-MB or 1000-Mb network. However, backup software that supported media servers could attach a tape library to each of

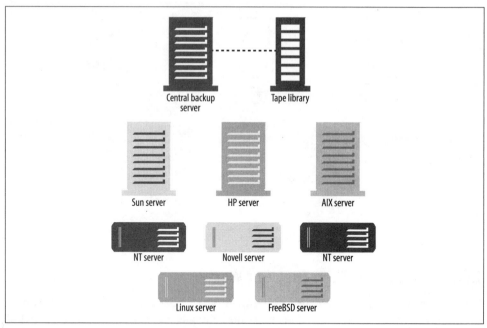

Figure 1-4. Centralized backups in the good old days

the large database servers, allowing these servers to back up to their own locally attached tape drives, instead of sending their data across the network.

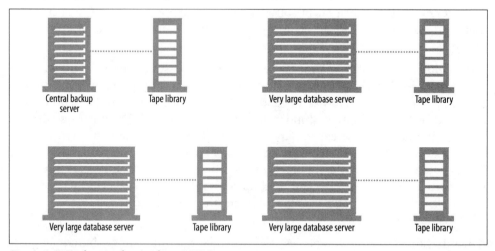

Figure 1-5. Backups today (without SANs)

Media servers solved the immediate bandwidth problem but introduced significant costs and inefficiencies. Each server needed a tape library big enough to handle a full backup. Such a library can cost from $50,000 to more than $500,000, depending on the size of the database server. This is also inefficient because, many servers of this size don't need to do a full backup every night. If the database software can perform incremental backups, you may need to perform a full backup only once a week or even once a month, which means that for the rest of the month, most tape drives in this library go unused. Even products that don't perform a traditional full backup have this problem. These products create a *virtual* full backup every so often by reading the appropriate files from scores of incremental backups and writing these files to one set of tapes. This method of creating a full backup also needs quite a few tape drives on an occasional basis.

Another thing to consider is that the size of the library (specifically, the number of drives that it contains) is often driven by the restore requirements—not the backup requirements. For example, one company had a 600-GB database they needed backed up. Although they did everything in their power to ensure that a tape restore would never be necessary, they knew they might need to in a true disaster. However, the restore requirement was still three hours. If the restore required reading from tape, the restore requirement didn't change; it still had to be done in less than three hours. Based on that, they bought a 10-drive library that cost $150,000. Of course, if they could restore the database in three hours, they could back it up in three hours. This meant that this $150,000 library was going unused approximately 21 hours per day.

Enter the SAN

Some backup software vendors attempted to solve the cost problem by allowing a single library to connect to multiple hosts. If you purchased a large library with multiple SCSI connections, you could connect each one to a different host. This allowed you to share the tape library but not the drives. While this ability helped reduce the cost by sharing the robotics, it didn't completely remove the inefficiencies discussed earlier.

What was really needed was a way to share the drives. And as long as the tape drives were shared, disk drives could be shared too. What if:

- A large database server could back up to a locally attached tape drive, but that tape drive could also be seen and used by another large server when it needed to back up to a locally attached tape drive?

- The large database server's disks could be seen by another server that backed up its disks without sending the data through the CPU of the server that's using the database?

- The disks and tape drives were connected in such a way that allowed the data to be sent directly from disk to tape without going through any server's CPU?

Fibre Channel and SANs have made all of these "what ifs" possible, including many others that will be discussed in later chapters. SANs are making backups more manageable than ever—regardless of the size of the servers being backed up. In many cases, SANs are making things possible that weren't conceivable with conventional parallel SCSI or LAN-based backups.

From NFS and SMB to NAS

NAS has roots in two main areas: the Server Message Block (SMB) and the Network File System (NFS) protocols. Interestingly enough, these two file-sharing protocols were developed by two of the biggest rivals in the computer industry: Microsoft and Sun Microsystems, and they both appeared in 1984! (IBM and Microsoft developed SMB, and Sun developed NFS.)

SMB/CIFS

When you use your Windows browser to go to "Network Neighborhood" and can read from and write to drives that are actually on other computers, you are probably using the SMB protocol.* The first mention of the SMB protocol was in an IBM technical reference in 1984, and it was originally designed to be a network naming and browsing protocol. Shortly thereafter, it was adapted by Microsoft to become a file sharing protocol. Several versions of the SMB protocol have been released throughout the years, and it has become the common file sharing protocol for all Microsoft Windows operating systems (Windows 3.1, 95, 98, Me, NT, 2000, and XP) and IBM OS/2 systems. Microsoft recently changed its name to the Common Internet File System (CIFS).

Like many Microsoft applications, CIFS was designed for simplicity. To allow others to access a drive on your system, simply right-click on a drive icon and select "Sharing." You then decide whether the drive should be shared read-only or read-write, and what passwords should control access. You can share a complete drive (e. g., *C:*) or just a part of the drive (e.g., *C:\MYMUSIC*).

Please note that I didn't say that CIFS was originally designed for performance. Actually, as covered later in the book, it was designed with multiple-user access in mind—at the expense of performance. However, Microsoft and other companies have made a number of performance improvements to CIFS in recent years.

The popularity of CIFS has led to many companies installing large, centralized CIFS servers that share drives to hundreds or thousands of PC clients. The most common reason to do this is to centralize the storage of important files. Users are encouraged to save anything important on the "network drive" because many don't back up their desktops. The administration staff, however, backs up the CIFS server.

---

* I say "probably" only because you can buy an NFS client for your Windows desktop as well.

Another type of CIFS server is a Unix/Linux box running Samba, which gets its name from the SMB protocol. Such a system can also share its drives with hundreds or thousands of PC clients, who will see it as nothing other than another PC sharing drives. Since both Linux and Samba are free, this solution has become quite popular.

To summarize, SMB has evolved into CIFS and become the predominant way to share files between Windows-based desktops and laptops. CIFS has a few limitations, which are covered in more detail later in this book.

NFS

Like many Unix projects, the Network File System (NFS) began as a pet project of a few engineers at Sun Microsystems. Sun introduced it to the public in 1984, and all Unix vendors subsequently added it to their suite of base applications. Via NFS, any Unix box can read from or write to any filesystem on any other Unix box—provided it has been shared.

NFS is used in a variety of ways. One of the most common uses is to have a central NFS server contain everyone's home directory. In Unix, a *home directory* is where users store files. In fact, a properly configured Unix system requires users to store files in their home directories (except for files that are obvious throwaways, such as files placed in */tmp*). If everyone's home directory is on an NFS file server, then all a company's data is in one place. This offers the same advantages as the CIFS server discussed earlier. With third-party software, PC systems can also access directories on a Unix server that have been shared via NFS.

NFS may have originally been designed with simplicity in mind, but it's certainly not as easy to use as Windows file sharing.* Each implementation of Unix has a command that is used to share a filesystem from the command line and a file that can share that filesystem permanently. For example, BSD derivatives typically use */etc/exports* and the *exportfs* command, while System V derivatives use */etc/dfs/dfstab* and the *share* command. As with all Unix commands, you must learn the command's syntax to share filesystems, because the syntax is also used in the *exports* file. Of course, a command's syntax varies between different versions of Unix.

Another difficulty with NFS is that it was originally based on UDP, rather than TCP. (Even though NFS v3 allows using TCP, most NFS traffic still runs across UDP.) The biggest problem with UDP and NFS is how retransmits are handled. NFS sends 8K packets that must be split into six IP fragments (based on a typical frame size of 1500 bytes). All six fragments must be retransmitted if any fragment is lost. UDP also has no flow control, so a server can ask for more data than it can receive, and excessive UDP retransmits can easily bring a network to its knees.

---

* As with many other difficult things about Unix, Unix administrators don't seem to mind. They might even argue that NFS is easier to configure than CIFS, because they can easily script it.

This is why NFS v3 allows for NFS on top of TCP. TCP has well-established flow control, and TCP requires retransmission only of lost packets—not the entire NFS packet like UDP. Of course, the decision to use UDP or TCP makes managing such servers even more complicated.

NFS and CIFS: Before NAS

Both NFS and CIFS servers have been around for several years and have gained quite a bit of popularity. This isn't to say that either is perfect. There are a number of issues associated with managing NFS and CIFS in the real world.

The first problem with both NFS and CIFS is that a server is usually dedicated to be an NFS or a CIFS server. Each server then represents just another system to manage. Patch management alone can be quite a hassle. Also, just because an environment has enough users to warrant an NFS or CIFS server doesn't mean they have the expertise necessary to maintain an NFS or CIFS server.

The next problem is that few environments are strictly Unix or strictly Windows; most environments are a mixture of both. Such environments find themselves in a predicament. Do they incur the extra cost of loading PC NFS software on their Windows desktops? Do they use Samba on their Unix boxes to provide CIFS services to PCs? If they do that, will their NT-savvy administrators understand how to administer Samba? Or will their Unix-savvy administrators understand Windows ACLs? The result is that such environments usually end up with a Unix NFS server and an NT CIFS server; now there are two boxes to manage instead of one.

The final problem involves performance. Disks that sit behind a typical NFS or CIFS server are simply not as fast to users as local disk. When saving large files or many files, this performance hit can be quite costly. It persuades people to save their files locally, which defeats the purpose of having network-mounted drives in the first place.

The reason both NFS and CIFS suffer from performance issues is that both were afterthoughts. Unix was developed in the late 60's, and DOS in the early 80's. It took both groups several years to realize they needed an easier way to share files and invented NFS and CIFS as a result. Although some tweaks have been made to the kernel to make these protocols faster, the fact is that they are simply another application competing for CPU and network resources. The only way to solve all these problems was to start from scratch, and network attached storage was born.

Enter NAS

If you think about it a moment, the NAS industry is based on selling boxes to do something any Unix or Windows system can do out of the box. How is it, then, that NAS vendors have been so successful? Why is it, then, that many are predicting a predominance of NAS in the future? The answer is that they have done a pretty good job of removing the issues people have with NFS and CIFS.

One thing vendors tried was to make NFS or CIFS servers easier to manage. They created packaged boxes with hot-swappable RAID arrays that significantly increased their availability and decreased the amount of time needed for corrective maintenance. Another novel concept was a single server that provided both NFS and CIFS services—reducing the total number of servers required to do the job. You can even mount the same directory via both NFS and CIFS. NAS vendors also designed user interfaces that made sharing NFS and CIFS filesystems easier. In one way or another, NAS boxes are easier to manage than their predecessors.

NAS vendors have also successfully dealt with the performance problems of both NFS and CIFS. In fact, some have actually made NFS faster than local disk!

The first NAS vendor, Auspex, felt that performance problems happened because the typical NFS[*] implementation forces each NFS request to go through the host CPU. Their solution was to create a custom box with a separate processor for each function. The host processor (HP) would be used only to get the system booted up, and NFS requests would be the responsibility of the network processor (NP) and the storage processor (SP). The result was an NFS server that was much faster than any of its predecessors.

Network Appliance was the next major vendor on the scene, and they felt that the problem was the Unix kernel and filesystem. Their solution was to reduce the kernel to something that would fit on a 3.5-inch floppy disk, completely rewriting the NFS subsystem so that it was more efficient, and including an optimized filesystem designed for use with NVRAM. Network Appliance was the first NAS vendor to publish benchmarks that showed their servers were faster than a locally attached disk.

Note that NAS filers use the NFS or CIFS protocol to transfer *files*. In contrast, SANs use the SCSI-3 protocol to share *devices*. (A side-by-side comparison of NAS and SAN can be found at the end of this chapter.)

Let me conclude this section with a definition of network attached storage:

> Network attached storage (NAS) is a computer (or device) dedicated to sharing files via NFS, CIFS, or DAFS.

SAN Versus NAS: A Summary

Table 1-1 compares NAS and SAN and should clear up any confusion regarding their similarities and differences.

---

[*] All early NAS vendors started with NFS first and added CIFS services later.

Table 1-1. Differences between SAN and NAS

	SAN	NAS
Protocol	Serial SCSI-3	NFS/CIFS
Shares	Raw disk and tape drives	Filesystems
Examples of shared items	/dev/rmt/0cbn	\\filer\C\directory\filename.doc
	/dev/dsk/c0t0d0s2	/nfsmount/directory/filename.txt
	\\.\Tape0	
Allows	Different servers can access the same raw disk or tape drive (not typically seen by the end user)	Different users can access the same filesystem or file
Replaces	Replaces locally attached disk and tape drives; with SANs, hundreds of systems can now share the same disk or tape drive	Replaces Unix NFS servers and NT CIFS servers that offer network shared file-systems

In this book, you will see how SANs and NAS relate to backup and recovery. SANs are an excellent way to increase the value of your existing backup and recovery system and can help you back up systems more easily than would otherwise be possible. I will also talk about NAS appliances and the challenges they bring to your backup and recovery system. I will cover ways to back up such boxes if you can't afford a commercial backup and recovery product, as well as go into detail about NDMP—the supported way to back up NAS filers.

Which Is Right for You?

One reason this book includes both SANs and NAS is that many people are starting to see filers as a viable alternative to a SAN. While filers were once perceived as "NFS in a box," people are now using them to host large databases and important production data. Which is right for you? The last section of this chapter attempts to explain the pros and cons of each architecture, allowing you to answer this question.

 Many comments made in the following paragraphs are summaries of statements made in later chapters. For the details behind these summary statements, please read Chapter 2 and Chapter 5.

The Pros and Cons of NAS

As mentioned earlier, NAS filers have become popular with many people for many reasons. The following is a summary of several:

Filers are fast enough for many applications

Many would argue that SANs are simply more powerful than NAS. Some would argue that NFS and CIFS running on top of TCP/IP creates more overhead on the client than SCSI-3 running on top of Fibre Channel. This would mean that a single host could sustain more throughput to a SAN-based disk than a

What About NAS Backups?

At one time, I felt that NAS had a rather distinct disadvantage. While it did significantly reduce system administration requirements, it created a challenge in one particular area—backup and recovery. (Of course, this didn't go over well with Mr. Backup.
) Since most NAS filers usually involve a stripped-down (or significantly customized) version of the operating system, normal backup and recovery client software often isn't applicable. With a few exceptions, you can't simply buy client software from your backup vendor for your filer. Although this has gotten better, there was a time when the only way to back up your NAS appliance was to use *rdump* or to back it up via an NFS mount.

Even the advent of the network data management protocol (NDMP, to be covered in detail in later chapters), didn't seem to help things at first. It usually meant locally attaching a tape drive to a filer and backing up that server's data to that tape drive. This often meant a significant reduction in automation. It didn't help that software vendors were slow to support NDMP, because they saw it as competition to their own client software.

However, a lot has changed in recent years. All major backup-software vendors support NDMP, and you can even use SAN technology to share a tape library between your filers and your other backup servers. Even if you're backing up your filers across the network, gigabit NICs that offload the TCP/IP processing from the host CPU make data transfer over the network much easier and faster. Jumbo frames also helped some vendors.

Another reason that backup and recovery of filers is now less a problem is that some NAS vendors introduced data-protection options equivalent to (and sometimes easier to use than) the options available on many Unix or NT systems—including built-in snapshots, mirroring, and replication. Therefore, for what it's worth, my respect for NAS has grown significantly in recent years.

NAS-based disk. While this may be true on very high-end servers, most real-world applications require much less throughput than the maximum available throughput of a filer.

NAS offers multihost filesystem access

A downside of SANs is that, while they do offer multihost access to devices, most applications want multihost access to files. If you want the systems connected to a SAN to read and write to the same file, you need a SAN or cluster-based filesystem. Such filesystems are starting to become available, but they are usually expensive and are relatively new technologies. Filers, on the other hand, offer multihost access to files using technology that has existed since 1984.

NAS is easier to understand

Some people are concerned that they don't understand Fibre Channel and certainly don't understand fabric-based SANs. To these people, SANs represent a significant learning curve, whereas NAS doesn't. With NAS, all that's needed to implement a filer is to read the manual provided by the NAS vendor, which is usually rather brief; it doesn't need to be longer. With Fibre Channel, you first need to read about and understand it, and then read the HBA manual, the switch manual, and the manuals that come with any SAN management software.

Filers are easier to maintain

No one who has managed both a SAN and NAS will argue with this statement. SANs are composed of pieces of hardware from many vendors, including the HBA, the switch or hub, and the disk arrays. Each vendor is new to an environment that hasn't previously used a SAN. In comparison, filers allow the use of your existing network infrastructure. The only new vendor you need is the manufacturer of the filer itself. SANs have a larger number of components that can fail, fewer tools to troubleshoot these failures, and more possibilities of finger pointing. All in all, a NAS-based network is easier to maintain.

Filers are much cheaper

Since filers allow you to leverage your existing network infrastructure, they are usually cheaper to implement than a SAN. A SAN requires the purchase of a Fibre Channel HBA to support each host that's connected to the SAN, a port on a hub or switch to support each host, one or more disk arrays, and the appropriate cables to connect all this together. Even if you choose to install a separate LAN for your NAS traffic, the required components are still cheaper than their SAN counterparts.

Filers are easy to protect against failure

While not all NAS vendors offer this option, some filers can automatically replicate their filesystems to another filer at another location. This can be done using a very low bandwidth network connection. While this can be accomplished with a SAN by purchasing one of several third-party packages, the functionality is built right into some filers and is therefore less expensive and more reliable.

Filers are here and now

Many people have criticized SANs for being more hype than reality. Too many vendors' systems are incompatible, and too many software pieces are just now being released. Many vendors are still fighting over the Fibre Channel standard. While there are many successfully implemented SANs today, there are many that aren't successful. If you connect equipment from the wrong vendors, things just won't work. In comparison, filers are completely interoperable, and the standards upon which they are based have been around for years.

Filers aren't without limitations. Here's a list of the limitations that exist as of this writing. Whether or not they still exist is left as an exercise for the reader.

Filers can be difficult to back up to tape

Although the snapshot and off-site replication software offered by some NAS vendors offers some wonderful recovery possibilities that are rather difficult to achieve with a SAN, filers must still be backed up to tape at some point, and backing up a filer to tape can be a challenge. One of the reasons is that performing a full backup to tape will typically task an I/O system much more than any other application. This means that backing up a really large filer to tape will create quite a load on the system. Although many filers have significantly improved the backup and recovery speeds, SANs are still faster when it comes to raw throughput to tape.

Filers can't do image-level backup of NAS

To date, all backup and recovery options for filers are file-based, which means the backup and recovery software is traversing the filesystem just as you do. There are a few applications that create millions of small files. Restoring millions of small files is perhaps the most difficult task a backup and recovery system will perform. More time is spent creating the inode than actually restoring the data, which is why most major backup/recovery software vendors have created software that can back up filesystems via the raw device—while maintaining file-level recoverability. Unfortunately, today's filers don't have a solution for this problem.

The upper limit is lower than a SAN

Although it's arguable that most applications will never task a filer beyond its ability to transfer data, it's important to mention that theoretically a SAN should be able to transfer more data than NAS. If your application requires incredible amounts of throughput, you should certainly benchmark both. For some environments, NAS offers a faster, cheaper alternative to SANs. However, for other environments, SANs may be the only option. Just make sure to test your system before buying it.

Pros and Cons of SANs

Many people swear by SANs and would never consider using NAS; they are aware that SANs are expensive and represent cutting edge technology. They are willing to live with these downsides in order to experience the advantages they feel only SANs can offer. The following is a summary of these advantages:

SANs can serve raw devices

Neither NFS nor CIFS can serve raw devices via the network; they can only serve files. If your application requires access to a raw device, NAS is simply not an option.

SANs are more flexible

What some see as complexity, others see as flexibility. They like the features available with the filesystem or volume manager that they have purchased, and those features aren't available with NAS. While NFS and CIFS have been around for several years, the filesystem technology that the filer is using is often new, especially when compared to *ufs*, *NTFS*, or *vxfs*.

SANs can be faster

As discussed above, there are applications where SANs will be faster. If your application requires sustained throughput greater than what is available from the fastest filer, your only alternative is a SAN.

SANs are easier to back up

The throughput possible with a SAN makes large-scale backup and recovery much easier. In fact, large NAS environments take advantage of SAN technology in order to share a tape library and perform LAN-less backups.

SANs are also not without their foibles. The following list contains the difficulties many people have with SAN technology:

SANs are often more hype than reality

This has already been covered earlier in this chapter. Perhaps in a few years, the vendors will have agreed upon an appropriate standard, and SAN management software will do everything it's supposed to do, with SAN equipment that's completely interoperable. I sure hope this happens.

SANs are complex

The concepts of Fibre Channel, arbitrated loop, fabric login, and device virtualization aren't always easy to grasp. The concepts of NFS and CIFS seem much simpler in comparison.

SANs are expensive

Although they are getting less expensive every day, a Fibre Channel HBA still costs much more than a standard Ethernet NIC. It's simply a matter of economies of scale. More people need Ethernet than need Fibre Channel.

It All Depends on Your Environment

Which storage architecture is appropriate for you depends heavily on your environment. What is more important to you: cost, complexity, flexibility, or raw throughput? Communicate your storage requirements to both NAS and SAN vendors and see what numbers they come up with for cost. If the cost and complexity of a SAN isn't completely out of the question, I'd recommend you benchmark both.

Make sure to solicit the help of each vendor during the benchmark. Proper configuration of each system is essential to proper performance, and you probably will not get it right on the first try. Have the vendors install the test NAS or SAN—even if you have to pay for it. It will be worth the money, especially if you've never configured one before.

I hope the rest of this book will prove helpful in your quest.

CHAPTER 2
Fibre Channel Architecture

Before jumping headfirst into using storage area networks, you need to understand something about the technology upon which most of them are based: Fibre Channel. You need to know answers to questions such as:

- Just what is Fibre Channel, anyway?
- What are the different variations (topologies) of Fibre Channel?
- What are the different parts of a Fibre Channel SAN?

Although this chapter is limited in size, it should explain Fibre Channel enough that you can understand the rest of the SAN chapters in this book. If you need to learn more about the inner workings of Fibre Channel, there are plenty of good books to help you.

Fibre Channel: An Overview

SANs certainly qualify as leading-edge technology. Some things being done with SANs can even be considered "bleeding edge." It's no surprise, then, that many people don't fully understand them yet. However, Fibre Channel has been around for years, and it is also a mystery. Why is that? Perhaps the reason Fibre Channel is so unknown is that you really didn't need to know too much about it up to this point. For most people, Fibre Channel meant plugging in a Fibre Channel disk to a host, and that was the end of it. They didn't know that they were creating a point-to-point Fibre Channel network when they did that. Even more people didn't realize that they were creating an arbitrated loop when they daisy-chained a few storage arrays together on the back of a server.

You don't need to know a whole lot about Fibre Channel when using it on such a small network. However, if you're trying to build even a reasonably sized SAN, not knowing Fibre Channel can greatly increase your confusion, frustration, and the total cost of the project.

Why Fibre Channel?

As covered in Chapter 1, the purpose of Fibre Channel was to remove the performance and logistical barriers of legacy LANs and the parallel SCSI architecture. The features of Fibre Channel include:

- Support for other, typically "non-network" protocols, such as SCSI. (This will be important for our discussion.)
- Confirmed delivery, thereby enhancing the reliability of the network.
- True quality of service (QOS) features, including fractional bandwidth and connection-oriented virtual circuits to guarantee bandwidth for critical backups or other operations.
- Extremely low-latency connection and connectionless service.
- Support for three different network topologies (point-to-point, arbitrated loop, and fabric), including auto-discovery of each topology and of all nodes placed on the network.
- Efficient, high-bandwidth, low-latency transfers using variable length (0 to 2KB) frames. This allows efficient transfer regardless of the payload size.
- Hot pluggable device support, which enables devices to be installed or removed without impacting the host system. This ability is critical to high availability systems and reduces downtime.

As shown in Table 2-1, Fibre Channel is the best technology for applications that require high-bandwidth, reliable solutions that scale from small to very large.

Table 2-1. Fibre Channel technology comparison

	Fibre Channel	Gigabit Ethernet	ATM
Technology application	Storage, network, video, clusters	Network	Network, video, SWAN
Topologies	Point-to-point, loop, hub, switched	Point-to-point hub, switched	Switched
Baud rate	1 Gb/s, 2Gb/s	1 Gb/s	622 Mb/s
Scalability to higher data rates	4 Gb/s	10 Gb/s	2.43 Gb/s (OC48)
Guaranteed delivery	Yes	No	No
Congestion data loss	None	Yes	Yes
Frame size	Variable, 0 to 2KB	Variable, 0 to 1.5KB	Fixed, 53B
Physical media	Copper and fiber	Copper and fiber	Copper and fiber
Protocols supported	Network, SCSI, video	Network, SCSI	Network, voice, video

What Is Fibre Channel?

Although a Fibre Channel network can be as simple as a Fibre Channel disk drive plugged into a Fibre Channel card or host bus adapter on the back of a server, it's

Who Is Fibre Channel?

Unfortunately, there are several groups that are attempting to standardize Fibre Channel, which concerns some industry analysts. Among those trying to standardize and/or influence Fibre Channel and SANs are the Storage Networking Industry Association (*http://www.snia.org*), the Fibre Channel Industry Association (*http://www.fibrechannel.com*), the EMC-led Fibre Alliance (*http://www.fibrealliance.org*), and the Sun-led Jiro platform expert group (*http://www.jiro.com*).

There are also at least two independent laboratories for Fibre Channel testing. The Interoperability Laboratory at the University of New Hampshire (*http://www.iol.unh.edu*) develops test suites for vendors to check compliance with the Fibre Channel standard. The Computational Science and Engineering Laboratory at the University of Minnesota (*http://www.lcse.umn.edu*) is focused on functionality and extending the application of Fibre Channel.

The SAN/Fibre Channel community seems to be developing the same way the Unix community developed. Each major vendor seems to want to put their stamp on how SANs operate, thinking that this will somehow result in more hardware and software sales of their platform. Although it seems to be the way of things, I think it's unfortunate. However, I do see that the platform-independent storage vendors (Brocade, Crossroads, etc.) tend to belong to all these organizations. Hopefully, the platform-dependent vendors (EMC, HP, IBM, Sun) will listen to these voices of reason when discussing interoperability issues. As of this writing, it appears that they are.

more than that. Fibre Channel is a set of standards that define a multilayered architecture that transfers data. Figure 2-1 shows the five layers are numbered FC-0 to FC-4 (thus not mapping directly to the seven-layered OSI networking model.)

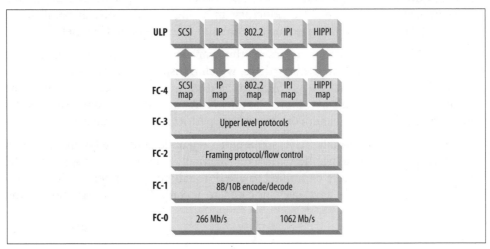

Figure 2-1. Fibre Channel layers

FC-4 (Mapping) defines how a Fibre Channel network communicates with upper-level protocols, such as SCSI and IP.* Each upper-level protocol (ULP) that is transportable over Fibre Channel has a map for it in FC-4. FC-3 (Common Services) is currently under development and will be used by applications requiring more than one port, such as data striping. FC-2 (Framing) is similar to the Media Access Control (MAC) layer in the OSI model, and defines how data from upper level applications is split into frames for transport over the lower layers. FC-0 and FC-1 are similar to the physical layer in the OSI model. FC-1 (Ordered Set) defines how frames are encoded and decoded for transport across those media types, and FC-0 (Physical) defines the various media types that can carry Fibre Channel data.

So, how does data get from a SCSI tape drive to a SCSI disk via a Fibre Channel network? First, a server requests that the data be retrieved from tape. SCSI and other protocols define how the data is initially retrieved from the tape drive. The SCSI *application* (as defined by the SCSI-3 protocol) then passes the data to the SCSI map of the Fibre Channel network, which receives the data from the SCSI application (as defined in FC-4). It then segments the data into frames (FC-2), encodes the frames (FC-1), and sends them across the various types of media (FC-0) that comprise the physical portion of the network.

Depending on the type of network, the Fibre Channel frames may travel over fiber optic or copper cables. They may also travel over one or more switches, hubs, or routers, depending on the type of Fibre Channel topology that is used. The frames eventually arrive at the port to which the disk drive is attached (typically after going into and out of the server's CPU). The frames are then decoded (FC-1), reassembled (FC-2), and given back to the SCSI-3 application for transfer to disk.

This is made possible by the SCSI-3 version of the SCSI protocol. One of the things defined in this specification is the concept of *serial SCSI*. That is, instead of sending SCSI data across multiple SCSI conductors (in a single SCSI cable) in parallel, the entire SCSI stream is sent through one transmission line in a Fibre Channel cable.

As far as the application that requested this transfer is concerned, it sent a SCSI request that went directly to the tape drive, which transferred the data via SCSI to its CPU so that it could transfer it via SCSI to the disk drive. In this case, however, the SCSI commands were sent to a Fibre Channel HBA capable of speaking serial SCSI, which uses a Fibre Channel network to actually perform the data transfer.

This allows the servers to talk SCSI, something they understand well, while the HBA uses Fibre Channel to change how the data is actually transferred. It's similar to the way millions of servers have continued to use IP to talk to each other, while the various lower network levels have been updated to include FDDI, ATM, and Gigabit

---

* Both SCSI and IP traffic can be sent across a Fibre Channel network.

Ethernet. (In fact, these lower layers now include Fibre Channel, since IP can also travel via a Fibre Channel network just like SCSI.)

One surprise from the data path just described is that Fibre Channel can run over both fiber and copper media. Fiber can run longer distances than copper, but copper cables (including video cable, miniature cable, and twisted pair) are perfectly viable (and less expensive) alternatives for shorter networks. The most common copper cable is twisted pair and uses a DB-9 connector. The cable lengths can run up to 30 meters, depending on the type of cabling, shielding, and components used, but copper is obviously highly susceptible to electromagnetic interference (EMI) problems. Fiber optic cables, on the other hand, can run up to 175, 500, and 10,000 meters— or even longer, based on the type of cabling and equipment being used.

Fiber or Fibre?

Please note the different spelling between the phrases *Fibre Channel* and *fiber optics*. Originally, Fibre Channel was intended to run only on fiber optic cables. However, once support for copper cabling had been added, the standards committee found themselves in a quandary. People already knew what Fiber Channel was, but the committee wanted to somehow show that Fiber Channel didn't necessarily mean fiber optic cables. The result was to use the European spelling of *fibre*, resulting in the current spelling of Fibre Channel. At least they tried!

When deciding the type of fiber to use, the first choice to make is between *multimode* and *single-mode* fiber. Multimode fiber can carry multiple light rays (known as *modes*) simultaneously by transmitting each mode at a slightly different reflection angle within the fiber core. Since the modes disperse over longer lengths (referred to as *modal dispersion*), multimode fiber is used for shorter distances (under 500 meters). Single-mode fiber, on the other hand, has a much thinner core that is designed to only transmit one light ray, or mode. This allows it to go much greater distances than multimode fiber, up to 10 kilometers. If you decide on multimode fiber, the second decision you need to make is the diameter of the core.* With multimode fiber, there are also two core diameters to choose from. The larger, 62.5-micron core can be used up to a length of 175 meters, but the 50-micron core is able to extend to 500 meters. This information is summarized in Table 2-2.

---

* The only reason that two types exist is to allow for you to use older fiber optic cable that ran for, say, a FDDI network. Most new cabling is 50 microns.

Table 2-2 . *Fiber optic cable types*

Diameter (microns)	Mode	Maximum length
62.5	Multimode	175 meters
50	Multimode	500 meters
9	Single mode	10 kilometers

Fibre Channel Ports

Before I explain the different Fibre Channel topologies, you need to know the names of the different types of Fibre Channel ports that are used in those topologies. There are three basic types of ports: the N_Port, the F_Port, and the E_Port. Then as you add arbitrated loop capabilities to these basic ports, they take the combined names of NL_Port, FL_Port, and G_Port.

N_Port
> An N_Port is a *node* port, or a port on a disk or computer. If a port is only an N_Port (and not an NL_Port), it can communicate only with another N_Port on a second node or to an F_Port on a switch.

F_Port
> An F_Port is a *fabric* port, which is found only on a switch. If a port is only an F_Port (and not an FL_Port), it can connect only to another N_Port via a point-to-point connection.

L_Port
> An L_Port implies it can participate in an arbitrated loop. If a port was only an L_Port, it could connect only to arbitrated loops, but ports that are exclusively L_Ports don't exist. The L is added to the end of an N_Port or F_Port to create an NL_Port or an FL_Port.

NL_Port
> A *node* port with arbitrated loop capabilities; that is, a port on a node that can connect to another node, to a switch (see N_Port) or to an arbitrated loop (see the L_Port definition).

FL_Port
> A *fabric* port with arbitrated *loop* capabilities; that is, a port on a switch that can connect to a node (see F_Port) or an arbitrated loop (see L_Port).

E_Port
> An E_Port is an *expansion* port on a switch that connects one switch to other switches via their E_Ports to form a large fabric.

G_Port
> A G_Port is a *generic* port on a switch that can act as an E_Port, an FL_Port, or an F_Port, depending on what connects to it.

Another term that's used in this book is HBA, for host bus adapter. This is the industry term for a Fibre Channel interface card that plugs into a host, such as a PCI or Sbus card (see the section "Host Bus Adapters (HBAs)" later in this chapter).

Addressing

The IEEE works with each manufacturer of Fibre Channel equipment to assign a fixed, unique, 64-bit address to each port and is referred to by its World Wide Name, or WWN. This is similar to the way MAC addresses are assigned to network interface cards (NICs). Then there are two dynamic addresses that may be assigned when this port connects to a Fibre Channel network. (This is similar to the way a desktop or laptop is given a dynamic IP address when it connects to a new network.) If a node connects to an arbitrated loop, it's assigned a dynamic 8-bit address, referred to as its *arbitrated loop physical address*, or AL_PA. If it connects to a fabric, it will be assigned a dynamic 24-bit address, referred to as its *native address identifier*, or S_ID. When a port is connected to both an arbitrated loop and a fabric, it's assigned a 24-bit address, and the lowest eight bits of the native address identifier become the AL_PA.

Fibre Channel Topologies

There are three Fibre Channel network topologies, the simplest and least expensive of which is *point-to-point*. The most expensive and complex Fibre Channel topology is the *fabric* topology, but it also has the greatest amount of functionality. The remaining topology is *arbitrated loop*, which fits right between point-to-point and fabric with regards to cost and functionality.

Point-to-Point

A point-to-point Fibre Channel network is the simplest and least expensive of the three topologies, and is simply two N_Ports communicating via a point-to-point connection.* As seen in Figure 2-2, a Fibre Channel array connected to a host is an example of a point-to-point connection.

Fabric

An illustration of a basic fabric network can be found in Figure 2-3. In a true fabric-only environment, each N_Port plugs into one F_Port on the switch. Each node is then assigned its native address identifier by the switch when it "logs into" the fabric.

---

* Actually, an N_Port connected to an F_Port on a switch is also a point-to-point connection. However, since that is really a part of a much larger fabric network, it's not thought of as such.

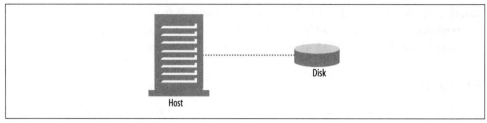

Figure 2-2. Point-to-point topology

(This is why this topology is sometimes referred to as "fabric login.") This 24-bit address allows for up to 16 million unique addresses within a single fabric, which should be enough for even the biggest SANs. (At this point, I can't possibly imagine a SAN with 16 million nodes on it, but then I keep thinking about what the popularity of the Internet did to the original IP specification.)

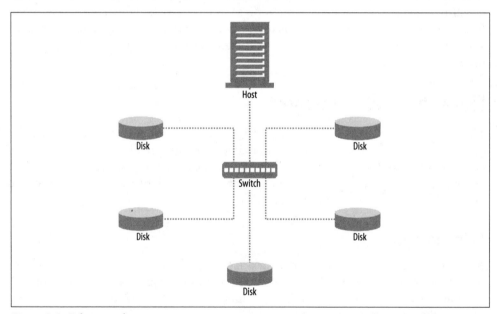

Figure 2-3. Fabric topology

When an N_Port is connected to a switch, it and other N_Ports connected to that switch can use the entire bandwidth of the port to which they are attached. Just as four nodes in a 100-Mb switched Ethernet environment can hold two simultaneous 100-Mb/s "conversations," every port in a Fibre Channel switch can supply the connected node with as much bandwidth as it needs—up to 100 MB/s. (That is, if the switch has been designed with the proper internal bandwidth. Not all switches are created equal.)

Of course, the switch in Figure 2-3 can connect to other switches via its E_Port, allowing the network to grow as much as needed, up to 16 million nodes. Unfortunately, the per-port cost of building a completely fabric-only environment has historically been quite high. (The cost-per-port of fabric switches decreases every day.)

Arbitrated Loop

The Fibre Channel arbitrated loop (FC-AL) was actually an add-on to the original Fibre Channel specification, which included only point-to-point and fabric topologies. However, the per-port cost of the fabric topology was prohibitively high, so the arbitrated loop topology was offered as a topology without the limits of point-to-point or the cost of fabric.

FC-AL quickly became the most dominant Fibre Channel topology, so much so that many people still refer to *all* Fibre Channel as "*f-kal*" (a common pronunciation of FC-AL). However, FC-AL's dominance is starting to disappear now that the per-port cost of fabric is coming down.

Arbitrated loops can appear in two physical layouts. As seen in Figure 2-4, a "true" arbitrated loop starts with several NL_Ports (either hosts or storage devices) configured in an actual loop, which requires splitting the transmit and receive wires of the connecting cables. Most Fibre Channel equipment isn't designed to be used this way, but it can be done with fiber optic cables with SC connectors that can be split, as illustrated in Figure 2-5.

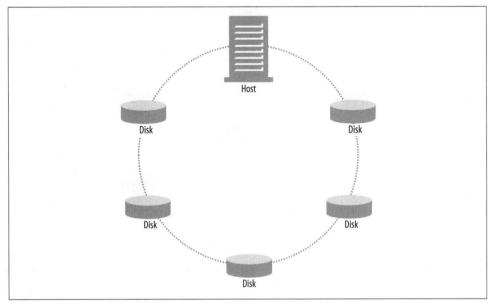

Figure 2-4. Arbitrated loop topology

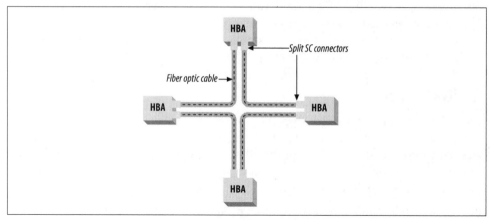

Figure 2-5. A "true" Fibre Channel loop using fiber optic cables

True loops as illustrated in Figures 2-4 and 2-5 typically are practical only with short distances due to logistical problems, but can be an inexpensive way to connect several Fibre Channel disk arrays to a single host. Another major limitation of this physical layout is that one bad HBA or cable connection can take out the entire network, since each HBA creates part of the loop. Therefore, the most common FC-AL physical layout is the "star" layout seen in Figure 2-6.

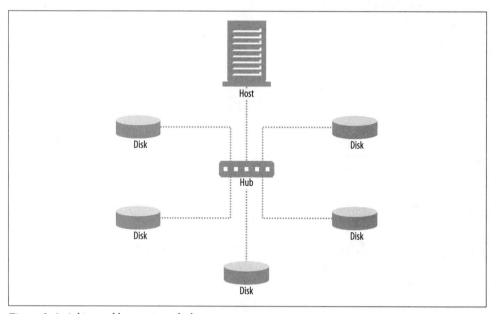

Figure 2-6. Arbitrated loop using a hub

An FC-AL star layout is accomplished by connecting each NL_Port to a Fibre Channel hub, and is electrically and logically the same as the loop layout in Figures 2-4 and 2-5, without forcing you to split the transmit and receive wires as shown in Figure 2-5. As you can see in Figure 2-7, the hub does the work of creating the loop. A managed hub can also prune the node in the event of a failure.

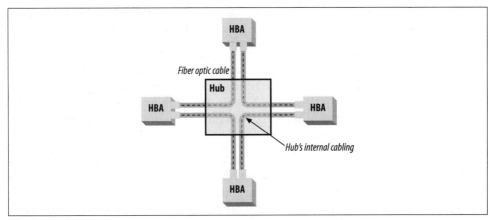

Figure 2-7. "Virtual" loop provided by hub

FC-AL Versus Fabric

Now that we know why it's called a loop, why is it called an *arbitrated* loop? The answer to that question is actually the first of two differences between arbitrated loop and fabric. Unlike fabric, FC-AL is a shared medium, in which nodes that wish to transmit on the loop must arbitrate for the right to do so. (The second difference between FC-AL and fabric is that nodes on a loop select their own address, rather than having it assigned by a switch.)

Arbitration

The first difference between FC-AL and fabric is that FC-AL is a shared medium. Only one port may communicate at once, significantly reducing its bandwidth when compared to the fabric topology—especially as the number of nodes increases. Ports that wish to transmit data must therefore arbitrate for the right to do so, thus the name *arbitrated* loop. The arbitration process can be quite complex, so the following should be considered a high-level summary.

A node begins arbitration by transmitting the ARB (arbitrate) frame. If no other ports are communicating, the ARB frame is received by the port that transmitted it, causing it to win arbitration and begin communicating. If two or more ports are arbitrating simultaneously, the port with the lowest AL_PA wins the arbitration.

Whenever a device wins arbitration, its access variable is set to 0. As long as this access variable is set to 0, the device can't request arbitration. Obviously, if it can't arbitrate, it can't win arbitration. This is what allows ports with lower priority (higher AL_PAs) to eventually win arbitration and be able to transmit. This and other types of logic built into FC-AL constitute what's called the *fairness algorithm*.

One of the reasons the fairness algorithm is so important is that once a port wins arbitration, it can transmit data until it's finished. This is different from a token ring network, where the token must be passed on after a set period of time.

While the winning port has control of the loop, obviously other ports may wish to arbitrate, but they are told to wait by the current arbitration winner until it's done. Once the winning FC-AL port completes its transmission, the arbitration progress starts again. The port with the next highest priority that has been trying to arbitrate while this device had control of the loop then immediately wins arbitration, it sets its access variable to 0 and begins transmitting.

This process continues until all devices that were trying to talk (while other devices already had control of the loop) are allowed to talk. Once all devices that need to talk have been allowed to talk, the last port to talk transmits an IDLE frame, telling other ports that the loop is idle. This causes them to set their access variable to 1, and the process starts all over again. Without getting into detail on the different types of frames that are sent, I'll give an example with a loop of three devices, with AL_PAs of 1, 2, and 3.

1. Ports 1 and 3 try to arbitrate at the same time by sending the ARB frame. Port 1 wins, since its AL_PA is lowest.

2. Port 1 sets its access variable to 0 and begins transmitting.

3. While Port 1 is transmitting, Port 3 continues trying to arbitrate. It's told to "wait."

4. While Port 3 is waiting, Port 2 also tries to begin arbitration. It's also told to wait.

5. Port 1 completes transmitting, at which point, Port 2 and 3 arbitrate. Port 2 will win arbitration since it's the port with the lowest AL_PA that is awaiting arbitration.

6. While Port 2 is transmitting, Port 3 continues to wait.

7. Port 1 now has something else to transmit, but it isn't allowed to arbitrate because its access variable is set to 0. Therefore, it must wait for now.

8. Port 2 completes transmitting, at which time Port 3 wins arbitration, since it's the only port that has requested arbitration at this point.

9. Port 3 sets its access variable to 0 and begins its transmission.

10. Once Port 3 completes its transmission, it "notices" that there are no other ports awaiting arbitration. It sends the IDLE frame, which notifies all nodes that the loop is free, causing them to reset their access variable to 1.

11. Since it's been waiting, Port 1 now begins and wins arbitration again.

Address selection

The second difference between FC-AL and fabric is how addressing is selected. Recall that when a node connects to a fabric, the switch assigns its address. In an arbitrated loop, however, each port selects its address from a list of available addresses. This is done in several steps:

1. The first step in loop initialization happens when an L_Port (either an NL_Port or an FL_Port) transmits a *loop initialization primitive* (LIP) frame, which is a special type of frame transmitted during loop failure, when a node powers on, or when a new node connects to the loop. This causes every other node to also transmit a LIP frame, at which point the loop becomes unusable until all nodes have received the *close* (CLS) frame, which will be transmitted later.

2. Once each node has transmitted the LIP frame, the loop needs to select a loop master, which will be important in the next step of initialization. This is done by continually transmitting the *loop initialization select master* (LISM) frame. If the loop is also connected to a fabric (via an FL_Port, as discussed later), the fabric port (FL) becomes the loop master. If not, the port with the lowest port name is chosen as loop master.

3. The next step is that every node must select an *arbitrated loop physical address*, or AL_PA. The loop master sends a *loop initialization select AL_PA* (LISA) frame "around the loop." Each L_Port on the loop selects a free AL_PA, sets its AL_PA to that value, and changes that AL_PA's "free" status in the LISA frame so that other L_Ports will not select it. It then passes the LISA frame to the next L_Port in the loop. (In the case of a reinitialization of a previously initialized loop, a particular port that already had an AL_PA assigned will attempt to select the same AL_PA again. If that fails, it selects a new one.)

4. Once the LISA frame has returned to the loop master, it sends the CLS frame to notify all nodes that the initialization process has completed. At this point, the loop is ready for use.

Combining Fabric and Arbitrated Loop Topologies

Arbitrated loop is inexpensive but has a physical limitation of 126 devices and a practical limitation of even less than that. Fabric can expand up to 16 million devices, but is extremely expensive. Therefore, it's common to combine several small arbitrated loops via a fabric. The network shown in Figure 2-8 gives you the best of both worlds.

The network in the figure connects an FL_Port or G_Port on a fabric switch to an arbitrated loop, typically via a hub. Remember that all devices in a fabric are assigned a 24-bit address, and the lowest 8 bits of that address becomes a device's AL_PA, if it's a member of an arbitrated loop. A loop that is connected to a fabric in this way is referred to as a *public loop*.

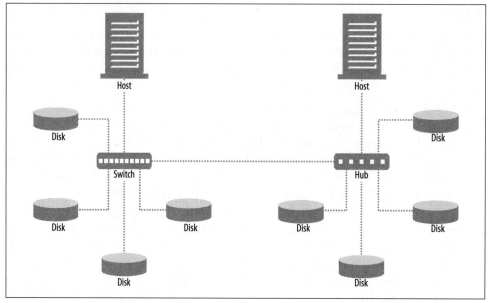

Figure 2-8. Fabric connected to an arbitrated loop

Here's an analogy that might help you understand how a public loop works: think of the AL_PA as the last octet of an IP address, where the higher 16-bits of the 24-bit address show which arbitrated loop a device is on, and the lower 8 bits show its address within that loop.

SAN Building Blocks

Let's now discuss the elements of a SAN and how they work together. The main elements of a SAN are servers, HBAs, switches, hubs, routers, disk systems, tape systems, cabling, and software. These are all illustrated in Figure 2-9.

Servers

No storage area network would have any reason for being if there weren't servers connected to it. The servers use the SAN to share storage resources. These servers can be anything from a traditional server to a high-end graphics workstation.

Host Bus Adapters (HBAs)

Servers connect to the SAN via their host bus adapter. This is often referred to as a "Fibre Channel card" or "Fibre Channel NIC." It's simply the Fibre Channel equivalent of a SCSI card (i.e., a SCSI HBA). As I've already mentioned, some HBAs may

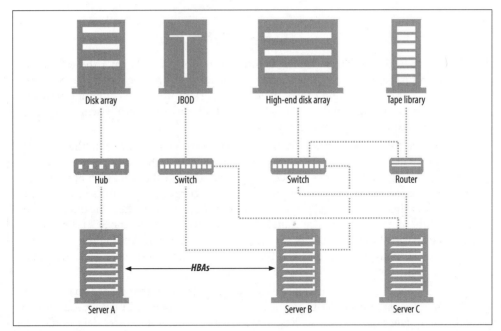

Figure 2-9. Elements of a SAN

use fiber, and some HBAs may use copper. Regardless of the physical layer, the HBA connects the servers to the SAN.

An iSCSI HBA is a standard, Ethernet NIC whose drivers have been updated to allow the transmission of serial SCSI-3 data across IP. Although theoretically this can be done with any Ethernet NIC, it's usually done with newer, hardware-accelerated Gigabit Ethernet NICs.

Figure 2-9 shows that two servers actually have two connections to the SAN via two HBAs. Although this configuration is used quite a bit, I should explain that just because you are using Fibre Channel and multiple connectors doesn't mean you will have redundant paths to a given device. This is true for a lot of reasons. Notice in Figure 2-9 that since the storage resources aren't connected to multiple switches, each path coming out of each server can access only one device.

Another reason you may not have redundant paths involves the limitations of the drivers. Remember that Fibre Channel disks are simply running the SCSI-3 protocol that has been adapted to work in a serial architecture. Since SCSI was historically written to understand one device that plugs into one bus, it's understandable that SCSI-3 doesn't understand the concept of a storage device that could appear on more than one HBA. Therefore, if you would like redundant paths, you also need some sort of redundant path management software. Its job is to stand between the kernel

SAN or LAN?

Many people look at the networks depicted here and say, "What's the difference between a LAN and a SAN?" The answer is really easy: the protocol they use. Systems on the LAN use IP, IPX, and other "typical" network protocols to communicate with other systems. Systems on the SAN use the SCSI-3 protocol (typically sent over Fibre Channel) to communicate with storage devices.

The term "SCSI" can be a bit confusing because the acronym refers to both the physical medium (a parallel SCSI cable) and the protocol that carries the traffic. Perhaps a comparison will help. IP traffic is sent over copper twisted-pair cables and fiber optic cables via the Ethernet protocol. SCSI[a] traffic is sent over copper SCSI[b] cables via the SCSI protocol. In this case, the SCSI protocol is performing essentially the same duties as the IP and Ethernet protocols. SCSI traffic also travels over fiber via the SCSI-3 protocol running on top of the Fibre Channel protocol. In this case, the SCSI-3 protocol is performing essentially the same duties as IP, and the Fibre Channel protocol is performing essentially the same duties as the Ethernet protocol.

A LAN is a collection of servers, clients, switches, and routers that carry data traffic via IP, IPX, Ethernet and similar protocols, usually IP running over Ethernet. A SAN is a collection of storage devices, servers, switches, and routers that carry data traffic via the SCSI and Fibre Channel protocols, usually SCSI-3 running over Fibre Channel.

a. In this case, SCSI refers to the protocol.

b. Here, SCSI refers to physical copper cable, also known as a parallel SCSI cable.

and the SAN, so that requests for storage resources are monitored and directed to the appropriate path. This software may be provided by a third-party or included in the operating system.

Watch Those Eyes!

There are two types of lasers in today's HBAs: optical fiber control (OFC) and non-OFC. OFC devices use a hand-shaking method to ensure they don't transmit a laser pulse if there is nothing connecting to the HBA. (This is for safety reasons, since a high-powered laser can cause permanent damage to your eyesight.) Non-OFC devices employ no such handshaking and will transmit even if a device isn't connected. Believe it or not, non-OFC devices are actually quite common. Therefore, please don't look directly into an HBA. You may regret it! It's also important to note that the laser light is invisible and can't be seen by the human eye. Also, the damage caused by such a laser might not be noticeable immediately but accumulates over time.

Switches

Figure 2-9 shows two servers connected to two Fibre Channel switches. Remember that when you connect to a switch, you use the switched fabric topology—not the arbitrated loop topology. That is, of course, unless the device you're connecting to the switch doesn't support fabric login, and the port on the switch is an FL_Port that supports arbitrated loop. (See the definitions in the previous section "Fibre Channel Ports.") In this case, the switch creates an arbitrated loop on the port to which you connect that device.

Switches are "intelligent" and have many possible configurations. Using software provided by the switch vendor, you can create zones that allow only certain servers to see certain resources. This configuration is usually done via a serial or Ethernet interface. As will be discussed in Chapter 3, this is analogous to a VLAN in Ethernet.

Where Fibre Channel networks require dedicated switches that use a proprietary protocol, iSCSI can use standard IP switches. However, as will be mentioned in Appendix A, it's likely that iSCSI SANs will still use dedicated switches. The difference is that they will be able to be the same make and model as all your other LAN switches and can be maintained by the same people without any additional training.

Security

A major difference between parallel SCSI and Fibre Channel is that most Fibre Channel devices have an RJ-45 port, allowing you to connect your SAN devices to a LAN. This allows for much easier configuration and out-of-band management than what is possible through the serial interface. It also allows your SAN devices to be monitored via SNMP-capable monitoring software. *However, this also opens up a major security hole.* If you simply connect the RJ-45 port of your SAN devices directly to your corporate LAN (or even worse, the Internet), it creates a way for malicious people (a.k.a. *black hats*) to take down your enterprise. This is why I suggest placing all LAN connections for SAN devices on a separate, well protected LAN. To do otherwise is to invite disaster. Also remember to change the default administrator passwords on these devices!

Another interesting security ramification of SANs is the configuration software that runs on servers connected to the SANs. Depending on the product and its capabilities, a black hat breaking into the wrong box can also wreak havoc on your SAN. Ask your configuration software vendor how to protect yourself from such a disaster. They will probably tell you to limit the number of boxes that run the configuration software and to isolate them on a separate LAN, securing them as much as possible. It's easy to consider putting your management and configuration software in multiple places, because it makes management of the SAN much easier. However, think about the security implications of this before doing so!

Hubs

Hubs understand only the arbitrated loop topology. When you connect a device to a hub, it causes the arbitrated loop that hub is managing to reinitialize, the device is then assigned an AL_PA (arbitrated loop physical address), and it begins arbitration when it needs to communicate with another device on the loop.

There are *managed* (i.e., "smart") hubs and *unmanaged* (i.e., "dumb") hubs. An unmanaged hub can't close the loop when a device on the loop is malfunctioning; a single bad device can disable the entire loop. A managed hub detects the bad device and removes it from the loop, allowing the rest of the loop to function normally. Although there are plenty of unmanaged hubs available, the cost difference between managed and unmanaged hubs is minimal, and the functionality difference between them is quite great. If you're going to use arbitrated loop, my advice would be to stay with managed hubs.

When planning a new SAN, you should also consider whether a hub is even appropriate. The cost difference between hubs and switches gets smaller every day, and the functionality difference is even greater than the difference between managed and unmanaged hubs. Since arbitrated loop is cheaper than fabric is, I have seen a number of sites build SANs based on hubs and arbitrated loop—only to rip out the hubs and replace them with switches a year or two later. Please consider purchasing a switch if at all possible.

Hub Switches

A hub switch is a type of box that crosses the bridge between a hub and a switch. Think of this box as multiple hubs plugged into a switch—all in one box. For example, a 24-port hub switch probably has three 8-port arbitrated loop hubs, with a switched fabric backbone for interloop communication. Communication within a hub is handled via standard arbitrated loop rules. However, if a device on one of the three "virtual" hubs within the switch needs to talk to a device on another virtual hub within the switch, the communication is carried from hub to hub via a switched fabric network. Of course, if this hub switch is connected to another switch, it communicates with that switch via a switched fabric connection. The purpose for this configuration is cost; hub switches cost less than a switch but more than a managed hub.

Routers and Bridges

There are two types of Fibre Channel routers. The first is sometimes referred to as a bridge and is what is depicted in Figure 2-9. This type of router converts the serial data stream into a parallel data stream and vice versa. It allows you to plug parallel SCSI devices, such as tape and optical drives, into your SAN. Once you have done this, you can share them just as you would share a device that speaks Fibre Channel natively. That is why, in Figure 2-9, you see a tape library connected to the SAN via a router.

 Router is a more appropriate name for this piece of equipment than bridge. The difference between a router and a bridge in IP networking is that a bridge communicates on Layer 2 and a router on Layer 3. When mapped to the OSI model, the Fibre Channel specification puts SCSI at Layer 3, because SCSI addresses, like IP addresses, are changeable, and WWN names and MAC addresses aren't. Also, a number of these routers possess intelligent routing capabilities (e.g., extended copy), which enable some important technologies (server-free backup). In addition, the major manufacturers of these devices call them routers.

The second type of router (that isn't pictured in Figure 2-9) goes between the HBAs and the switches. This type of router can actually route traffic based on load and finds alternate paths when necessary. This is a relatively new type of router but one that shows a lot of promise.

Disk Systems

As you can see in Figure 2-9, disk systems come in many shapes and sizes. While many people think it's necessary to buy a high-end disk array to enter the SAN space, you can see that there are two other types of disk on the SAN in Figure 2-9. The first is a "disk array," sometimes referred to as "RAID in a box." These types of arrays can typically be configured as a RAID 0+1, RAID 1+0, or RAID 5 array, and can present the disks to the SAN in a number of ways. (See Appendix B for definitions of the various levels of RAID.) They will often automatically pick a hot spare and perform other tasks JBOD just can't do without third-party software.

The second type of disk system is JBOD, which stands for Just a Bunch Of Disks. (No, I didn't make that up.) These disks are either parallel SCSI disks plugged into a SAN router or Fibre Channel disks plugged directly into the switch. You can also plug several JBOD disks into a hub and then plug the hub into the switch. This is a more cost-effective way to plug several smaller disks into the SAN. However, as discussed earlier, you should perform a cost-benefit analysis when deciding whether to just plug the disks into the switch or to plug them into a hub that gets plugged into the switch.

The final type of disk system is the high-end disk array. These typically offer significant advantages over JBOD or "RAID in a box" systems, but they do cost quite a bit more than the other systems. Features that may be available in such systems are:

- Creation of additional mirrors that can be split for backup purposes
- Server-free remote copy (to another frame)

- Proactive monitoring and notification of failed (or failing) components
- Multiple server connections (32, 64, or more servers connected directly to a single array)
- Internal zoning capabilities
- Multipathing and failover software
- Redundant internal paths for data and commands
- Advanced caching capabilities
- Advanced software features, such as off-site replication, automatic performance tuning, and virtualization of resources

Although some of these features may be available in the "RAID in a box" products, a high-end array will probably offer all of them in one box.

 In order to use iSCSI, both disk and tape systems need to have iSCSI adapters added to them, or the existing Fibre Channel HBAs needs to be upgraded to support both Fibre Channel or IP.

Cabling

Often overlooked in discussions about SAN architecture, cabling is obviously an important part of the system. These cables are typically fiber optic cables with SC connectors. (This is the same type of cables used for Gigabit Ethernet.) As discussed previously, there are also DB9-style connectors, which are less expensive and may be more appropriate for some environments. Please remember that fiber optic cables are fragile, and should be treated as such. I have heard this described more than once as an advantage over SCSI. Fiber optic cables either work, or they don't. Either no data gets through, or all the data gets through. In contrast, a SCSI cable may work fine under some conditions, but not others. (Don't you hate it when that happens?)

Software

There are many products in this category, and this is one of the fastest growing areas of SAN products. This category of SAN building blocks includes both traditional software and firmware. This means it may be found in numerous places, including server, routers, other hardware devices, or on a high-end disk array. Among other things, these products offer the following features:

Protocol conversion

Suppose you'd like to address SSA disks[*] and Fiber Channel disks from a single host. A product offering protocol conversion can make this happen.

Zoning

Zoning is an important aspect of SANs. Without zoning, every host connected to the SAN can read and write to every disk in the SAN. By separating the servers and disks into zones, you solve this problem.

Device/path failover

Suppose you have multiple Fibre Channel paths to the same device. By default, Fibre Channel will not use one of those links as a failover link if the other one fails. Software can make this happen.

Load balancing

This is similar to the failover feature. If you have multiple paths to a single storage resource, wouldn't it be nice to distribute the load between those paths? This is often combined with the failover feature, where traffic is load balanced during normal operations but will failover in case of device failure.

Backup and recovery management

These products perform such tasks as creating third mirrors that can be split off for backup, allowing you to share robotic tape libraries, and even transferring data between devices on the SAN without going through anyone's CPU.

Fibre Channel and SANs: A Summary

To share resources, you need a network. To share computing resources, the industry developed the LAN, which enabled access to any computing resource (computer) from any other computing resource. This introduced the concept of a *shared* resource, in which one computing resource could be shared by multiple clients.

Just as the LAN allowed the introduction of NFS (a shared filesystem that was a revolutionary concept when it first appeared), the SAN has introduced a new concept: a shared *storage device*. A shared storage device is a raw storage device (such as a disk, optical, or tape drive) that is connected to a SAN and appears as a locally attached device to any computer connected to the SAN. To put it in simpler terms, connecting a tape drive to a SAN allows any computer attached to that SAN to perform a backup to that tape drive just as if that tape drive were physically attached to that computer via a SCSI cable. And with this wonderfully new concept, we can accomplish wonderful things.

---

[*] SSA stands for serial storage architecture. SSA is a competing architecture to Fibre Channel, but it has been around for a while and has not gained much acceptance. That isn't to say that there aren't SSA devices out there, though.

CHAPTER 3
Managing a SAN

What's it like to manage a SAN? What kind of applications lend themselves to SANs? What kind of tasks do you find yourself performing once you've decided to actually purchase a SAN? Why does a SAN require more management than traditional, parallel SCSI? What can you do with a SAN that you can't do without a SAN? These are all important questions.

The Different Uses for SANs

Many of the reasons you would want to use a SAN are the same as the reasons for using NAS. Those reasons are covered primarily in Chapter 1. Chapter 6 covers the applications where NAS systems perform exceptionally well. Therefore, this section of this chapter covers only the applications in which SANs tend to perform better than NAS.

Large, High-Performance Databases

SANs perform well with large, high-performance databases. While some databases support placing their datafiles on a NAS filer, many don't. Even if the database doesn't specifically support NAS, there may be performance issues with running a large, high-performance database on NAS. Therefore, many environments chose to run their databases on SAN-attached disks. SAN-attached disks offer two distinct advantages to NAS filers:

High-performance backups

When you talk about terabyte-sized databases, it's hard to beat the backup and recovery performance of SAN-attached disks, especially if you start talking about server- or client-free backups. Such backups allow you to back up a large amount of data in a short period of time, without any performance impact to the application. There are parallels to some of these backup types in the NAS world, but SAN-based backups are almost always faster than NAS-based backups. Whether or not you need that additional speed is your decision.

Faster database performance

If your budget is unlimited, you can't beat SAN-attached disks for performance. If cost is a factor, though, some NAS systems may actually be faster than equivalently priced SAN systems. But, if you've got the money, SAN-attached disks will be fastest.

Filesystems with Many, Many Files

There are some applications that generate hundreds of thousands, or even millions of files—even within the same filesystem. Why is this an issue? The issue is that it's almost impossible to back up such a filesystem via standard, filesystem-based backup software. This is why most of the major backup software vendors have developed image-level backup and recovery for such filesystems. This allows them to back up the filesystem via its raw device. Recovery can be done at the file level for individual files or at the raw device level for high-performance recoveries.

However, this technology isn't possible with most of today's NAS filers. Almost all filers don't support this type of backup and recovery. Therefore, if you are forced to do a recovery of a NAS filesystem with many, many files, it will take significantly longer than the same filesystem if it were on a SAN. How much faster an image-level recovery would be depends on your application, of course. But a 10-fold performance improvement during such restores isn't uncommon, and 100-fold improvement isn't unheard of.

Databases Requiring Raw Device Access

There are a few databases that require access to the raw device. There are many more databases that support both raw and cooked files, but are run by DBAs who prefer using raw files for their performance and integrity issues. Only SAN-attached disks can provide raw device access. NAS filers can only share files—not devices.

Vendors That Don't (or Won't) Support NAS

There are some vendors who refuse to support their database products on NAS-attached storage. This lack of support comes in various forms. Some companies just don't want to know that their database is running on a NAS filer. If you tell them that, they won't support you. Other vendors go so far as to prevent their databases from being put on a filer. For example, current versions of SQL Server and Exchange won't even run if their database files appear to be placed on a CIFS-mounted filesystem.

Many statements made in this section are generalizations based on past or current experiences with SANs. Before deciding which type of network storage to use, you should definitely verify anything you find relevant. Test it yourself.

SAN Issues to Be Managed

There is no question that SANs bring significant advancements to the storage industry. However, taking advantage of this technology requires a major shift in how you think about and manage your storage. On one hand, Fibre Channel, the technology on which most SANs are based, is simply a new physical layer upon which SCSI data can travel. On the other hand, Fibre Channel has broken the SCSI mold in so many ways that it challenges a number of assumptions many of us have had for years about our SCSI-based storage devices. Since some of these assumptions are no longer true, it creates new issues that must be addressed—issues that must be managed.

Access to storage resources in a Fibre Channel network is accomplished using *channels* (thus the name Fibre Channel) through a *loop* (arbitrated loop), or a *fabric* (a network of SAN fabric switches) to connect one or more hosts to one or more storage devices. Each individual channel, or data path, in a SAN provides a virtual end-to-end connection between a server or host through the SAN to any intended and assigned storage resource, including all physical components and logical connections. Each path can be thought of, both physically and logically, as a virtual representation of a singular SCSI connection or cable. However, unlike the SCSI cable, this cable can create a channel from any SAN-connected server to any SAN-connected storage device. This results in many interesting differences between SANs and parallel SCSI.

iSCSI SANs will have all of these issues as well.

Multiple Paths to a Single Device

The first assumption about SCSI-based storage that isn't true with SANs is that each SCSI device will appear only on one SCSI bus. With SANs, it's perfectly normal to connect more than one Fibre Channel HBA on the same host to the same SAN, resulting in multiple paths to the same device. Since switches and some storage devices can also accept multiple Fibre Channel connections, the number of physical paths to each device may actually be quite high. These paths are managed by a routing protocol on the switches, and software running on the operating system of each client using the SAN.

One of the strengths of the Fibre Channel *fabric* topology is the use of *multipath routing* between SAN switches. This is the ability to simultaneously route multiple channels through interconnected switches. SAN fabric switches are closer to Ethernet routers than switches. Ethernet switches use a spanning tree-type protocol to identify redundant paths in the network. Such a protocol enables only one path and blocks all other redundant paths. An Ethernet router, on the other hand, will probably use a link state routing protocol such as OSPF (open shortest path first) to handle multiple paths. OSPF assigns weighted metrics to each potential data path and uses the shortest path for each connection.

A SAN fabric switch uses the FSPF protocol (Fibre Channel shortest path first), which considers all concurrent data paths to be of equal value or cost and doesn't require blocking redundant connections. Instead, two or more redundant paths in a SAN lets the administrator load-balance SAN traffic by distributing I/O across all available paths. This allows the SAN to take advantage of the additional bandwidth provided by each concurrent physical connection.

Redundant paths also provide failover capability in the event of a failure of any of the components in the data path. SANs with redundant paths may also incorporate advanced antithrashing features to prevent the possibility of continual and constant load redistribution due to errors at either end of the data path.

Although redundant paths provide for load balancing and link failover, they also create a problem. Because each device on the SAN will appear as a SCSI ID on each HBA connected to the SAN, a system with multiple HBAs connected to the SAN will actually think that each device on each path is a separate device. This presents the operating system with what appears to be multiple storage resources, when in reality they're only multiple paths to the same resource. Therefore, a logical layer needs to be inserted to mask these paths and present the operating system with the appearance of a single SCSI connection.

This task is usually performed by multipathing software that runs on each server connected to the SAN. This software can come from a number of places. Some of the enterprise storage array vendors, such as Compaq, EMC, and Hitachi offer such software with their storage arrays. Independent software vendors also offer multipathing software. Multipathing functionality has also been incorporated into some operating systems, Solaris 8, for example. Multipathing is discussed in more detail later in this chapter.

Multiple Servers Accessing the Same Device

The second assumption about SCSI-based storage that isn't true with SANs is that a single storage resource will be seen only by one host. This comes from practice, rather than the SCSI protocol. The SCSI specification allows a single device to connect to multiple hosts, but this is usually not done in practice. Therefore, many operating systems believe that any SCSI device that is visible to them is available for their exclusive access. However, SANs allow multiple hosts to access the same storage device.

The solution to this problem is *zoning*. A *zone* is a virtual private SAN within a SAN, similar to Ethernet VLANs, and there are two main types of zoning. By separating the SAN into several smaller SANs, you limit the number of hosts that can see a given storage resource. Similar to zoning is the concept of *LUN masking*, in which each host is given a list of LUNs it's permitted to see. (Zoning and LUN masking are covered in more detail later in this chapter.) The second kind of zoning is *hard zoning*, where a zone is created using a list of physical ports on a switch. Every host connected to those ports is a member of that VLAN. *Soft zoning* is the third (and most common) type of zoning, and it uses a list of World Wide Names (WWNs) to determine who is a member of the zone. Any host whose WWN appears on the list is a member of the zone. Zoning is discussed in more detail later in this chapter.

Storage Devices with Changing Addresses

Another assumption about SCSI-based storage that isn't true with SANs is that a given device's SCSI address never changes. The way that some operating systems assign SCSI addresses to SAN devices may cause their SCSI address to change after a reboot. This is especially true if the storage resources that were available at the last reboot are different than the ones available during a subsequent reboot. If the operating system assigns SCSI IDs to storage resources in the order they appear, the SCSI ID of any given resource may change from time to time. Depending on the volatility of your SAN and your operating systems, this could become a nightmare.

The solution to this problem is called *persistent binding*. A persistent binding is a permanent relationship between a SCSI ID and a WWN. This relationship is part of the HBA driver configuration and essentially says "associate any LUNs from this WWN to this SCSI target." Since WWNs never change, the SCSI ID remains permanent— no matter what happens with the SAN. Binding is explained in more detail later in this chapter.

Lack of Interoperability

Another assumption many people have about SCSI-based storage devices is that any SCSI device can be connected to any other SCSI device of the same generation. For example, any LVD Ultra-2 device can connect with any other LVD Ultra-2 device. Within certain, well-documented limits, you can even connect devices with different speeds together, and they will negotiate a common speed in much the same way as modems negotiate the speed at which they will communicate. Many people therefore falsely assume that "Fibre Channel is Fibre Channel," and buy what they feel is the best HBA, disk array, and switch, and then connect them together and expect the system to work. Sadly, it doesn't work that way.

An early-adopter mind set helps a lot when using new technology such as SANs. Early adopters tend to look at things a little differently.

Ask a lot of questions

Talk to people that have already done what you want to do. Talk to an integrator that has implemented the exact type of SAN you are trying to implement. Ask them what HBAs, switches, and SAN management software they recommend. What kind of configuration changes did they need to make to the Fibre Channel driver? What kind of kernel tweaks did they make? Did they try another vendor's HBA, switch, or software and have problems?

Expect a lot of difficulty during initial testing

Maybe you will have trouble, and maybe you won't. Maybe you won't misconfigure a zone and accidentally overwrite one server's storage with another server. Maybe you won't connect the wrong device to your server and cause it to panic. Maybe you will connect your switch to your servers and storage, and everything will work right the first try. But *expecting* everything to work out of the box is completely unrealistic.

Interoperability will happen, but not at first

Again, ask an integrator which components will work together, and buy the components the integrator recommends. Don't assume all Fibre Channel devices work together, because they don't yet. All the vendors have gotten the message that interoperability is important, and they will make their products more interoperable with time. Every day, more and more Fibre Channel products work together. But assuming that they all work together today is also unrealistic.

Access to Storage Resources

If all your SAN devices are functioning properly, you will be spending much of your SAN management time allocating storage resources and giving access to them. First, you will create virtual disk and tape devices through a process called *virtualization*. Second, you will create zones or use LUN masking to create data paths between the virtual storage resources and the servers that need them. Third, you can use persistent binding to create a permanent relationship between each virtual resource and a SCSI ID on a server. Finally, you use multipathing software to take advantage of the multiple physical paths between each storage resource and each server.

Storage Virtualization

A SAN may consist of hundreds or thousands of physical disks inside one or more storage arrays, and many tape drives inside one or more tape libraries. The first task of the SAN administrator is to turn these physical resources into virtual ones that may be used by the servers. This is done by dividing a single physical resource into multiple resources (i.e., *slicing*), or by aggregating many physical resources into one virtual resource (i.e., *striping/RAID*). There isn't much to do with tape libraries, because you can't create slices of a tape drive or stripe many tape drives together.* However, with disk arrays, there's quite a bit of work to do, and the virtualization of disk storage can take place on either the storage array or the server level.

Slicing

All storage consists of a number of individual disks. These disks can be treated as complete units or can be sliced into smaller sections. One reason for doing this is the performance characteristics of the various sections of the disk. Each disk is made of several platters, and each platter contains three sections, or *bands*, each with different performance characteristics. This is because the speed at which the read/write head is passing over the data is greater when it's closer to the outer edge of the platter, and lesser when it's closer to the inner edge of the platter.

Here's a real-world example from one company with two applications. One application required frequent, high-speed access to its disks; another required infrequent, lower-speed access to its disks. The company had a series of large disks, and needed to create two equally sized RAID partitions. They could have striped half of the disks together and created the first RAID volume, then striped the other half of the disks into the second RAID volume. However, they used slicing to increase the performance for the first application (that really needed the best performance it could get), and sacrifice some performance for the second application (that really didn't need that much performance).

First, they sliced each disk into two slices. The first slice consisted of half of the capacity of the disk, but it used only the outer band of the disk. The second slice used the other half of the disk, but it resided on the two inner bands of the disk. Therefore, they have two equally sized stripes on each disk—one slower and one faster.

Next, they striped all the faster stripes consisting of the outer band. This created a faster RAID partition. Then they striped together all the slower stripes from the inner two bands. This created a slower RAID partition.

Since the application that needed faster performance also accessed the disk much more than the other application, it was given two performance increases. The first performance increase was because all its data was on the outer slice of the disk—the fastest section of the disk. The second performance increase was due to the fact that the read/write head only needed to seek within the outer band of the disk to access the faster application's data. Of course, when the slower application needed to access its data, the read/write head needed to seek to the inner bands of the disk, but this application only accessed the disk occasionally. This meant that the read/write

---

* Actually, there are tape RAID units, but they exist only as standalone units.

head spent most of its time in the outer band—significantly reducing seek times and increasing the speed of the disk for the faster application.

Striping/RAID

Whether you create large virtual disks from individual disks, virtual disks provided by a disk vendor, or slices of physical disks, you're creating these large, virtual disks using RAID. The amount of availability you have is based on the level of RAID you choose. Common numbered examples of RAID are RAID 0, RAID 1, RAID 0+1, RAID 1+0, RAID 10 (1+0 and 10 refer to the same thing), RAID 2, RAID 3, RAID 4, RAID 5, and RAID 6. (See Appendix B for descriptions of the various levels of RAID.)

Implementations of Virtualization

There are two ways to implement RAID: hardware and software. Each has its advantages and disadvantages.

Controller-based implementation

Controller-based (i.e., hardware-based) RAID is usually found in mid- to high-level storage arrays. It's generally accepted that controller-based RAID is faster than software-based RAID, but this assumption is challenged on a regular basis.

A storage array capable of hardware RAID will usually be able to virtualize their disks in a number of ways. The first thing you can do, of course, is create a virtual disk consisting of many smaller physical disks using RAID 0. You can also usually create RAID 5 disk groups and RAID 1 mirrors, and can sometimes create multiple mirrors for a single disk or group of disks. Often, you can create multiple levels of RAID, such as creating several large virtual disks using RAID 0, and then creating a RAID 5 disk group from those disks. However, when this is done, all the operating system sees is the end result. If you used 100 30-GB disks to create 50 RAID 1 mirrors, and then used RAID 0 to stripe them together, the operating system would see one, large 1500-GB volume.

With controller-based RAID, there needs to be some way to notify administrators of disk failures. This can be accomplished a couple of different ways. The first is for the disk array to have a LAN port that can issue SNMP traps or accept SNMP queries, which allows the controller to do its own failure notifications. This is referred to as *outofband* management.

Some controllers require the installation of software on one of the systems that has Fibre Channel access to the array. Such a controller sends its notifications to this software via the Fibre Channel interface, and the software is responsible for notifying others via the server's network interface. This can be done via email, pages, SNMP traps, or a number of other methods. This method is referred to as *in-band* management.

Software-based implementation

Software-based RAID is more common and works with any type of disk array, including disks that aren't in an array (i.e., JBOD). You can also create multiple levels of RAID and additional RAID 1 mirrors using software-based RAID. In fact, software-based RAID usually has more functionality and flexibility than its hardware-based counterparts.

Failure reporting is relatively simple, since there is already software running on each server that knows when a disk fails and must be replaced. This software simply needs to be told how to perform its notification. The default setup usually uses the system's default messaging facility, such as Unix's *syslog* or the Windows NT Event Log. Some products also support SNMP traps, emails, or pages.

Zoning

One of the biggest differences between Fibre Channel and parallel SCSI is that an unrestricted SAN allows all devices on the SAN to be seen by all servers connected to the SAN, just as all hosts on a LAN can see all other hosts on that LAN. This, of course, will cause lots of problems if you allow it to happen. The solution to this problem is the use of zoning and LUN masking. Before describing how zoning works, let's look at a similar technology—Virtual LANs or VLANs.

When a LAN administrator needs to restrict traffic to certain hosts, they create a VLAN. A VLAN can be created using a list of switch ports, MAC addresses, or protocols. A VLAN created using switch ports causes any host that connects to one of those ports to belong to the VLAN. A VLAN created using MAC addresses acts differently. Whether the VLAN spans one or many switches, a MAC address that belongs to a particular VLAN will be put into that VLAN no matter which port or which switch it plugs into. A protocol-based VLAN goes one step farther, creating a VLAN of those hosts that communicates with a particular protocol. For example, you might want to support AppleTalk on your LAN but limit AppleTalk traffic to those ports that happen to have a machine talking AppleTalk connected to them. If a machine connects to any port and starts using the AppleTalk protocol, it's automatically added to the AppleTalk VLAN.

Figure 3-1 illustrates a single LAN with three VLANs. If an NIS domain is created in VLAN 1, any broadcast messages for that domain are limited to Servers B, C, G, and H. If VLAN 2 is the Apple Talk VLAN, only Servers D, E, and F see AppleTalk traffic. VLAN 3 looks a little odd, of course, with only one host in it, but that prevents any broadcast traffic sent by Server A from being seen by any other servers on the LAN.

Zones are similar to VLANS. Like VLANs, zones can span multiple switches and limit traffic to those ports or addresses that belong to them. Servers and storage resources can also exist in more than one zone. One difference is that VLANs are

---

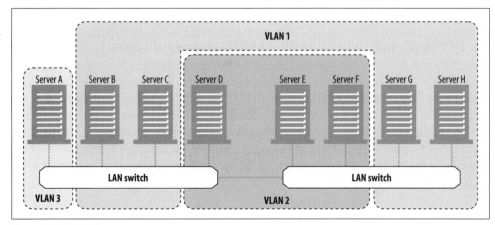

Figure 3-1. VLANs

primarily intended to increase the aggregate throughput of a LAN, not prevent the different servers from communicating with each other. Zones, on the other hand, serve exactly that purpose. Consider the SAN depicted in Figure 3-2, which looks a lot like Figure 3-1. The LAN switches have been replaced by SAN switches, the VLANs have been replaced by zones, and four storage arrays have been placed on the other side of the switches.

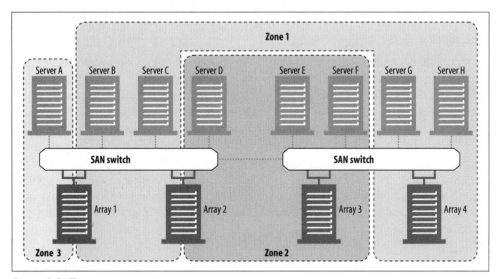

Figure 3-2. Zones

Servers B, C, G, and H can all access and share the right half of Array 1, the left of Array 2, and all of Array 4. However, Servers A, D, E, and F don't see those disks at all. Only Server A can access the left half of Array 1, and Servers D, E, and F can access and share the right half of Array 2 and all of Array 3.

Creating zones

Zones are created using several steps. The first step is to assign an alias to each port on each switch and to each node on the SAN. Assigning aliases makes the later steps of creating a zone much easier. Instead of having to recognize or enter the entire WWN of each switch port or node on the SAN, the SAN administrator can use a name that makes sense, such as "Switch1_Port1," "Elvis_HBA," or "Disk_Array1." Once these aliases have been created, a SAN administrator may create either a *hard* or *soft* zone. (The difference between hard and soft zones is covered in the next section.) Once a particular zone configuration has been created, it's pushed out to every switch in the SAN. The point at which all switches have the same configuration is referred to as the *point of convergence*.

Hard zones

A hard zone is created using the names of switch ports, just as a VLAN can be created using ports on a switch. Perhaps an example would help explain how a hard zone works. First, assume that you have a SAN consisting of three switches, as well as several hosts and disk arrays, and you want to create a zone consisting of the first port on each switch. You create aliases for each port (e.g., *Switch1_Port1, Switch2_Port1, Switch3_Port1*). Then you create a zone (e.g., *Hard1*) with these aliases as members. Any server or storage resource that connects to port 1 on any of these three switches is automatically placed in the *Hard1* zone.

Soft zones

A soft zone is created using a list of the WWNs of the HBAs on the servers or storage resources connected to the SAN, much like a VLAN that is created using a list of MAC addresses. The following example will help explain how a soft zone works. First, assume that you have a SAN consisting of many switches, as well as several hosts and disk arrays, and you want to create a zone consisting of two of the servers (e.g., *Elvis* and *Apollo*) and one disk array. You now create aliases for the two servers and the disk array (e.g., *Elvis_HBA1, Apollo_HBA2, Array1_Controller1*). Then you create a zone (e.g., *Soft1*) with these aliases as members. As long as this zone configuration is pushed out to all switches on the SAN, these two servers and the disk array can connect to any port on any switch, and they are automatically placed into the *Soft1* zone.

 One side effect of creating soft zones is that they are tied to the WWN. If you change or upgrade any of your HBAs, you need to update your soft-zone configuration.

Broadcast zones

A broadcast zone behaves similarly to a VLAN that is created using a protocol such as the AppleTalk VLAN discussed previously. Since Fibre Channel can carry both SCSI and IP traffic, you can create a zone that consists only of those HBAs that support (or wish to carry) IP traffic. However, unlike protocol-based VLANs that can automatically add a server to a VLAN if it's using a particular protocol, a broadcast zone is merely a functional classification. Current zoning technology doesn't support automatically adding a member to a zone based on its protocol. A broadcast zone is merely a soft zone that contains the HBAs that communicate with a particular protocol.

Naming your zones

Just as creating aliases for the ports on your switches and arrays helps you identify them, using an appropriate naming convention for your zones can help too. You should pick a name that reflects how the zones are being used. Two common naming conventions are called *server-centric* and *storage-centric*.

Server-centric
> If you've got a SAN that consists of many storage arrays connected to one server, the zone should be named after the server. This is referred to as a server-centric zone-naming convention.

Storage-centric
> If you've got one storage cabinet attached to many servers, name the zone after the storage cabinet. This is referred to as a storage-centric zone-naming convention.

LUN Masking

Although logical unit number (LUN) masking isn't technically a type of zoning, it does perform a similar function. It keeps different servers from seeing or using each other's storage on the SAN. However, before explaining how LUN masking and zoning are different, we must define LUN masking. And before we do that, we must first define a LUN.

A LUN is a logical representation of a physical unit of storage and may represent any of the following:

- Physical disk
- Physical tape drive
- Robotic control device
- Logical disk consisting of many physical disks striped together
- Logical disk consisting of two mirrored stripes

Each Fibre Channel storage array or tape library may have multiple ports that can be connected to the SAN, each with its own WWN. The array will also be configured to represent its storage as LUNs attached to these WWNs. Therefore, each array will appear to the hosts on the SAN as one or more LUNs attached to one or more WWNs.

LUN masking hides, or *masks*, LUNs so that each server sees only the LUNs you want it to see. LUN masking is actually performed at a level just above zoning. A zone grants or restricts access only to a given *port* on a storage array, but LUN masking can take that port and grant one server access to some of its LUNs and grant another server access to the rest of its LUNs.

Suppose you have a single-ported storage array with a number of disks, some of which you want to use on one host and some you want to use on a second host. In order for this to work, you need to create a zone that gives both servers access to the storage array. However, nothing prevents the first server from using the second server's disks, which is what LUN masking is for. LUN masking allows you to selectively present half the LUNs to the first server and half to the second server.

Depending on which vendors you use, LUN masking can be performed on one of three levels:

Storage array
> A storage array can be configured to present certain LUNs to certain hosts. One way this is done is through offsets. Suppose a storage array has a total of 100 LUNs. Connected to that storage array via a switch are five hosts, and you want each host to see 20 of the 100 LUNs. You configure the array so that LUNs 1 through 20 are displayed to the first server, LUNs 21 through 40 are displayed to the second server, and so on. The first server then sees LUNs 1 through 20 and doesn't see LUNs 21 through 100; they have been masked from its view.

Intelligent bridges and routers
> If you use a storage array that doesn't support LUN masking, another way to accomplish it is to place an intelligent bridge or router between the servers and the storage. Then follow steps similar to the ones just described.

HBA drivers
> LUN masking performed on the HBA level places the responsibility for masking the undesirable LUNs on the HBA driver itself. Although the HBA can see all the LUNs available on the SAN, you configure the driver to mask the LUNs you don't want it to see. Once this has been done, the driver presents to the operating system only the LUNs you want it to see.

Designing Your SAN for Availability

One issue with traditional parallel SCSI that can be solved by SANs is that of having a single point of failure. Everyone knows that the failure of a single SCSI card, cable, or terminator can render your parallel-based SCSI devices useless. With SANs, you can use multiple paths to ensure that no single device can do this. However, many people design their SANs just as they design their parallel based SCSI systems—one path to each device. Consider the SAN depicted in Figure 3-3.

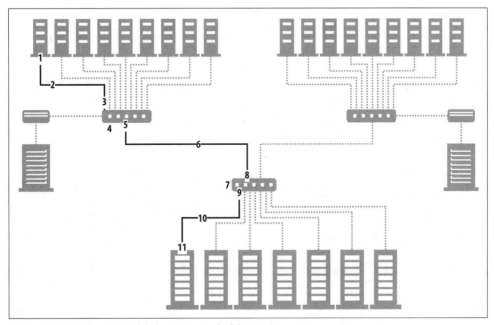

Figure 3-3. Single points of failure in a single fabric

In the figure, each server has only one path to each storage array and tape library. Each path has at least 11 single points of failure, as shown by the numbered arrows:

1. The server's HBA
2. The Fibre Channel conductor from the server to the first switch
3. The incoming GBIC on the first switch
4. The first switch
5. The outgoing GBIC on the first switch
6. The Fibre Channel conductor from the first switch to the second switch
7. The second switch
8. The incoming GBIC on the second switch
9. The outgoing GBIC on the second switch
10. The Fibre Channel conductor from the second switch to the storage array
11. The controller on the storage array

Besides having 11 single points of failure, there are several pieces of equipment that need preventative maintenance at various times, such as firmware upgrades, driver updates, and hardware replacement. The only way to do any of these things is to take down at least one system's storage. If the piece of equipment that needs maintenance is one of the switches, then several systems will be without storage during the upgrade.

You can create a SAN that has no single points of failure and can be maintained without a service interruption by designing a SAN that looks more like the one in Figure 3-4. You can see that every server has two completely separate paths to each storage resource, as depicted by Path A and Path B for the server on the left side of the drawing. If any piece of equipment along Path A fails or needs preventative maintenance, Path B will take over immediately until that piece of equipment is returned to full functionality.

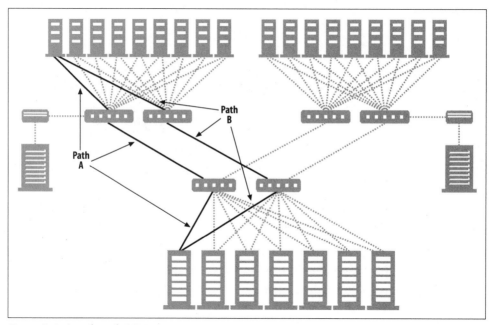

Figure 3-4. A multipath SAN

Multipathing

Once you've designed a SAN with multiple paths, you need some type of software that understands you have multiple paths and knows how to use them. The reason for this is that deep inside every SAN is the SCSI protocol, and SCSI was never designed with multiple paths in mind. This means you need a piece of software to sit between the SAN and the operating system and present only one path to the operating system at any one time. This is the job of multipathing software, and there are dozens of such products now on the market. Here are a few examples in alphabetical vendor order:

- Compaq's Secure Path
- EMC's Power Path
- Solaris 8 has native multipathing support
- Veritas' Volume Manager has multipathing support
- Vicom's Storage Virtualization Engine

Multipathing software actually performs two functions: automatic failover and load balancing.

Automatic failover

Perhaps the most important job for multipathing software is to automatically redistribute I/O to another channel in the case of fabric failure. This should be done in such a way that the operating system never realizes there was an interruption in service. This, of course, needs to be done within the limits of a SCSI timeout.

Load balancing

The second important job multipathing software performs is dynamic load balancing. Many administrators perform this task manually using *static* load balancing. That is, they take an inventory of the various paths a particular server has to its SAN-attached disks and then use the different names of the disks to balance the load between the various paths. Dynamic load balancing, however, can be done only with multipathing software, because such software sends a given stream of data down the least-used path. This allows you to fully utilize all paths when the SAN is completely functional. Then, of course, if a given path becomes nonfunctional, there is simply one less path for the load balancing software to use.

Preventing thrashing

What happens when a given path goes up and down multiple times? Without some type of antithrashing setup, multipathing software might just go a little crazy. There are a few different ways to keep the system from thrashing in this manner. The first is to configure the software to reenable a previously failed link only after a certain amount of time. If the link goes back down while the software is waiting to reenable it, the clock starts over again. Another common method is to set up the SAN in such a way that a failed link must be reenabled by an administrator after she is convinced that link is healthy again.

Persistent Binding

Once zones and LUN masking have been set up, each server should see its storage—and only its storage. Once this has been done, one initial setup task remains. It's already been mentioned that one of the issues with SANs is that servers can sometimes change the SCSI address of a particular unit of SAN-based storage. This is particularly true if the configuration of the SAN changes between reboots. Again, this is caused by the assumptions the SCSI drivers make about targets they see.

The upper levels of all device drivers used in a SAN environment are designed for SCSI. The SCSI I/O model assumes a small number of targets on a single bus and a small number of LUNs on each target. In order for SCSI addresses to remain permanent, they need to be bound to an address that doesn't change.

As discussed in Chapter 2, when a device logs into a fabric, it's also assigned a source ID (S_ID) by the fabric switch. When a device connects to an arbitrated loop, it selects an arbitrated loop physical address (AL_PA) during the initialization process. The S_ID and AL_PA are similar to IP addresses in a DHCP environment. They are dynamic, and so therefore shouldn't be used to generate SCSI addresses.

The unchanging target address of a SAN-based storage device is the 64-bit WWN. Similar to the MAC address with Ethernet devices, the WWN is a permanent number assigned to each port on a storage array or an HBA on a server. However, as mentioned previously, a SAN-connected RAID array may have hundreds of disks that need to be individually addressed by servers. Therefore, the RAID controller creates LUNs for each device. Each LUN has a corresponding WWN assigned, which is a subset of the master WWN assigned to the RAID controller. These LUNs are used by the operating system as a SCSI address and mask the underlying use of RAID technology.

Binding is the process of associating the operating system's controller, target, and LUN value to the WWN of the LUN created on the RAID array controller. Binding takes place on the device driver level; the unique WWN value is *bound* to an operating-system controller-target value. When this bind is persistent from boot to boot and across hardware changes and failures in the SAN, it's called a *persistent bind*. To establish a persistent bind, the driver must save this association in nonvolatile memory or a configuration file.

Ongoing Maintenance

Once the SAN is installed, configured, and doing what you designed it to do, things get much better. Even so, there's still plenty of work to be done. The rest of the work involves managing, monitoring, and maintaining the storage.

Managing (Storage Resource Management)

Few SANs live on using their initial design. Even the one shown in Figure 3-4 can be outgrown with time. At some point, someone will want to change the SAN in order to:

Increase or decrease the number of servers

If a SAN is successful, it becomes popular. Everybody wants to put their storage on the SAN. This results in more HBAs, more ports, and more switches. Another common occurrence in SANs is no different than parallel based SCSI: somebody gets the bright idea of consolidating servers. This, of course, changes the design of the SAN.

Increase or decrease the number of storage arrays

Whether you're adding more servers to the SAN or not, the need for additional storage capacity will inevitably drive you to purchase more storage. Will you buy additional storage arrays of the size you are using, or will you look at larger, more centralized storage arrays? Even if you don't grow your storage dramatically, what about centralizing all your storage into one or more large storage arrays anyway? What affect will these changes have on the number of ports and switches required for your SAN?

Increase or decrease the number of switches, hubs, or routers

This change, of course, is driven by the previous two changes. Whether you increase or decrease the number of servers or storage arrays, it will change the number of ports that you need. Will you buy additional switches and use inter-switch links, or ISLs? As you gain experience with your SAN, you will probably also want to increase its level of availability. What about purchasing a director class switch? What does the SAN look like now that you've changed it?

You will find yourself asking such questions as you spend more time with your SAN. The process of asking and answering these questions is now referred to as *storage resource management* (SRM), and there are a number of SRM products now on the market. Due to the volatility of this market, I don't list the vendors here, but an updated list of SRM products is available at *http://www.storagemountain.com*. However, here's a list of features that are beginning to be typical with SRM products:

Automatic discovery

Instead of having to enter the hundreds of devices that reside on your SAN, these products can automatically query what devices exist on your SAN. This is an incredible time saver!

Graphical and command line interfaces

Although being able to view the SAN graphically is one of the best features of SRM products, it's also helpful to be able to administer things via the command line. Many of the products allow you to use all their features via a command line or graphical interface.

Status reporting

> As will be mentioned in the next section, your SAN must be monitored. Most SRM products incorporate in-band monitoring into their products, allowing you to monitor the status of the devices on your SAN as well as configure them.

SAN visualization

> Once the SRM product has discovered all the devices on your SAN and checked their status, it can show you a network map of all the devices, with each device type having an icon of a different color and shape. These drawings resemble the network diagrams network administrators have grown used to in LAN-based products.

Storage allocation

> Many of these products can create and modify zones and create and modify LUN masking properties, allowing you to administer these attributes from a single source. Often they allow you to do this even on heterogeneous hardware.

Storage array configuration (virtualization)

> Some products have worked with the various storage array vendors, and they are able to create RAID volumes of various levels on the storage arrays in the SAN from a central point.

Relatively speaking, the storage resource management industry is in its infancy. As mentioned previously, there are a lot of vendors vying for this open market. However, SANs will have fully arrived only when these products are mature.

Monitoring

Including redundant paths and using multiple levels of RAID keeps a single component failure from causing you any severe grief, but if you don't monitor your SAN, you'll never know the component failed and won't be able to replace it before the next component fails.

This attribute of ongoing maintenance has already been mentioned in the previous section, and the easiest way to monitor a SAN is to purchase and install an SRM product. What if you don't have the budget yet? The easiest answer is to build your own out-of-band management system using SNMP.

Almost all switches and storage arrays include an Ethernet port you can plug into your LAN or into a dedicated LAN for reporting purposes. You can then monitor them passively or actively. A passive monitoring system waits for the switch or array to notify you of a failure via an SNMP trap. An active monitoring system involves creating your own monitoring application that issues SNMP queries against your switches and arrays.

LAN administrators and enterprise management applications can come in handy here. They are used to this kind of monitoring and can assist you in entering the SNMP world, especially if you aren't that familiar with it.

Maintenance

No matter how good your equipment is, you will need to perform maintenance on it. This maintenance can take various forms:

Hardware failures

Every disk drive, switch, hub, HBA, cable, or RAID controller fails at some time. Your best defense against this is to monitor your SAN.

Software/firmware failure

All new software and firmware should be tested in a development area prior to going into production. If that isn't possible, make sure your vendor provides you with a backup and restore procedure for your system should it fail due to software or firmware.

 Be very sure of your SRM software company. Depending on how it's implemented, SRM software could become a single point of failure in your SAN.

Software/firmware upgrades

Over time, you will need to upgrade your SRM software, the firmware on your switch, or the drivers on your HBAs. The best defense against this is dual pathing, as discussed in the availability section.

Hardware upgrades

At some point, you will want a bigger switch, a different HBA, or a faster disk drive. Again, the best way to make maintenance of this nature a nonevent is to have redundant paths.

Using SANs to Maximize Your Storage

Although they do create additional management issues, SANS can allow you to maximize your investment in both online (disk) and offline (tape and optical) storage.

When speaking rather broadly, there are essentially three things the SAN in Figure 3-5 makes possible:

- Online storage maximization
- Offline storage maximization
- Truly highly available systems

Online storage maximization allows you to create a pool of disk systems that can be allocated to the servers that need them—as well as many other things. Because a SAN allows for multiple servers to access multiple physical disks via multiple physical paths, it also allows for truly highly available systems. Offline storage

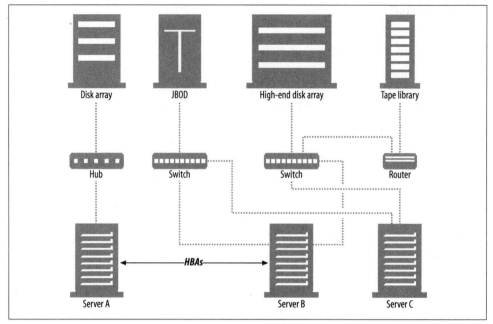

Figure 3-5. Elements of a SAN

maximization means being able to configure your backup and recovery system in ways that you were never able to do before.

Online Storage Maximization

Many large data centers have thousands of discrete disks between all of their servers. There are a lot of disadvantages to this that can be overcome by SANs.

When one disk fails, the server often has to be taken down in order to repair it. While this can be solved by buying RAID arrays with hot-swappable disks and at least one hot spare for each array, allocating a hot spare for each array can be expensive. Also, if the hot spare has already been used and not been replaced, you can't automatically use the spare from one server to fix a bad drive in another server. You wouldn't even want to do this manually, since doing so degrades the integrity of the server you borrowed the drive from.

Consider aging or decrepit disk drives. I remember one client that had an entire set of servers that could not afford down time. Behind these servers were disk drives with a known problem that wasn't discovered until the servers had been in production for a long time. They would occasionally leak swag oil on the disk, rendering it useless. The vendor was offering free replacements, but doing so took over a year due to the downtime and hassle required to make the swap. Although this is similar to the last problem, it's slightly different. Using discrete disks doesn't easily allow for preventive replacement of drives you know are old or potentially faulty.

Another manageability issue is space allocation. It's common to have one server starving for disk space, while another has disks to spare. I know of one large data center where they had individual servers that were out of space, but the entire data center was actually only using 10% of its total capacity. They had over 40 TB of available spinning disk, but couldn't allocate a single disk to the servers that needed them—because doing so required physically moving the disk from one server to another—and downtime for both servers.

Putting your disks behind a SAN can solve all three problems—and many others just like them. Consider the first two problems. One way to solve them is to put all your storage on a rather large storage array behind the SAN. This array can have redundant power supplies, paths, and disks. This array can also contain a small common pool of hot spare disks. This arrangement requires far fewer disks than having a hot spare for each system. When any disk in the array fails, it can be automatically replaced by the storage array, and the array notifies you to replace the bad drive. The bad drive can then be replaced online. This is the "hardware" solution and is the most tested method for solving those problems. You don't have to have an expensive array, though; simply place your JBOD disk behind your SAN, and use enterprise volume management software to fix these issues. (This would be a "software solution.)

Either solution also makes proactive maintenance much easier. You simply buy the new disk, connect it to the array (or the SAN), and use the appropriate volume manager to make the new disks active and the old disks inactive. The old or failing disks can then be moved out of service.

Perhaps the greatest benefit of consolidating your storage behind a SAN is dynamic space allocation. Just as tape drives can be allocated to the servers that need them, disk drives need be allocated only to the servers that need more storage. If you find that you've allocated too much storage for a given server, simply deallocate that storage from that server, and return it to the pool of storage that is available for servers that need it. If a given server is out of storage, and you don't have any more disk available in the spare storage pool, you can just buy more disk, attach it to the SAN, and voila! Buying disks this way also allows you to buy bigger arrays that are cheaper per GB. If you were using discrete disks and only need 10 GB, you might be able to justify a 20-GB array, but not a 200-GB array, which would be much cheaper per GB. Someone will ask you to prove that the server will soon need 200 GB. However, if you were putting that 200 GB behind the SAN, allowing any server to use it when it needs it, you can do just that. It's much easier to justify that the entire data center will soon need 200 new gigabytes of disk.

Is This for Real?

It should be noted that the concept of online storage consolidation and maximization is perhaps the most oversold feature of SANs. The degree to which you can take advantage of the features mentioned earlier depends on the number and type of platforms you are running. Each platform brings with it unique challenges, so the chances of having problems with your configuration increase with the number of different platforms you're running.

Once you've gotten each host to see each disk you want it to see, now what? Another real challenge with online storage maximization is the idea of managing all these disks in a completely new way. Putting the disks on a SAN may increase the number of things you can do with them, but it also creates a whole new layer of management. Ask yourself questions like these:

- How are you going to keep track of all those disks?
- How will you know which disks are failing or are about to fail?
- How will you replace the disks when they fail?
- How are you going to manage the volumes and filesystems on those disks?
- How will you handle the operating systems that want to lay claim to every disk they can see?

Probably the most common answer to all these questions has been to purchase large, enterprise-class storage arrays, like those from Compaq, EMC, Hitachi, and IBM. Such vendors have made sure their arrays can communicate with a number of platforms and already have software to handle these management issues.

This isn't to say you can't take advantage of these features without such an array. You will probably save yourself quite a bit of money if you do. There are dozens of new hardware and software vendors that can help you do this, but you'll probably need to do a little more homework.

Offline Storage Maximization

In the upper right corner of Figure 3-5 you can see a tape library connected to the SAN via a SAN router. Assume there is a zone that contains the tape library and the three servers. Server A, Server B, and Server C will all see each tape drive in that tape library as if it were physically attached via a standard parallel SCSI cable. In this configuration, the robotic device is also connected to one of the SCSI buses on the back of the SAN router, which makes the robotic device visible to all three servers. Each server can then build device files just as they would for a parallel SCSI-attached tape drive or robotic device.

This configuration allows each server to attempt to control of both the robotics and the tape drives! If you allow each server to attempt control them independently, chaos would result. This is where the robot and drive sharing software from your backup software vendor comes into play. It acts as a traffic cop, allocating tape drives to the servers that need them. This is referred to as *LAN-free* backups.

LAN-free backups allow each server connected to the SAN to back up its entire dataset directly to its own tape drive. It can do this without transferring the data via the LAN and without forcing the administrator to allocate one or more tape drives to its exclusive use.

LAN-free backups allow you to maximize the return on your investment in tape libraries. Instead of being forced to buy many smaller libraries and connect a few drives to each server, you can buy one or two really large tape libraries and dynamically allocate the tape drives to the servers that need them. What a savings! By buying two libraries and connecting them both to the SAN, you also increase the availability of tape drives to all servers. In the pre-SAN days, a given media server could rely only on the tape library that was physically attached to it. Now, every time you buy a new library, you can add a new level of availability to your backup system, because every server can use every library.

More details on LAN-free backups are provided in Chapter 4.

Online and Offline Storage Maximization Combined

If you move some of your online storage onto the SAN, you get more ways to maximize your offline storage. Consider the storage array in Figure 3-5. With proper zoning, it's visible to all three servers. What if you could make a copy of Server A's data and make it visible to Server B? This allows Server B to back up Server A's data without creating any load on Server A. What if you had dozens of servers you wanted to back up this way? If you can make a copy of each dataset available on the SAN, you can have one server dedicated to backing them up. That allows you to back up terabytes of data without impacting the servers using that data. This book refers to this type of backup as a *client-free backup,*[*] because the backup data doesn't travel through the backup client that's using it. Such backups are being done today in data centers across the country.

There is also a relatively new technology that allows you to send the data directly from disk to tape without going through any CPU. This technology is called *extended copy*, or *third-party copy*, and backups performed in this manner are referred to as *server-free backups*, since the data path moves directly from disk to tape without going through any servers.

---

[*] There are many terms for this type of backup. I prefer this one, for reasons that are covered in Chapter 4.

Because many people feel that LAN-free, client-free, and server-free backups represent the best ways to take immediate advantage of SAN technology today, each is covered in detail in Chapter 4.

Truly Highly Available Systems

Another area that has benefited quite a bit from the advent of SANs has been highly available (HA) systems. Since SANs allow for multiple paths from multiple servers to multiple physical devices, it's much easier to build a truly HA system using SANs.

Consider Server B and Server C from Figure 3-5. You can see that both have an independent path to the right two switches. Each switch also has an independent path to the two disk arrays. If you used an enterprise volume manager and a high-availability application, you can mirror the two disk arrays and mirror the application on both servers, and there would be no single point of failure in the system. This model can be expanded to clusters of many systems, all sharing a common function.

Clustered systems present a unique challenge to backup and recovery systems. Different people take different tactics to meet these challenges. The first is to back up both nodes as clients. The upside to this is that everything is backed up. The downside is that you back up the shared data twice. (Actually, you back it up as many times as you have nodes in the cluster.) The other tactic is to back up only the cluster entity. The downside to this is that you might not back up some of the operating-system configuration files on the individual nodes. The upside, of course, is that you only back up shared data once.

The true difficulty with any method of backing up a cluster is when the cluster supports individual application failover. Such clustering software allows each application to failover from one node to another, without affecting other applications. The upside to this is that you can load balance applications across multiple nodes in the cluster. The difficulty lies in knowing which node of the cluster has the active Oracle database. Here's what happens:

1. You attempt to back up the entity known as *clustera*.
2. The backup application logs into *clustera*, but in reality, it's actually logged into *nodea* or *nodeb*.
3. Either *nodea* or *nodeb* is actually running Oracle. The other node can see the Oracle database files but can't put the database in backup mode.
4. Your job is to figure out which node the application is actually running on, and then *rsh/ssh* to that system to put the database into backup mode.

   As you can see, clusters present a unique challenge to the backup and recovery folks! Although the topic of HA is an important one, it's beyond the scope of this book.

Summary

Don't assume that the SAN will manage itself, and you'll be doing better than most! Besides having a good initial design and implementation of your SAN, the best thing you can do to make life in your SAN-box better is to evaluate and select a good storage resource management product, then test it over and over before you put it in production. Also, having a SAN can also allow you to do some really wonderful things, including online and offline storage management and truly highly available systems.

SAN Backup and Recovery

Overview

A SAN typically consists of multiple servers, online storage (disk), and offline storage (tape or optical), all of which are connected to a Fibre Channel switch or hub—usually a switch. You can see all these SAN elements in Figure 4-1. Once the three servers in Figure 4-1 are connected to the SAN, each server in the SAN can be granted full read/write access to any disk or tape drive within the SAN. This allows for *LAN-free*, *client-free*, and *server-free* backups, each represented by a different-numbered arrow in Figure 4-1.

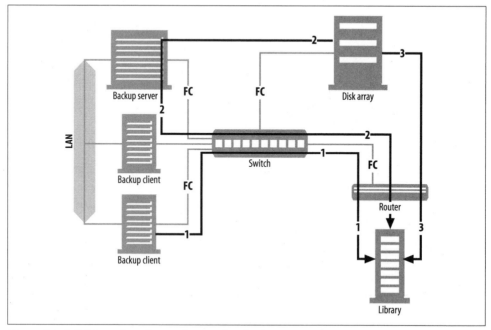

Figure 4-1. LAN-free, client-free, and server-free backups

Pretty much anything said in this chapter about Fibre Channel-based SANs will soon be true about iSCSI-based SANs. To visualize how an iSCSI SAN fits into the pictures and explanations in this chapter, simply replace the Fibre Channel HBAs with iSCSI-capable NICs, and the Fibre Channel switches and hubs with Ethernet switches and hubs, and you've got yourself an iSCSI-based SAN that works essentially like the Fibre Channel-based SANs discussed in this chapter. The difficulty will be in getting the storage array, library, and software vendors to support it.

LAN-free backups

LAN-free backups occur when several servers share a single tape library. Each server connected to the SAN can back up to tape drives it believes are locally attached. The data is transferred via the SAN using the SCSI-3 protocol, and thus doesn't use the LAN.* All that is needed is software that will act as a "traffic cop." LAN-free backups are represented in Figure 4-1 by arrow number 1, which shows a data path starting at the backup client, traveling through the SAN switch and router, finally arriving at the shared tape library.

Client-free backups

Although an individual computer is often called a server, it's referred to by the backup system as a *client*. If a client has its disk storage on the SAN, and that storage can create a mirror that can be split off and made visible to the backup server, that client's data can be backed up via the backup server; the data never travels via the backup client. Thus, this is called *client-free* backup. Client-free backups are represented in Figure 4-1 by arrow number 2, which shows a data path starting at the disk array, traveling through the backup server, followed by the SAN switch and router, finally arriving at the shared tape library. The backup path is similar to LAN-free backups, except that the backup server isn't backing up its own data. It's backing up data from another client whose disk drives happen to reside on the SAN. Since the data path doesn't include the client that is using the data, this is referred to as client-free backups.

To my knowledge, I am the first to use the term *client-free* backups. Some backup software vendors refer to this as server-free backups, and others simply refer to it by their product name for it. I felt that a generic term was needed, and I believe that this helps distinguish this type of backups from server-free backups, which are defined next.

---

* This term may be changed in the near future, since iSCSI-based SANs will, of course, use the LAN. But if you create a separate LAN for iSCSI, as many experts are recommending, the backups will not use your production LAN. Therefore, the principle remains the same, and only the implementation changes.

Server-free backups

If the SAN to which the disk storage is connected supports a SCSI feature called *extended copy*, the data can be sent directly from disk to tape, without going through a server. There are also other, more proprietary, methods for doing this that don't involve the *extended copy* command. This is the newest area of backup and recovery functionality being added to SANs. Server-free backups are represented in Figure 4-1 by arrow number 3, which shows a data path starting at the disk array, traveling through the SAN switch and router, and arriving at the shared tape library. You will notice that the data path doesn't include a server of any kind. This is why it's called *server-free* backups.

 No backup is completely LAN-free, client-free, or server-free. The backup server is always communicating with the backup client in some way, even if it's just to get the metadata about the backup. What these terms are meant to illustrate is that the bulk of the data is transferred without using the LAN (LAN-free), the backup client (client-free), or the backup server (server-free).

Client-Free or Server-Free?

I am well aware that some vendors refer to client-free backups as server-free backups. I find their designation confusing, and I'm hoping that my term *client-free backups* will catch on. The reason that they refer to client-free backups as server-free is that the backup world turns things around. What you refer to as a server, the backup system refers to as a client. Although you consider it a server, it's a client of the backup and recovery system. When it comes to the backup and recovery system, the server is the system that is controlling all of the backups. I am trying to keep things consistent by referring to backups that don't go through a client (but do go through the backup server) as client-free backups. In order for me to call something server-free, the data path must not include any server of any kind. The only backup like that is an extended copy backup as described in the previous section. Therefore, I refer only to extended copy backups as server-free backups. That's my story and I'm sticking to it.

LAN-Free Backups

As discussed in Chapter 1, LAN-free backups allow you to use a SAN to share one of the most expensive components of your backup and recovery system—your tape or optical library and the drives within it. Figure 4-2 shows how this is simply the latest evolution of centralized backups. There was a time when most backups were done to locally attached tape drives. This method worked fine when data centers were small, and each server could fit on a single tape. Once the management of dozens (or even hundreds) of individual tapes became too much or when servers would no longer fit on a tape, data centers started using backup software that allowed them to use a central backup server and back up their servers across the LAN. (The servers are now referred to by the backup system as clients.)

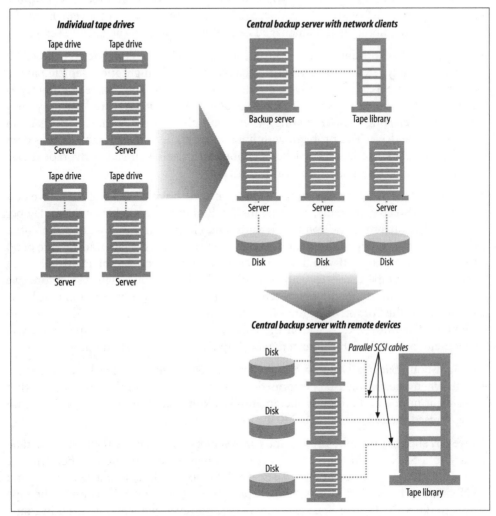

Figure 4-2. The evolution of backup methodologies

This methodology works great as long as you have a LAN that can support the amount of network traffic such backups generate. Even if you have a state-of-the-art LAN, you may find individual backup clients that are too big to back up across the LAN. Also, increasingly large amounts of system resources are required on the backup server and clients to back up large amounts of data across the LAN. Luckily, backup software companies saw this coming and added support for remote devices. This meant that you could again decentralize your backups by placing tape drives on each backup client. Each client would then be told when and what to back up by the central backup server, but the data would be transferred to a locally attached tape drive. Most major software vendors also allowed this to be done within a tape library. As depicted in Figure 4-2, you can connect one or more tape drives from a tape library to each backup client that needs them. The physical movement of the media within the library is then managed centrally—usually by the backup server.

Although the backup data at the bottom of Figure 4-2 isn't going across the LAN, this isn't typically referred to as LAN-free backups. The configuration depicted at the bottom of Figure 4-2 is normally referred to as *library sharing*, since the library is being shared, but the drives aren't. When people talk about LAN-free backups, they are typically referring to *drive sharing*, where multiple hosts have shared access to an individual tape drive. The problem with library sharing is that each tape drive is dedicated to the backup client to which it's connected.* The result is that the tape drives in a shared library go unused most of the time.

As an example, assume we have three large servers, each with 1.5 TB of data. Five percent of this data changes daily, resulting in 75 GB of incremental backups per day per host.† All backups must be completed within an eight-hour window, and the entire host must be backed up within that window, requiring an aggregate transfer rate of 54 MB/s‡ for full backups. If you assume each tape drive is capable of 15 MB/s,§ each host needs four tape drives to complete its full backup in one night. Therefore, we need to connect four tape drives to each server, resulting in a configuration that looks like the one at the bottom of Figure 4-2. While this configuration allows the servers to complete their full backups within the backup window, that many tape drives will allow them to complete the incremental backup (75 GB) in just 20 minutes!

An eight-hour backup window each night results in 240 possible hours during a month when backups can be performed. However, with a monthly full backup that takes eight hours, and a nightly incremental backup that takes 20 minutes, they are going unused for 228 out of their 240 available hours.

However, suppose we take these same three servers and connect them and the tape library to a SAN as illustrated in Figure 4-3. When we do so, the numbers change drastically. As you can see in Figure 4-3, we'll connect each host to a switched fabric SAN via a single 100-MB Fibre Channel connection. Next, we must connect the tape drives to the SAN. (For reasons explained later, however, we will only need five tape

---

* As mentioned later in this chapter, SCSI devices can be connected to more than one host, but it can be troublesome.

† This is actually a high rate of change, but it helps prove the point. Even with a rate of change this high, the drives still go unused the majority of the time.

‡ 1.575 TB ÷ 8 hours ÷ 60 minutes ÷ 60 seconds = 54.6 MB/s

§ There are several tape drives capable of these backup speeds, including AIT-3, LTO, Mammoth, Super DLT, 3590, 9840, and DTF.

drives to meet the requirements discussed earlier.) If the tape drives supported Fibre Channel natively, we can just connect them to the SAN via the switch. If the tape drives can connect only via standard parallel SCSI cables, we can connect the five tape drives to the SAN via a Fibre Channel router, as can be seen in Figure 4-3. The routers that are shipping as of this writing can connect one to six SCSI buses to one or two Fibre Channel connections. For this example, we will use a four-to-one model allowing us to connect our five tape drives to the SAN via a single Fibre Channel connection. (As is common in such configurations, two of the drives will be sharing one of the SCSI buses.)

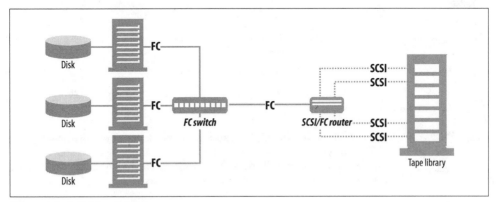

Figure 4-3. LAN-free backups

With this configuration, we can easily back up the three hosts discussed previously. The reason that we only need only five tape drives is that in the configuration shown in Figure 4-3, we can use dynamic drive sharing software provided by any of the major backup software companies. This software performs the job of dynamically assigning tape drives to the hosts that need them. When it's time for a given host's full backup, it is assigned four of the five drives. The hosts that aren't performing a full backup will share the fifth tape drive. By sharing the tape drives in this manner, we could actually backup 25 hosts this size. Let's take a look at some math to see how this is possible.

Assume we have 25 hosts, each with 1.5 TB of data. (Of course, all 25 hosts need to be connected to the SAN.) With four of the five tape drives, we can perform an eight-hour full backup of a different host each night, resulting in a full backup for each server once a month. With the fifth drive, we can perform a 20-minute incremental backup of the 24 other hosts within the same eight-hour window.* If this was done with directly connected SCSI, it would require connecting four drives to each host, for a total of 100 tape drives! This, of course, would require a really huge library. In

---

* 20 minutes × 24 hosts = 480 minutes, or 8 hours

fact, as of this writing, there are few libraries available that can hold that many tape drives. Table 4-1 illustrates the difference in the price of these two solutions.

Table 4-1. 25-host LAN-free backup solution

	Parallel SCSI solution		SAN solution	
	Quantity	Total	Quantity	Total
Tape drives	100	$900K	5	$45K
HBAs	25	$25K	25	$50K
Switch	None		2	$70K
Router	None		1	$7K
Device server software	Same		Same	
Tape library	Same		Same	
Total		$925K		$172K

 Whether or not a monthly full backup makes sense for your environment is up to you. Unless circumstances require otherwise, I personally prefer a monthly full backup, nightly incremental backups, followed by weekly cumulative incremental backups.

Each solution requires some sort of HBA on each client. Since Fibre Channel HBAs are more expensive, we will use a price of $2,000 for the Fibre Channel HBAs, and $1,000 for the SCSI HBAs.* We will even assume you can obtain SCSI HBAs that have two SCSI buses per card. The SCSI solution requires 100 tape drives, and the SAN solution requires five tape drives. (We will use UHrium LTO drives for this example, which have a native transfer speed of 15 MB/s and a discounted price of $9,000.) Since the library needs to store at least one copy of each full backup and 30 copies of each incremental backup from 25 1.5-TB hosts, this is probably going to be a really large library. To keep things as simple as we can, let's assume the tape library for both solutions is the same size and the same cost. (In reality, the SCSI library would have to be much larger and more expensive.) For the SAN solution, we need to buy two 16-port switches, and one four-to-one SAN router. Each solution requires purchasing device server licenses from your backup software vendor for each of the 25 hosts, so this will cost the same for each solution. (The SAN solution licenses might cost slightly more than the SCSI solution licenses.) As you can see in Table 4-1, there is a $700,000 difference in the cost of these two solutions.

What about the original requirements above, you ask? What if you only need to back up three large hosts? A three-host SAN solution requires the purchase of a much

---

* These are Unix prices. Obviously, Windows-based cards cost much less.

smaller switch and only one router. It requires 12 tape drives for the SCSI solution but only five for the SAN solution. As you can see in Table 4-2, even with these numbers, the SAN solution is over $40,000 cheaper than the SCSI solution.

Table 4-2. Three-host LAN-free backup solution

	Parallel SCSI solution		SAN solution	
	Quantity	Total	Quantity	Total
Tape drives	12	$108K	5	$45K
HBAs	3	$3K	3	$6K
Switch	None		1	$8K
Router	None		1	$7K
Device server software	Same		Same	
Tape library	Same		Same	
Total		$111K		$66K

How Does This Work?

The data in the previous section shows that sharing tape drives between servers can be a Good Thing. But how can multiple servers share the same physical tape drive? This is accomplished in one of two ways. Either the vendor uses the SCSI *reserve* and *release* commands, or they implement their own queuing system.

SCSI reserve/release

Tape drives aren't the first peripherals that needed to be shared between two or more computers. In fact, many pre-SAN high availability systems were based on disk drives that were connected to multiple systems via standard, parallel SCSI. (This is referred to as a multiple-initiator system.) In order to make this possible, the commands *reserve* and *release* were added to the SCSI-2 specification. The following is a description of how they were intended to work.

Each system that wants to access a particular device issues the SCSI *reserve* command. If no other device has previously reserved the device, the system is granted access to the device. If another system has already reserved the device, the application requesting the device is given a *resolution conflict* message. Once a reservation is granted, it remains valid until one of the following things happen:

- The same initiator (SCSI HBA) requests another reservation of the same device.
- The same initiator issues a SCSI release command for the reserved device.
- A SCSI bus reset, a hard reset, or a power cycle occurs.

If you combine the idea of the SCSI reserve command with a SCSI bus that is connected to more than one initiator (host HBA), you get a configuration where multiple hosts can share the same device by simply reserving it prior to using it. This device can be a disk drive, tape drive, or SCSI-controlled robotic arm of a tape library. The following is an example of how the configuration works.

Each host that needs to put a tape into a drive attempts to reserve the use of the robotic arm with the SCSI *reserve* command. If it's given a *resolution conflict* message, it waits a predetermined period of time and tries again until it successfully reserves it. If it's granted a reservation to the robotic arm, it then attempts to reserve a tape drive using the SCSI *reserve* command. If it's given a *resolution conflict* message while attempting to reserve the first drive in the library, it continues trying to reserve each drive until it either successfully reserves one or is given a *resolution conflict* message for each one. If this happens, it issues a SCSI *release* command for the robotic arm and then waits a predetermined period of time and tries again. It continues to do this until it successfully puts a tape into a reserved drive. Once done, it can then back up to the drive via the SAN.

This description is how the designers *intended* it to work. However, shared drive systems that use the SCSI reserve/release method run into a number of issues, so many people consider the SCSI reserve/release command set to be fundamentally flawed. For example, one such flaw is that a SCSI bus reset releases the reservation. Since SCSI bus resets happen under a number of conditions, including system reboots, it's highly possible to completely confuse your reservation system with the reboot of only one server connected to the shared device. Another issue with the SCSI reserve/release method is that not all platforms support it. Therefore, a shared drive system that uses the SCSI reserve/release method is limited to the platforms on which these commands are supported.

Third-party queuing system

Most backup software vendors use the third-party queuing method for shared devices. When I think of how this works, I think my two small daughters. Their method of toy sharing is a lot like the SCSI reserve/release method. Whoever gets the toy first gets it as long as she wants it. However, as soon as one of them has one toy, the other one wants it. The one who wants the toy continually asks the other one for it. However, the one that already has the toy issues a resolution conflict message. (It sounds like, "Mine!") The one that wants the toy is usually persistent enough, however, that Mom or Dad have to intervene. Not very elegant, is it?

A third-party queuing system is like having Daddy sit between the children and the toys, where each child has full knowledge of what toys are available, but the only way they can get a toy is to ask Daddy for it. If the toy is in use, Daddy simply says, "You can't have that toy right now. Choose another." Then once the child asks for a toy that's not being used, Daddy hands it over. When the child is done with the toy, Daddy returns it to the toy bin.

There are two main differences between the SCSI reserve/release method and the third-party queuing method:

Reservation attempts are made to a third-party application

In the SCSI reserve/release method, the application that wants a drive has no one to ask if the drive is already busy—other than the drive itself. If the drive is busy, it simply gets a *resolution conflict* message, and there is no queuing of requests. Suppose for example, that Hosts 1, 2, and 3 are sharing a drive. Host 1 requests for and is issued a reservation for the drive and begins using it. Host 2 then attempts to reserve the drive and is given a resolution conflict message. Host 3 then attempts to reserve the drive and is also given a resolution conflict message. Host 2 then waits the predetermined period of time and requests the drive again, but it's still being used. However, as soon as it's given a resolution conflict message, the drive becomes available. Assuming that Host 2 and Host 3's waiting time is the same, Host 3 will ask for the drive next, and is granted a reservation. This happens despite the fact that it's actually Host 2's "turn" to use the drive, since it asked for the drive first.

However, consider a third-party queuing system. In the example, Host2 would have asked a third-party application if the drive was available. It would have been told to wait and would be placed in a queue for the drive. Instead of having to continually poll the drive for availability, it's simply notified of the drive's availability by the third-party application. The third-party queueing system can also place multiple requests into a queue, keeping track of which host asked for a drive first. The hosts are then given permission to use the drive in the order the requests were received.

Tape movement is accomplished by the third party

Another major difference between third-party queuing systems and the SCSI reserve/release method is that, while the hosts do share the tape library, they don't typically share the robotic arm. When a host requests a tape and a tape drive, the third-party application grants the request (if a tape and drive are available) and issues the robotic request to one host dedicated as the robotic control host.*

Levels of Drive Sharing

In addition to accomplishing drive sharing via different methods, backup software companies also differ in how they allow libraries and their drives to be shared. In order to understand what I mean, I must explain a few terms. A main server is the

---

* Although it's possible that some software products have also implemented a third-party queuing system for the robotic arm as well, I am not aware of any that do this. As long as you have a third-party application controlling access to the tape library and placing tapes into drives that need them, there is no need to share the robot in a SCSI sense.

central backup server in any backup configuration. It contains the schedules and indexes for all backups and acts as a central point of control for a group of backup clients. A device server has only tape drives that receive backup data from clients. The main server controls its actions. This is known as a *three-tiered backup system*, where the main server can tell a backup client to back up to the main server's tape drives or to the tape drives on one of its device servers. Some backup software products don't support device servers and require all backups to be transmitted across the LAN to the main server. This type of product is known as a *two-tiered backup system*. (A *single-tiered* backup product would support only backups to a server's own tape drives. An example of such a product would be the software that comes with an inexpensive tape drive.)

Sharing drives between device servers
> Most LAN-free backup products allow you to share a tape library and its drives only between a single main server and/or device servers under that main server's control. If you have more than one main server in your environment, this product doesn't allow you to share a tape library and its drives between multiple main servers.

Sharing drives between main servers
> Some LAN-free backup products allow you to share a library and its drives between multiple main servers. Many products that support this functionality do so because they are two-tiered products that don't support device servers, but this isn't always the case.

Restores

One of the truly beautiful things about sharing tape drives in a library via a SAN is what happens when it's time to restore. First, consider the parallel study illustrated in Table 4-2. Since only three drives are available to each host, only three drives will be available during the restores as well. Even if your backup software had the ability to read more than three tapes at a time, you wouldn't be able to do so.

However, if you are sharing the drives dynamically, a restore could be given access to all available drives. If your backups occur at night, and most of your restores occur during the day, you would probably be given access to all drives in the library during most restores. Depending on the capabilities of your backup software package, this can drastically increase the speed of your restore.

 Few backup software products can use more drives during a restore than they did during a backup, but that isn't to say that such products don't exist.

Other Ways to Share Tape Drives

As of this writing, there are at least three other ways to share devices without using a SAN. Although this is a chapter about SAN technology, I thought it appropriate to mention them here.

NDMP libraries

The Network Data Management Protocol (NDMP), originally designed by Network Appliance and PDC/Intelliguard (acquired by Legato) to back up filers, offers another way to share a tape library. There are a few vendors that have tape libraries that can be shared via NDMP.

Here's how it works. First, the vendors designed a small computer system to support the "tape server" functionality of NDMP:

- It can connect to the LAN and use NDMP to receive backups or transmit restores via NDMP.
- It can connect to the SCSI bus of a tape library and transmit to (or receive data from) its tape drives.

They then connect the SCSI bus of this computer to a tape drive in the library, and the Ethernet port of this computer to your LAN. (Current implementations have one of these computers for each tape drive, giving each tape drive its own connection to the LAN.) The function of the computer system is to convert data coming across the LAN in raw TCP/IP format and to write it as SCSI data via a local device driver which understands the drive type. Early implementations are using DLT 8000s and 100-Mb Ethernet, because the speed of a 100-Mb network is well matched to a 10-MB/s DLT. By the time you read this, there will probably be newer implementations that use Gigabit Ethernet and faster tape drives.

Not only does this give you a way to back up your filers; it also offers another option for backing up your distributed machines. As will be discussed in Chapter 7, NDMP v4 supports backing up a standard (non-NDMP) backup client to an NDMP-capable device. Since this NDMP library looks just like another filer to the backup server, you can use it to perform backups of non-NDMP clients with this feature. Since the tape library does the job of tracking which drives are in use and won't allow more than one backup server to use it at a time, you can effectively share this tape library with any backup server on the LAN.

SCSI over IP

SCSI over IP, also known as iSCSI, is a rather new concept when compared to Fibre Channel, but it's gaining a lot of ground. A SCSI device with an iSCSI adapter is accessible to any host on the LAN that also has an iSCSI interface card. Proponents of iSCSI say that Fibre Channel-based SANs are complex, expensive, and built on standards that are still being finalized. They believe that SANs based on iSCSI will solve these problems. This is because Ethernet is an old standard that has evolved slowly in such a way that almost all equipment remains interoperable. SCSI is also another standard that's been around a long time and is a very established protocol.

The one limitation to iSCSI today is that it's easy for a host to saturate a 100-MB/s Fibre Channel pipe, but it's difficult for the same host to saturate a 100-MB/s (1000 Mb or 1 Gb) Ethernet pipe. Therefore, although the architectures offer relatively the same speed, they aren't necessarily equivalent. iSCSI vendors realize this and are therefore have developed network interface cards (NICs) that can communicate "at line speed." One way to do this is to offload the TCP/IP processing from the host and perform it on the NIC itself. Now that vendors have started shipping gigabit NICs that can communicate at line speed, iSCSI stands to make significant inroads into the SAN marketplace. More information about iSCSI can be found in Appendix A.

Shared SCSI

There are some vendors that provide shared access to SCSI devices via standard parallel SCSI. Since all the LAN-free implementations that I have seen have used Fibre Channel, it's unclear how well such products would be supported by drive-sharing products.

Problems Caused by Reboots

I have heard reports of difficulties caused by an individual host rebooting while a drive on the SAN is in use by another host. On some operating systems, busy drives aren't seen by the operating system, and thus aren't available to use. Even worse, it sometimes causes the available drives' names to be changed, resulting in a completely inoperable set of drives. Some vendors have worked around the missing-drives problems using intelligent SAN routers. Some vendors have worked around name-change problems by tying the virtual name of the drive to the drive's actual serial number. Make sure you talk to your SAN hardware and software vendors about how they handle this situation.

A Variation on the Theme

LAN-free backups solve a lot of problems by removing backup traffic from the LAN. When combined with commercial interfaces to database backup APIs, they can provide a fast way to back up your databases. However, what happens if you have an application that is constantly changing data, and for which there is no API? Similarly, what if you can't afford to purchase the interface to that API from your backup software company? Usually, the only answer is to shut down the application during the entire time of the backup.

One solution to this problem is to use a client-free backup solution, which is covered in the next section. However, client-free backups are expensive, and they are meant to solve more problems (and provide more features) than this. If you don't need all the functionality provided by client-free backups, but you still have the problem described earlier, perhaps what you need is a *snapshot*. In my book *Unix Backup and Recovery*, I introduced the concept of snapshots as a feature I'd like to see integrated into commercial backup and recovery products, and a number of them now offer it.

What is a snapshot?

A snapshot is a virtual copy of a device or filesystem. Think of it as a Windows shortcut or Unix symbolic link to a device that has been frozen in time. Just as a symbolic link or shortcut isn't really a copy of a file or device that it points to, a snapshot is a symbolic (or virtual) representation of a file or device. The only difference between a snapshot and a shortcut or symbolic link is that the snapshot always mimics the way that file or device looked at the time the snapshot was taken.

In order to take snapshots, you must have snapshot software. This software can be found in any of the following places:

Advanced filesystems
> There are filesystems that let you create snapshots as part of their list of advanced features. These filesystems are usually not the filesystem provided by the operating-system vendor and are usually only available at an extra cost.

Standard host-based volume managers
> A host-based volume manager is the standard type of volume manager you are used to seeing. They manage disks that are visible to the host and create virtual devices using various levels of RAID, including RAID 0 (striping), RAID 1 (mirroring), RAID 5, RAID 0+1 (striping and mirroring), and RAID 1+0 (mirroring and striping). (See Appendix B for descriptions of the various levels of RAID.) Snapshots created by a standard volume manager can be seen only on the host where the volume manager is running.

Enterprise storage arrays
> A few enterprise storage arrays can create snapshots. These snapshots work virtually the same as any other snapshot, with the additional feature that a snapshot made within the storage array can be made visible to another host that also happens to be connected to the storage array. There is usually software that runs on Unix or NT that communicates with the storage array and tells it when and where to create snapshots.

Enterprise volume managers
> Enterprise volume managers are a relatively new type of product that attempt to provide enterprise storage array type features for JBOD disks. Instead of buying one large enterprise storage array, you can buy SAN-capable disks and create

RAID volumes on the SAN. Some of these products also offer the ability to create snapshots that are visible to any host on the SAN.

Backup software add-on products

Some backup products have recognized the value provided by snapshot software and can create snapshots within their software. These products emulate many other types of snapshots that are available. For example, some can create snapshots only of certain filesystem types, just like the advanced filesystem snapshots discussed earlier. Others can create snapshots of any device that is available to the host, but the data must be backed up via that host, just like the snapshots provided by host-based volume managers. Some, however, can create snapshots that are visible to other hosts, emulating the functionality of an enterprise storage array or enterprise volume manager. This type of snapshot functionality is discussed in more detail later in this chapter.

Let's review why we are looking at snapshots. Suppose you perform LAN-free backups but have an application for which there is no API or can't afford the API for an application. You are therefore required to shut down the application during backups. You want something better but aren't yet ready for the cost of client-free backups, nor do you need all the functionality they provide. Therefore, you need the type of snapshots that are available only from an advanced filesystem, a host-based volume manager, or a backup software add-on product that emulates this functionality. An enterprise storage array that can create snapshots (that are visible from the host of which the snapshot was taken) also works fine in this situation, but it isn't necessary. Choose whichever solution works best in your environment. Regardless of how you take the snapshot, most snapshot software works essentially the same way.

When you create a snapshot, the snapshot software records the time at which the snapshot was taken. Once the snapshot is taken, it gives you and your backup utility another name through which you may view the snapshot of the device or filesystem. It looks like any other device or filesystem, but it's really a symbolic representation of the device. Creating the snapshot doesn't actually copy data from *diska* to *diska.snapshot*, but it appears as if that's exactly what happened. If you look at *diska.snapshot*, you'll see *diska* exactly as it looked at the moment *diska.snapshot* was created.

Creating the snapshot takes only a few seconds. Sometimes people have a hard time grasping how the software can create a separate view of the device without copying it. This is why it's called a snapshot; it doesn't actually copy the data, it merely took a "picture" of it.

Once the snapshot has been created, most snapshot software (or firmware in the array) monitors the device for activity. When it sees that a block of data is going to change, it records the "before" image of that block in a special logging area (often called the *snapshot device*). Even if a particular block changes several times, it only needs to record the way it looked before the first change occurred.[*]

For details on how this works, please consult your vendor's manual. When you view the device or filesystem via the snapshot virtual device or mount point, it watches what you're looking for. If you request a block of data that has not changed since the snapshot was taken, it retrieves that block from the original device or filesystem. However, if you request a block of data that has changed since the snapshot was taken, it retrieves that block from the snapshot device. This, of course, is completely invisible to the user or application accessing the data. The user or application simply views the device via the snapshot device or mount point, and where the blocks come from is managed by the snapshot software or firmware.

Problem solved

Now that you can create a "copy" of your system in just a few seconds, you have a completely different way to back up an unsupported application. Simply stop the application, create the snapshot (which only takes a few seconds) and restart the application. As far as the application is concerned, the backup takes only a few seconds. However, there is a performance hit while the data is being backed up to the locally attached tape library (that is being shared with other hosts via a LAN-free backup setup). The degree to which this affects the performance of your application will, of course, vary. The only way to back up this data without affecting the application during the actual transfer of data from disk to tape is to use client-free backups.

 One vendor uses the term "snapshot" to refer to snapshots as described here, and to describe additional mirrors created for the purpose of backup, which is discussed in the section "Client-Free Backups." I'm not sure why they do this, and I find it confusing. In this book, the term snapshot will always refer to a virtual, copy-on-write copy as discussed here.

Problems with LAN-Free Backups

LAN-free backups solve a lot of problems. They allow you to share one or more tape libraries between your critical servers, allowing each to back up much faster than they could across the LAN. It removes the bulk of the data transfer from the LAN, freeing your LAN for other uses. It also reduces the CPU and memory overhead of backups on the clients, because they no longer have to transmit their backup data via

---

[*] Network Appliance filers appear to act this way, but the WAFL filesystem is quite a bit different. They store a "before" image of every block that is changed every time they sync the data from NVRAM to disk. Each time they perform a sync operation, they leave a pointer to the previous state of the filesystem. A Network Appliance snapshot, then, is simply a reference to that pointer. Please consult your Network Appliance documentation for details.

TCP/IP. However, there are still downsides to LAN-free backups. Let's take a look at a LAN-free backup system to see what these downsides are.

A typical LAN-free backup system is shown in Figure 4-4, where the database resides on disks that are visible to the data server. These disks may be a set of discreet disks inside the data server, a disk array with or without mirroring, or an enterprise storage array. In order to back up the data, the data must be read from the disks by the data server (1a) and transferred across the data server's backplane, CPU, and memory via some kind of backup software. It's then sent to tape drives on the data server (1b). This is true even if you use the snapshot technology discussed earlier. Even though you've created a static view of the data to back up, you still must back up the data locally.

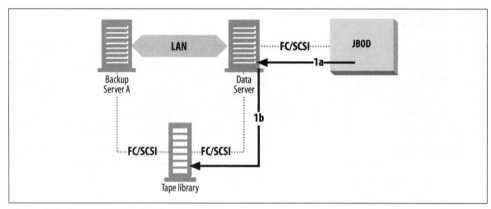

Figure 4-4. A typical LAN-free backup system

This, of course, requires using the CPU, memory, and backplane of the data server quite a bit. The application is negatively affected, or even shut down, during the entire time it takes to transfer the database from disk to tape. The larger the data, the greater the impact on the data server and the users. Also, traditional database recovery (including snapshot recovery systems like those described at the end of the previous section) requires transferring the data back across the same path, slowing down a recovery that should go as fast as possible.

With this type of setup, a recovery takes as long or longer than the backup and is limited by the I/O bandwidth of the data server. This includes only the recovery of the database files themselves. If it's a database you are recovering, the replaying of the transaction logs adds a significant amount of time on top of that.

Let's take a look at each of these limitations in more detail.

Application impact

You'd think that backing up data to locally attached tape drives would present a minimal impact to the application. It certainly creates much less of a load than typical LAN-based backups. In reality, however, the amount of throughput required to complete the backup within an acceptable window can sometimes create quite a load on the server, robbing precious resources needed by the application the server is running. The degree to which the application is affected depends on certain factors:

- Are the size and computing power of the server based only on the needs of the "primary" application, or are the needs of the backup and recovery application also taken into account? It's often possible to build a server that is powerful enough that the primary application isn't affected by the demands of the backup and recovery application, but only if both applications are taken into account when building the server. This is, however, often not done.
- How much data needs to be transferred from online storage (i.e., disk) to offline storage (i.e., tape) each night? This affects the length of the impact.
- What are the I/O capabilities of the server's backplane? Some server designs do a good job of computing but a poor job of transferring large amounts of data.
- How much memory does the backup application require?
- Can the primary application be backed up online, or does it need to be completely shut down during backups?
- How busy is the application during the backup window? Is this application being accessed 24×7, or is it not needed while backups are running?

Please notice that the last question asked about when the application is *needed*—not when it's being used. The reason the question is worded this way is that too many businesses have gotten used to systems that aren't available during the backup window. They have grown to expect this, so they simply don't try to use it at that time. They would use it if they could, but they can't—so they don't. The question is, "Would you like to be able to access your system 24×7?" If the answer is yes, you need to design a backup and recovery system that creates minimal impact on the application.

Almost all applications are impacted in some way during LAN-based or LAN-free backups. File servers take longer to process file requests. If you have a database and can perform backups with the database running, your database may take longer to process queries and commits. If your database application requires you to shut down the database to perform a backup, the impact on users is much greater.

Whether you are slowing down file or database services, or you are completely halting all database activity, it will be for some period of time. The duration of this period is determined by four factors:

- How much data do you have to back up?
- How many offline storage devices do you have available?
- How much can your backup software take advantage of these devices?
- How well can your server handle the load of moving data from point A to point B?

Recovery speed

This is the only reason you are backing up, right? Many people fail to take recovery speed into consideration when designing a backup and recovery system when they should be doing almost the opposite. They should design a backup and recovery system in such a way that it can recover the system within an acceptable window. In almost every case, this also results in a system that can back up the system within an acceptable window.

If your backup system is based on moving data from disk to tape, and your recovery system is based on moving data from tape to disk, the recovery time is always a factor of the questions in the previous section. They boil down to two basic questions: how much data do you have to move, and what resources are available to move it?

No other way?

Of course applications are affected during backups. Recovery takes as long, if not longer, than the backup. There's simply no way to get around this, right? That was the correct answer up until just recently; however, client-free backups have changed the rules.

What if there was a way you could back up a given server's data with almost no impact to the application? If there were any impact, it would last for only a few seconds. What if you could recover a multi-terabyte database instantaneously? Wouldn't that be wonderful? That's what client-free backups can do for you.

Client-Free Backups

Performing client-free backup and recovery requires the coordination of several steps across at least two hosts. At one point in time, none of the popular commercial backup and recovery applications had software that could automate all the steps without requiring custom scripting by the administrator. All early implementations of client-free backups involved a significant amount of scripting on the part of the administrator, and almost all early implementations of client-free backups were on Unix servers. This was for several reasons, the first of which was demand. Many people had really large, multi-terabyte Unix servers that qualified as candidates for client-free backups. This led to a lot of cooperation between the storage array vendors and the Unix vendors, which led to commands that could run on a Unix system and accomplish the tasks required to make client-free backups possible. Since many of these tasks required steps to be coordinated on multiple computers, the *rsh* and *ssh* capabilities of Unix came in handy.

Since NT systems lacked integrated, advanced scripting support, and communications between NT machines were easy for administrators to script, it wasn't simple to design a scripted solution for NT client-free backups. (As you will see later in this section, another key component that was missing was the ability to mount brand new drive letters from the command line.) This, combined with the fact that NT machines tended to use less storage than their monolithic Unix counterparts, meant that there were not a lot of early implementations of client-free backup on NT. However, things have changed in recent years. It isn't uncommon to find very large Windows machines. (I personally have seen one approaching a terabyte.) Scripting and intermachine communication has improved in recent years, but the limitation of not being able to mount drives via the command line has existed until just recently.* Therefore, it's good that a few commercial backup software companies are beginning to release client-free backup software that includes the Windows platform. Those of us with very large Windows machines can finally take advantage of this technology.

Windows isn't the only platform for which commercial client-free applications are being written. As of this writing, I am aware of several products (that are either in beta or have just been released) that will provide integrated client-free backup and recovery functionality for at least four versions of Unix (AIX, HP-UX, Solaris, and Tru64).

The next section attempts to explain all the steps a client-free backup system must complete. These steps can be scripted, or they can be managed by an integrated commercial client-free backup software package. Hopefully, by reading the steps in detail, you will have a greater appreciation of the functionality client-free backups provide, as well as the complexity of the application that provide them.

How Client-Free Backups Work

As you can see in Figure 4-5, there is SAN-connected storage that is available to at least two systems: the data server and a backup server. The storage consists of a primary disk set and a *backup mirror*, which is simply an additional copy of the primary disk set. (In the figure, the primary disk set is mirrored, as represented by the M1/M2.) Note that the SAN-connected storage is depicted as a single, large multi-hosted storage array with an internal, prewired SAN. The reason for this is that all early implementations of client-free backups have been with such storage arrays. As discussed earlier, there are now enterprise volume managers that will make it possible to do this with JBOD on a SAN, but I use the concept of a large storage array in this example because it's the solution that's available from the most vendors—even if it's the most expensive.

The normal status quo of the backup mirror is that it's left split from the primary disk set. Why it's left split will become clear later in this section.

At the appropriate time, the backup application performs a series of tasks:

---

* It was the Microsoft's partnership with Veritas that finally made this a reality. The volume manager for Windows 2000 is a "lite" version of Veritas Volume Manager.

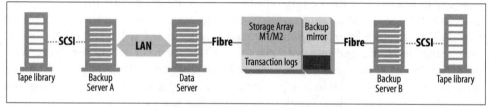

Figure 4-5. A client-free backup arrangement

1. Backup Server A, the main backup server, tells Backup Server B to begin the backup.

2. Unmounts the backup mirror (if it's a mounted filesystem) from Backup Server B.

3. Exports the volumes from the OS' volume manager on Backup Server B.

4. Establishes the backup mirror (i.e., "reconnects" it to the primary disk set) by running commands on Backup Server B that communicate with the storage array.

5. Backup Server B monitors the backup mirror, waiting for the establish to complete.

6. Backup Server B waits for the appropriate time to split off the backup mirror.

7. Backup Server B tells Data Server to put the application into backup mode.

8. Backup Server B splits the backup mirror.

9. Backup Server B tells Data Server to take the application out of backup mode.

10. Backup Server B imports the volumes found on the backup mirror.

11. Backup Server B mounts any filesystems found on the backup mirror.

12. Backup Server B now performs the backup of the backup mirror via its I/O backplane, instead of the data server's backplane.

13. After the backup, the filesystems are left mounted and imported on Backup Server B.

These tasks mean that the backup data is sent via the SAN to the backup server and doesn't travel through the client at all, which is why it's referred to as client-free backups. Again, some vendors refer to this as server-free backups, but I reserve that term for a specific type of backup that will be covered in the section, "Server-Free Backups."

You may find yourself asking a few questions:

- How do you put the application into backup mode?
- How do you import another machine's volumes and filesystems?
- Why is the backup mirror left split and mounted most of the time?
- This sounds really complicated. Is it?

Before explaining this process in detail, let's examine a few things that make client-free backups possible:

You must be able to put the application into backup mode

You are going to split off a mirror of the application's disk, and it has no idea you're going to do that. The best way to do this is to stop all I/O operations to the disk during the split. This is usually done by shutting down the application that is using the disk. However, some database products, such as Oracle and Informix, allow you to put their databases into a backup-friendly state without shutting them down. This works fine as well. Informix actually freezes all commits, and Oracle does some extra logging. If you're backing up a file server, you need to stop writes to the files during the time of the split. Otherwise, the filesystem can be corrupted during the process. If you perform an online, split-mirror backup of a SQL Server database, SQL Server's recovery mechanism is supposed to recover the database back to the last checkpoint. However, any transactions that aren't in the online transaction log are lost. (In other words, you can't issue a *load transaction* command after a split mirror recovery). Microsoft Exchange must normally be shut down during the split.

This isn't to say that a backup and recovery software company can't write an API that communicates with the SQL Server and Exchange APIs. This software product could tell SQL Server and Exchange that it performed a traditional backup, when in reality it's performing a split-mirror backup. In fact, this is already being done for Exchange in the NAS world with snapshots, which act like split mirrors as far as the application is concerned.

You have to be able to back up the application's data via a third-party application

If the application is a file server, this is usually not a problem. However, most modern databases are backed up by passing a stream of data to the backup application via a special API. Perhaps two examples will illustrate what I mean.

The standard way to back up Oracle is to use the RMAN (Recovery Manager) utility. Once configured, your backup software automatically talks to Oracle's RMAN API, which then passes streams of data back to the backup application. However, Oracle also allows you start *sqlplus* (a command-line utility you can script), issue the command *alter tablespace tablespace begin backup* and then back up that tablespace's datafiles in any way you want.* When it's time to recover, you shut down the database, restore those datafiles from backup, then use Oracle's archived redo logs to redo any transactions that have occurred since the backup.

Informix now offers similar functionality, but it didn't always do so. Prior to the creation of the *onbar* utility, you were forced to use the *ontape* utility to back up Informix. This backed up a database's datafiles or logical logs (transaction logs)

---

* Prior to 9i, this was done with the *suvrmgr* command, but this command has been removed from 9i.

to tape. If you didn't back up the datafiles with *ontape*, you couldn't restore the database to a point in time. For example, suppose you shut down the database and used a third-party backup tool to back up the database's datafiles. You then started up the database and ran it a while, making and recording transactions. If you then shut down the database, using your third-party tool to restore the datafiles, there would be no way within Informix to redo the transactions that occurred since the backup was taken. Therefore, third-party backups with these versions of Informix were useless, preventing you from doing client-free backups of these databases. Now, with the *onbar* utility, Informix supports what it calls an *external backup*. As you will see later, this is the tool that you now use to perform client-free backups of Informix.

Although Microsoft Exchange does have transaction logs, the only way to back them up is via the Microsoft-provided tools and APIs. Unless a backup product writes an application that speaks to Microsoft's API and tricks it into thinking that the split mirror backup is a "normal" backup, there is no way to perform an online third-party backup of it. However, you can perform an *offline* third-party backup of Exchange by shutting down the Exchange services prior to splitting the mirror. You can then restore the Exchange server back to the point the mirror was split, but you lose any messages that have been sent since then. (This is why there are few people performing client-free backups of Exchange.)

Microsoft's SQL Server has a sophisticated recovery mechanism that allows you to perform both online and offline backups, with advantages and disadvantages of both. If you split the mirror while SQL Server is online, you shouldn't suffer a service interruption because of backup, but the recovery process that SQL Server must perform when a restored database is restarted will take much longer. If you shut down SQL Server before splitting the mirror, SQL Server doesn't need to recover the database back to the last checkpoint before it can start replaying transaction logs. However, you will obviously suffer a service interruption whenever you perform a backup. Whether you shut down the database or not, you can't use the *dump transaction* and *load transaction* commands in conjunction with a split mirror backup of SQL Server.

You have to be able to establish to (and split the mirror from) the primary disk set
This functionality is provided by software on the backup server or data server that communicates with the volume manager of the storage array. With large, multihosted arrays (e.g., Compaq's Enterprise Storage Array, EMC Symmetrix, and Hitachi 9000 series), the client-side software is communicating with the built-in, hardware RAID controller. (An example of this is provided later in this chapter.) Other solutions use software RAID; in this situation, the client-side software is talking to the host that is managing the volumes.

You must be able to see the backup mirror from the backup server
Once you split the backup mirror from the primary disk set, you have to be able to see its disk on the backup server. If you can't, the entire exercise is pointless.

This is where Windows NT has typically had a problem. Once the mirror has been split, the associated drives just "appear" on the SCSI bus—roughly the equivalent to plugging in new disk drives without rebooting or running the Disk Manager or Computer Management GUIs. However, Windows 2000 now uses a light version of the Veritas Volume Manager. You can purchase a full-priced version for both NT and Windows 2000, which comes with command line utilities. By the time you read this, the full version of Volume Manager should support the necessary functionality. In fact, Veritas will reportedly have a script included with the product that is specifically designed to help automate client-free backups.

You normally have to have the same operating system on the data server and the backup server

The reason for this is that you are going to be reading one host's disks on another host. If Backup Server B in Figure 4-5 is to back up the data server's disks, it needs to understand the disk labels, any volume manager disk groups and volumes, and any filesystems that may reside on the disks. With few exceptions, this normally means that both servers must be running the same operating system. At least one client-free backup software package has gotten around this limitation by writing custom software that can understand volume managers and filesystems from other operating systems. But, for the most part, the data server and backup server need to be the same operating system. This can be true even if you aren't using a volume manager or filesystem and are backing up raw disks. For example, a Solaris system can't perform I/O operations on a disk that has an NT label on it.

Before continuing this explanation of client-free backups, I must define some terms that will be used in the following example. Please understand that there are multiple vendors that offer this functionality, and they all use different terminology and all work slightly differently.

 The lists that follow in the rest of this chapter give examples for Compaq, EMC, and Hitachi using Exchange, Informix, Oracle, and SQL Server databases, and the Veritas Volume Manager and File System. These examples are for clarification only and aren't meant to imply that this functionality is available only on these platforms or to indicate an endorsement of these products. These vendors are listed in alphabetical order throughout, and so no inferences should be made as to the author's preference for one vendor over another. There are several multihosted storage array vendors and several database vendors. Consult your vendor for specifics on how this works on your platform.

Primary disk set

The term *primary disk set* refers to the set of disks that hold the primary copy of the data server's data. What I refer to as a disk *set* are probably several independent disks or can be one large RAID volume. Whether the primary disk set uses RAID 0, 1, 0+1, 1+0, or 5 is irrelevant. I'm simply referring to the entire set of disks that contain the primary copy of the data server's data. Compaq calls this the *primary mirror*, EMC calls it the *standard*, and Hitachi, the *primary volume* or *P-VOL*.

Backup mirror

The *backup mirror* device is another set of disks specifically allocated for backup mirror use. When people say "the backup mirror," they are typically referring to a set of backup mirror disks that are associated with a primary disk set. It's often referred to as a "third mirror," because the primary disk set is often mirrored. When synchronized with the primary disk set, this set of disks then represents a third copy of the data—thus the term *third mirror*. However, not all vendors use mirroring for primary disk sets, so I've chosen to use the term backup mirror instead. Compaq and EMC both call this a BCV, or *business continuity volume*; Hitachi calls it the *secondary volume* or S-VOL.

Backup mirror application

This is a piece of software that synchronizes and splits backup mirror devices based on commands that are issued by the client-side version of the software running on the data or backup server. That is, you run the *backup mirror application* on your Unix or NT system, and it talks to the disk array and tells it what to do. Compaq has a few ways to do this. The more established way is to use the Enterprise Volume Manager GUI and the Compaq Batch Scheduler. The Batch Scheduler is a web-based GUI that is accessible via any web browser and can automate the creation of BCVs. For scripting, however, you should use the SAN-Works Command Scripter, which allows direct command-line access to the StorageWorks controllers. EMC's application for this is Timefinder; Hitachi's is Shadowimage.

Establish

To establish a backup mirror is to tell the primary disk set to copy its data over to the backup mirror, thus synchronizing it with the primary disk set. Many backup mirror applications offer an incremental establish, which copies only the sectors that have changed since the last establish. Some refer to this as *silvering* the mirror, a reference to the silver that is put on the back of a "real" mirror.

Split

When you split a backup mirror, you tell the disk array to break the link between the primary disk set and the backup mirror. This is typically done to back up the backup mirror. Once it's finished, you have a complete copy of the primary disk set on another set of devices, and those devices become visible on the backup server. This is also called *breaking* the mirror.

Restore

To restore the backup mirror is to copy the backup mirror to the primary disk set. Once the command to do this is issued, the restore usually appears to have been completed instantaneously. As will be explained in more detail later, requests for data that has not yet been restored is redirected to the mirror.

Main server

As discussed earlier in this chapter, a main server is the server in a backup environment that schedules all backups and stores in the database information about what backups went to what tape. It may or may not have tape drives connected to it.

Device server

A device server, as discussed earlier, is a server that has tape drives connected to it. The backups that go to these tape drives are scheduled by the main server. The main server also keeps track of what files went to what tapes on this device server.

Backing Up the Backup Mirror

This section explains what's involved in backing up a backup mirror to another server.

Setup

Figure 4-6 again illustrates a typical backup mirror backup configuration. There is a main backup server (Backup Server A) that is connected to a tape library (via SCSI or Fibre Channel) and connected to the data server via a LAN. The data server is connected via Fibre Channel to the storage array, and its datafiles and transaction logs reside on its primary disk sets. The datafiles have a backup mirror associated with them, and it's connected via Fibre Channel to a device server (Backup Server B), and that device server is connected via SCSI to another tape library.

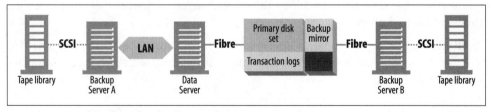

Figure 4-6. Another client-free backup configuration

 Multihosted storage arrays have a SAN built into them. You can put extra switches or hubs between the storage array and the servers connecting to it, but it isn't necessary unless the number of servers that you wish to connect to the storage array exceeds the number of Fibre Channel ports the array has.

To back up a database, you must back up its datafiles (and other files) and its transaction logs. The datafiles contain the actual database, and the transaction logs contain the changes to the database since the last time you backed up the datafiles. Once you restore the datafiles, the transaction logs can then replay the transactions that occurred between the time of the datafile backup and the time of the failure. Therefore, you must back up the transaction logs continually, because they are essential to a good recovery.

Back up the transaction logs

As shown in Figure 4-7, transaction logs are often backed up to disk (1), and then to tape (2). This is my personal preference, but it isn't required. The reason I prefer to back up to disk and then to tape is that replaying the transaction logs is the slowest part of the restore, and having the transaction logs available on disk significantly speeds up the process. The log disk may or may not be on the storage array and doesn't need a backup mirror.

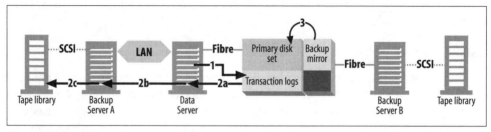

Figure 4-7. Backing up the transaction logs

You can also see in Figures 4-5 and 4-6 that the transaction logs don't need to be backed up via the split mirror. The reason for this is that there is no supported methods for backing up transaction logs this way. Therefore, there is no reason to put them on the backup mirror.

As discussed previously, the backup mirror is left split from the primary disk set (3). The following list details how transaction logs are backed with Exchange, Informix, Oracle, and SQL Server:

Exchange
> As discussed previously, the only way to back up Exchange's transaction logs is to write an application that communicates directly with Microsoft's API.

Informix
> Informix's transaction logs are called *logical logs* and can be backed up directly to tape or disk. Again, I recommend backing up to disk first, followed by a backup to tape, since recovering logical logs from disk is much faster than recovering them from tape. If you plan to perform client-free backups, you need to use Informix's *onbar* command, which provides the *log_full.sh* script to kick off the

backups of logical logs whenever one becomes full. Although the setup in the next section may look involved, once it's complete, logical log backup and recovery is actually easy with Informix.

Oracle

Oracle's transaction logs are called *redo logs*, and the backup to disk is accomplished with Oracle's standard archiving procedure. This is done by placing the database in *archive log mode* and specifying *automatic archiving*. As soon as one online redo log is filled, Oracle switches to the next one and begins copying the full log to the archived redo log location. To back up these archived redo logs to tape, you can use an incremental backup that runs once an hour or more often if you prefer.

SQL Server

As discussed previously, you will not be able to use SQL Server's dump transaction command in conjunction with a split backup. If you need point-in-time recovery, you need to choose another backup method.

Back up the datafiles

It's now time to back up the datafiles. In order to do that, you must:

1. Establish the backup mirror to the primary disk set.
2. Put the database in backup mode, or sync the filesystem.
3. Split the backup mirror.
4. Take the database out of backup mode.
5. Import and mount the backup mirror volumes to the backup server.
6. Back up the backup mirror volumes to tape.

The details of how these steps are accomplished are discussed next.

Establish the backup mirror. As shown in Figure 4-8, you must establish (reattach) the backup mirror to the primary disk set (1), causing the mirror to copy to the backup mirror any regions that have been modified since the backup mirror was last established (2).

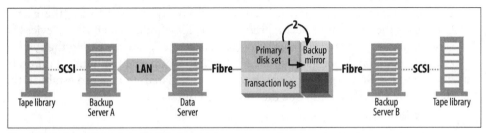

Figure 4-8. Establishing the backup mirror

The following list shows how this works for the various products:

Compaq

This functionality is available on the RAID Array 8000 (RA8000) and the Enterprise Storage Array 12000 (ESA12000) using HSG80 controllers in switch or hub configurations. The SANworks Enterprise Volume Manager and Command Scripter products support Windows NT/2000, Solaris, and Tru64.

Although Compaq uses the term BCV to refer to a set of disks that comprise a backup mirror, their arrays don't have any commands that interact with the entire BCV as one entity. All establishing and splitting of mirrors takes place on the individual disk level. Therefore, if you have a striped set of mirrored disks to which you want to assign a third mirror, you need assign a third disk to each set of mirrored disks that make up that stripe. In order to do this, you issue the following commands:

```
set mirrorset-name nopolicy
set mirrorset-name members=3
set mirrorset-name replace=disk-name
```

First, the *nopolicy* flag tells the mirror not to add members to the disk group until you do so manually. Then you add a member to the mirrorset by specifying that it has one more member than it already has. (The number 3 in this example assumes that there was already a mirrored pair to which you are adding a third member.) Then, you specify the name of the disk that is to be that third mirror.

Once this relationship is established for each disk in the stripe, it will take some time to copy the data from the existing mirror to the backup mirror. To check the status of this copy, issue the command *show mirrorset mirrorset-name*.

These commands can be issued via a terminal connected directly to the array, or via the Compaq Command Line Scripter tool discussed earlier.

EMC

On EMC, establishing the BCV (i.e., backup mirror) to the standard (i.e., primary disk set) is done with the *symbcv establish* command that is part of the EMC Timefinder package. (Timefinder is available on both Unix and Windows.) When issuing this command, you need to tell it which BCV to establish. Since a BCV is actually a set of devices that are collectively referred to as "the BCV," EMC uses the concept of *device groups* to tell Timefinder which BCV devices to synchronize with which standard devices. Therefore, prior to issuing the *symbcv establish* command, you need to create a device group that contains all the standards and the BCV devices to which they are associated. In order to establish the BCV to the standard, you issue the following command:

```
# symbcv establish -g group_name [-i]
```

The –g option specifies the name of the device group that you created above. If the BCV has been previously established and split, you can also specify the –i flag that tells Timefinder to perform an *incremental* establish. This tells Timefinder to look at both the BCV and the standard devices and copy over only those regions that have changed since the BCV was last established. It even allows you to modify the BCV while it's split. If you modify any regions on the BCV devices (such as when you overwrite the private regions of each device with Veritas Volume Manager so that you can import them to another system), those regions will also be refreshed from the standard, even if they have not been changed on the primary disk set.

Once the BCV is established, you can check the progress of the synchronization with the *symbcv verify –g device_group* command. This shows the number of "BCV invalids" and "standard invalids" that still have to be copied. It also sometimes lists a percentage complete column, but I have not found that column to be particularly reliable or useful.

Hitachi

On HDS, establishing the *shadow volume* (i.e., backup mirror) to the primary mirror is done with the *paircreate* command that is part of the HDS Shadowimage package. (Shadowimage is available on both Unix and NT.) When issuing this command, you need to tell it which secondary volume (S-VOL) to establish. Since an S-VOL is actually a pool of devices that are collectively referred to as "reserve pool," HDS uses the concept of *groups* to tell Shadowimage which S-VOL devices to synchronize with which primary volumes (P-VOL). Therefore, prior to issuing the *paircreate -g device_group* command, you need to create a device group that contains all the primary mirrors and the BCV devices to which they are associated.

In order to establish (i.e., synchronize) the S-VOL to the P-VOL, issue the following command:

```
# paircreate –g device_group
```

If the S-VOL has been previously established and split, you can also specify the *pairresync* command that tells Shadowimage to perform a resynchronization of the pairs. This tells Shadowimage to apply the writes to the P-VOL, which are logged in cache, to the S-VOL because it has been split. It even allows you to modify the S-VOL while it's split. If you modify any regions on the S-VOL devices (such as when you overwrite the private regions of each device with Veritas Volume Manager so that you can import them to another system), those regions are also refreshed from the primary, even if they have not been changed on the primary mirror.

Once the S-VOL is established, you can check the progress of the synchronization with the *pairdisplay –g device_group* or *–m all* command. This shows you the number of "transition volumes" that still have to be copied and the percentage of copying already done.

Put the database in backup mode. As shown in Figure 4-9, once the backup mirror is fully synchronized with the primary disk set, you have to tell the data server to put the database in backup mode (1). In most client-server backup environments, this is normally accomplished by telling the backup software to run a script prior to a backup. The problem here is the backup client, where the script is normally run, isn't the host where the script needs to run. The client in Figure 4-9 is actually the Backup Server B, not Data Server. This means that you need to use something like *rsh* or *ssh* to pass the command from Backup Server B to Data Server. There are now *ssh* servers available for both Unix and Windows. The commands you need to run on Data Server will obviously depend on the application.

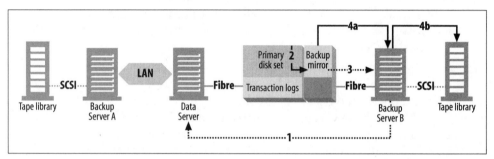

Figure 4-9. Backing up the backup mirror

Here are the steps for Exchange, Informix, Oracle, and SQL Server:

Exchange

Exchange must be shut down prior to splitting the mirror. This is done by issuing a series of *net stop* commands in a batch file:

```
net stop "Microsoft Exchange Directory" /y
net stop "Microsoft Exchange Event Service" /y
net stop "Microsoft Exchange Information Store" /y
net stop "Microsoft Exchange Internet Mail Service" /y
net stop "Microsoft Exchange Message Transfer Agent" /y
net stop "Microsoft Exchange System Attendant" /y
```

Informix

Informix is relatively easy. All you have to do is specify the appropriate environment variables and issue the command *onmode –c block*. Unlike Oracle, however, once this command is issued, all commits will hang until the *onmode –c unblock* command is issued.

Oracle

Putting Oracle databases in backup mode is no easy task. You need to know the names of every tablespace, and place each tablespace into backup mode using the command *alter tablespace tablespace_name begin backup*. Many people create a script to automatically discover all the tablespaces and place each in backup mode. Putting the tablespaces into backup mode causes a minor performance hit, but the database will continue to function normally.

SQL Server

As discussed previously, it isn't necessary to shut down SQL Server prior to splitting the mirror. However, doing so will speed up recovery time. To stop SQL Server, issue the following command:

```
net stop MSSQLSERVER
```

Split the backup mirror. As shown in Figure 4-9, once the database is put into backup mode, the backup mirror is split from the primary disk set (2).

This split requires a number of commands on the Compaq array. First, you set the *nopolicy* flag with the command *set mirrorset-name nopolicy*. Then you split the mirror by issuing the command *reduce disk-name* for each disk in the BCV. Then you create a *unit name* for each disk with the command *add unit unit-name disk-name*. Finally, you make that unit visible to the backup server by issuing the commands *set unit unit-name disable_access_path=all* and *set unit unit-name enable_access_path=(backupserver-name)*.

To do this on EMC, run the command *symbcv split -g device_group* on the backup server. To do this on Hitachi, run the command *pairsplit –g device_group*. (On both EMC and Hitachi, the backup mirror devices are made visible to the backup server as part of the storage array's configuration.)

Take the database out of backup mode. Now that the backup mirror is split, you can take the database out of backup mode. Here are the details of taking the databases out of backup mode:

Exchange

To start Exchange automatically after splitting the mirror, place the following series of commands in a batch file and run it:

```
net start "Microsoft Exchange Directory" /y
net start "Microsoft Exchange Event Service" /y
net start "Microsoft Exchange Information Store" /y
net start "Microsoft Exchange Internet Mail Service" /y
net start "Microsoft Exchange Message Transfer Agent" /y
net start "Microsoft Exchange System Attendant" /y
```

Informix

Again, Informix is relatively easy. All you have to do is specify the appropriate environment variables and issue the command *onmode -c unblock*. Any commits that were issued while the database was blocked will now complete. If you perform the block, split, and unblock fast enough, the users of the application will never realize that commits were frozen for a few seconds.

Oracle

Again, you must determine the name of each tablespace in a particular ORACLE_SID, and use the command *alter tablespace tablespace_name end backup* to take each tablespace out of backup mode.

SQL Server

To start SQL Server automatically after splitting the mirror, run the following command:

```
net start MSSQLSERVER
```

Import the backup mirror's volumes to the backup server. This step is the most OS-specific and complicated step, since it involves using OS-level volume manager and filesystem commands. However, the prominence of the Veritas Volume Manager makes this a little simpler. Veritas Volume Manager is now available for HP-UX, Solaris, NT, and Windows 2000. Also, the native volume manager for Tru64 is an OEM version of Volume Manager.

On the data server, the logical volumes are mounted as filesystems (or drives) or used as raw devices on Unix for a database. As shown in Figure 4-9, you need to figure out what backup mirror devices belong to which disk group, import those disk groups to the backup server (3), activate the disk groups (which turns on the logical volumes), and mount the filesystems if there are any. This is probably the most difficult part of the procedure, but it's possible to automate it.

It isn't possible to assign drive letters to devices via the command line in NT and Windows 2000 without the full-priced version of the Veritas Volume Manager. Therefore, the steps in the list that follows assume you are using this product. Except where noted, the commands discussed next should work roughly the same on both Unix and NT systems. If you don't want to pay for the full-priced volume manager product, there is an alternate, although much less automated, method discussed at the end of the Veritas-based steps.

You can write a script that discovers the names of the disk groups on the backup mirror and uses the command *vxdg -n newname -t import volume-group* to import the disk/volume groups from the backup server. (The *–t* option specifies that the new name is only temporary.) The following list is a brief summary of how this works. It's not meant to be an exact step-by-step guide; it gives you an overall picture of what's involved in discovering and mounting the backup mirror.

1. First, you need a list of disks that are on the primary disk set. Compaq's *show disks* command, EMC's *inq* command, and Hitachi's *raidscan* command provide this information.

2. To get a list of which disk groups each disk was in, run the command *vxdisk –s list devicename* on Unix or *vxdisk diskinfo disk_name* on Windows.

   You now have a list of disk groups that can be imported from the backup mirror.

3. Import each disk group with the *vxdg -n newname -t import disk-group* command.

4. A *vxrecover* is necessary on Unix to activate the volumes on the disk.

5. On Unix, you may also need to mount the filesystems found on the disk. On NT/2000, the Volume Manager takes care of assigning drive letters (i.e., mounting) the drives.

 It's wise to perform an *fsck* or *chkdisk* of the backup mirror's filesystems at this point.

As mentioned before, if you are running Windows and don't wish to pay for the full-priced version of Volume Manager, you can't assign the drive letters via the command line. Since it isn't reasonable to expect you to go to the GUI every night during backups, an alternative method is to perform the following steps manually each time there is a configuration change to the backup mirror:

1. Split the backup mirror as described in the previous section "Split the backup mirror." This makes the drives accessible to the backup server.

2. Start the Computer Management GUI in Windows 2000 and later (or the Disk Administrator GUI in NT), and tell it to find and assign drive letters to new disk drives.

3. A reboot may be necessary to effect the changes.

4. After the drive letters have been assigned, you may establish and split the backup mirror at will. However, bad things are liable to happen if you reboot the server (or try to access the backup mirror's disks) while the backup mirror is established.

 It's wise to perform a *chkdisk* of the backup mirror's disks at this point.

Back up the backup mirror volumes to tape.   This is the easy part. Define a backup configuration to back up the filesystems, drives, or raw devices that were found on the backup mirror. Since the volumes are actually imported and/or mounted on the backup server, the backup server should be listed as the client for this backup configuration. As shown in Figure 4-9, the data is sent from the backup mirror to the backup server (4a), and then to tape (4b).

The transaction logs should be backed up to disk and to tape (as shown in Figure 4-7) before, during, and after this operation.

And that's all there is to client-free backup!

Client-Free Recovery

Nobody cares if you can back up—only if you can recover. How do you recover from such a convoluted setup? This is really where the beauty of having the backup mirror stay split and mounted comes in. Unless the entire storage array is destroyed, it's available for an immediate restore. However, let's start with the worst-case scenario: the entire storage array was destroyed and has been replaced.

Recovering from complete destruction of the storage array

As shown in Figure 4-10, the worst possible thing that can happen is if something catastrophic happens to the storage array, destroying the primary disk set, backup mirror, and transaction log backup disk. Because of the extreme amount of proactive monitoring most of the enterprise storage arrays have, this is rather unlikely to happen. In fact, with the backup mirror left split most of the time, about the only probable way for both the backup mirror and the primary disk set to be damaged is complete destruction of the physical unit, such as by fire. The first step in this recovery is that the storage array must, of course, be repaired or reinstalled.

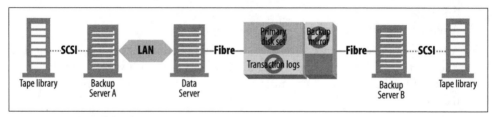

Figure 4-10. Loss of the storage array

Restore backup mirror from tape

Once the storage array is fully functional, you need to restore the backup mirror from tape as shown in Figure 4-11 (1a–b). While this is going on, the transaction log backups can also be restored from tape to disk (2a, b, and c). This allows them to be immediately available once the backup mirror is restored.

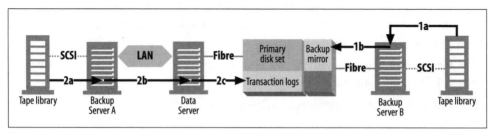

Figure 4-11. Recovering from backup

Once the recovery of the backup mirror has been completed from tape, we can move on to the next step. (Of course, if you don't have to recover the backup mirror from tape, you can start with the next step.)

Recovering after a tape recovery or if you lose the primary disk set and not the backup mirror

This recovery is much more likely to occur and will occur under the three following circumstances:

- If you lost the entire storage array, repaired it, and recovered the backup mirror from tape (as discussed in the previous section)
- If you lost both sides of the primary disk set but did not lose the backup mirror
- If the database or filesystem residing on the primary disk set was logically corrupted but the backup mirror was split at the time

The process now is to recover the primary disk set from the backup mirror, replay the transaction logs, and bring the database online.

Restore primary disk set from the backup mirror

You now need to tell the storage array to copy the data from the backup mirror back to the primary disk set. Here's how to do so:

Compaq

By running the Compaq EVM GUI you can easily connect the third mirror back to the primary mirror and restore the data to the first mirror set. If you want to do this via the command line, use the *unmirror* command to turn off the primary mirrors. Then use the *mirror* command to create a one-way mirror of each disk in the BCV, followed by *set mirrorset-name nopolicy*, and *set mirrorset-name members=[n+2]*. Now issue the command *set mirrorset-name replace=disk-name* for each disk from the primary mirror. This places the primary disks as additional disks in the temporary mirrorsets created for recovery, causing the data on the backup mirror disks to be copied to the primary disks. Then run the commands *add unit unit-name disk-name*, *set unit unit-name disable_access_path=all*, and *set unit unit-name enable_access_path=(primary-server-name)* to grant the primary server access to the new mirror. Once the copy had been completed, you can remove the additional mirror with the *reduce mirror* command.

EMC

To recover the primary disk set (standard) from the backup mirror (BCV), you must tell the backup mirror application to do so. With EMC, you issue the command *symbcv restore -g device_group*, which begins copying the BCV to the standard as shown in Figure 4-12. With EMC, the moment this command is executed, the primary disk set appears to have been restored and is immediately accessible. How does this work? Some people seem to think that the backup mirror is simply mounted as the primary disk set during a restore. That isn't what happens at all. The backup mirror isn't visible to the data server at any time, so this isn't even possible.

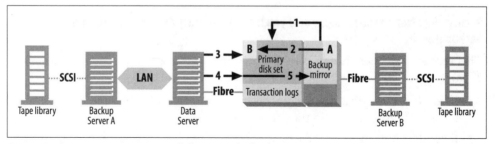

Figure 4-12. Recovering a primary disk set via the backup mirror

Take a look at Figure 4-12 and assume that some time has passed. The data in block "A" has been copied to block "B," (2) but the rest of the data on the BCV has not yet been copied. If the application asks for the data that has been restored from the BCV, it will receive it from the BCV (3). If the application requests data that has not yet been copied (4), Timefinder forwards the request to the BCV (5). The data is then presented to the application as if it was already on the standard.

Hitachi

To recover the primary mirror from the S-VOL, tell the Shadowimage application to do so. With HDS, issue the command *pairresync –restore –g device_ group*, which begins copying the S-VOL to the P-VOL. In this way, HDS and EMC are similar; the moment this command is executed, the primary mirror appears to have been restored and is immediately accessible.

Replay transaction logs

Since the disk-based transaction log dumps were recovered in a previous step, you can now start the transaction log restore from the disk-based transaction log backups (see Figure 4-13).

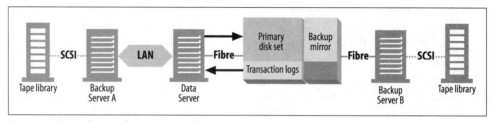

Figure 4-13. Replaying the transaction logs

Here's an overview of how to do this for Exchange, Informix, Oracle, and SQL Server:

Exchange

Since you can't restore any transaction logs, you will simply need to restart the Exchange services after the restore. You can do this via the Exchange GUI.

Informix

First, you need to tell Informix you've performed what it calls an "external recovery" of the chunks. To do this, issue the command *onbar –r –e –p*, which tells Informix to examine the chunks to make sure they've been recovered and to know which logical log it needs to start with. Once this completes successfully, you can tell Informix to perform the logical log recovery with the command *onbar –r –l*. (You can perform both steps with one command (*onbar –r –e*), but I prefer to perform each step separately. The *–p* option of the *onbar –r –e –p* command tells it to perform only the physical recovery.)

Oracle

Oracle recoveries can be quite complex and are covered in detail elsewhere in this book. Assuming that you have done a restore of one or more datafiles from the backup mirror to the primary disk set, the following commands replay the redo logs:

```
$ sqlplus /nolog
> connect /as sysdba
> startup mount ;
> recover database ;
```

SQL Server

You can't recover transactions that have occurred since the split-mirror backup was taken. If you need point-in-time recovery, use another backup method.

Bring the database online

Once the transaction log recovery is complete, the database is fully online, whether or not the backup mirror has been fully restored to the primary disk set (see Figure 4-14).

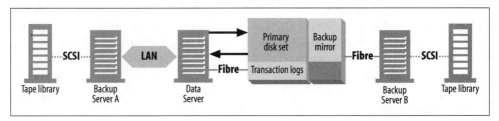

Figure 4-14. Database is online

Isn't that recovery scenario a beautiful thing? Imagine recovering a 10-TB database in under a minute. If you need the ultimate in instant recovery, it's difficult to beat the concept of client-free backup and recovery.

Other Variations on the Theme

Some people love to have an entire copy of their database or file server sitting there at all times just waiting for an instant restore. Others feel that this is a waste of money. All that extra disk can cost quite a bit. They like the idea of client-free backups—backing up the data through a system other than the system that is using the data. However, they don't want to pay for another set of disks to store the backup mirror. What do they do?

The first thing some do is to share the backup mirror. Whether the backup mirror is in an enterprise storage array or a group of JBOD that is made available on the SAN for that purpose, it's possible to establish this backup mirror to more than one primary disk set. Obviously you can't back up more than one primary disk set at one time using this method, but suppose you have primary disk sets A and B. Once you finish establishing, splitting, and backing up primary disk set A, you can establish the backup mirror to primary disk set B, split it, then back it up again. Many people rotate their backup mirrors this way.

However, some storage vendors have a solution that's less expensive than having a separate backup mirror for each primary disk set and is more elegant than rotating a single backup mirror between multiple primary disk sets: snapshots.

Again, let's start with an enterprise storage array or a group of JBOD being managed by an enterprise volume manager. Recall that in the previous section "LAN-Free Backups," some volume managers and storage arrays can create a virtual copy, or a snapshot. To another host that can see it, it looks the same as a backup mirror. It's a static "picture" of what the volumes looked like at a particular time.

Creating the snapshot is equivalent to the step where you split off the backup mirror. There is no step where you must establish the snapshot. You simply place the application into a backup status, create the snapshot, and then take the application out of backup status. After that, the storage array or enterprise volume manager software makes the device visible to another host. You then perform the same steps as outlined in the previous section "Backing Up the Backup Mirror," for importing and mounting the volumes on the backup server. Once that is accomplished, you can back it up just like any other device.

Recovery of a snapshot

Similar to the backup mirror backup, the snapshot can typically be left around in case of recovery. However, most snapshot recoveries aren't going to be as fast as the backup mirror recovery discussed earlier. Although the data can still be copied from disk to disk, the recovery may not be as instantaneous. However, since this section of the industry is changing so fast, this may no longer be the case by the time you read this.

It should also be noted that, unlike the backup mirror, the snapshot still depends on the primary disk set's disks. Since it's merely a virtual copy of the disks, if the original disks are physically damaged, the snapshot becomes worthless. Therefore, snapshots provide quick recovery only in the case of logical corruption of the data, since the snapshot still contains a noncorrupted copy of the data.

A valid option

This variation on client-free backup represents a valid option for many. Depending on your configuration, this method can be significantly less expensive than a backup mirror, while providing you exactly the level of recoverability you need.

Server-Free Backups

So far in this chapter, we have discussed LAN-free and client-free backups. LAN-free backups help speed backup and recovery by removing this traffic from the LAN. They allow you to purchase one or more really large tape libraries and share those tape libraries among multiple servers. This allows you to take advantage of the economies of scale that large libraries provide, as the cost per MB usually decreases as the size of a library increases. Backing up large amounts of data is much easier on the clients when that data is sent via Fibre Channel, instead of being sent across the LAN.* Therefore, LAN-free backups reduce the degree to which backups affect any applications that are running on the client.

Client-free backups also offer multiple advantages. They remove almost all application impact from the backup client, since all significant I/O operations are performed on the backup server. If you use a backup mirror for each set of primary disk sets, they also offer a virtually instantaneous recovery method. However, this recovery speed does come with a significant cost, since purchasing a backup mirror for each set of primary disk sets requires purchasing more disk capacity then would otherwise be necessary. If your primary disk set is mirrored, you need to purchase a backup mirror, requiring the purchase of 50% more disk. If the primary disk set is a RAID 4 or RAID 5 volume, you will need to purchase almost 100% more disk.†

---

* There are vendors that are shipping gigabit network cards that offload the TCP/IP processing from the server. They make LAN-based backups easier, but LAN-free backups are still better because of the design of most backup software packages.

† It's not quite 100%, since the second stripe doesn't have to be a RAID 5 set. If it were simply a RAID 0 set, you'd need about 90% more disk than you already have.

What about snapshots? You may remember that we have discussed snapshots as an alternate way to provide instantaneous recoveries. However, snapshots (that have not been backed up to tape) only protect against logical corruption, and the loss of too many drives on the primary disk set results in a worthless snapshot. Therefore, client-free backups that use a backup mirror are the only backup and recovery design that offers instantaneous recovery after the loss of multiple drives on the primary disk set.

The remaining disadvantage to client-free backups is that you still need a server to act as a data path for the data to be backed up. Let's say that you've got several large backup clients running the same operating system, and all of their storage resides on an enterprise storage array that can perform client-free backups. Chances are that you are now talking about a significant amount of storage to back up each night. In fact, many client-free backup designs use full backups every night, because every file they back up changes every night. This is the case with almost any database that uses "cooked" files on the filesystem for its data files and is always true of a database that uses raw devices for the same purpose. (While there are a few block-level incremental packages available, they aren't yet widely used.) This means that if you back up five 2-TB clients, you are probably backing up 10 TB every night. Even though you have offloaded the data transfer from the data servers to the backup server, you will need a reasonably large server to back up 10 TB every night, and that server can have no purpose other than that.

With LAN-free backups, you back up the data without using the LAN. With client-free backups, you back up the data without using the client. What if you could transfer the data directly from disk to tape, without going through any server at all? If you could, your backups would be completely server-free. As with client-free backups, applications are almost completely unaffected, because few I/O operations are performed on the backup client.

One significant difference between client-free backups and server-free backups is that there are no homegrown server-free backup designs. The reasons for this will become clear as you see how deep into the filesystem and device driver levels you must go to accomplish the task.

Look, Ma, No Server

A truly server-free backup has a data path that doesn't include a server. It uses a server, of course, to control the process, but the data moves directly from disk to tape without going through any server's CPU—including the backup server. There are three essential requirements of server-free backup. You must be able to:

- Present the backup application with a static view of the disk set
- Map the blocks of data on the disk set to the files to which they belong
- Move the data directly from disk to tape

Getting a static view of the data

In order to use a backup mirror setup to present a static copy to the backup application, you must perform the following steps:

1. Establish the mirror
2. Quiesce the application writing to the disk
3. Split the mirror

If you wish to use a snapshot to present a static copy to the backup application, you need to perform only two steps:

1. Quiesce the application writing to the disk
2. Create the snapshot

 Not all database applications permit online third-party backups.

The procedures performed during this step are essentially the same as those used for client-free backup. Therefore, if you need more detail about these steps, please refer to that section of this chapter.

Logically mapping the disk to the filesystem

Now that the backup application has a static view of the disks to back up, you must perform an additional step that is necessary because of the way you back up the data. LAN-free and client-free backups back up filesystem data in the traditional way—via the filesystem. However, the method server-free backup uses to transfer the data to tape has no knowledge of the filesystem. As you'll see in the next step, it will simply transfer blocks of data to tape.

Therefore, prior to transferring these blocks of data to tape, you must create a map of which blocks belong to which files. That way, when the backup application is asked to restore a certain file, it knows which blocks of data to restore. Figure 4-15 illustrates how this works. File A consists of data blocks A, B, and C. File B consists of data blocks D, E, and F. Once the snapshot or split mirror has been created, these mappings remain constant until the split mirror or snapshot is created again. While it's static, the backup application records the file associations for File A and File B. When the restore application asks for File A to be restored, the server-free backup software knows it needs to restore disk blocks A, B, and C.

Transferring the data directly from disk to tape

The reason for the step in the previous section is that the main difference between client-free and server-free backups is the path the data takes on its way to tape—as

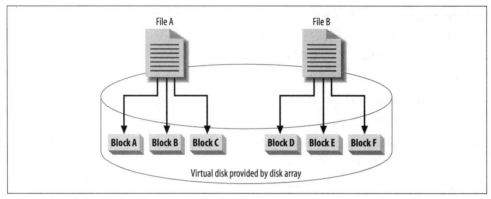

Figure 4-15. Logical file-to-disk mapping

illustrated in Figure 4-16. You'll note that Figure 4-16 looks much like Figure 4-9 with a few minor changes. First, you no longer need the dedicated backup server that is seen to the right of the storage array in Figure 4-9. This means that Backup Server A takes the responsibility of quiescing the application that is writing to the disk. Second, the tape library and backup mirror (or snapshot) must be connected to a SAN with support for *extended copy (xcopy)*. Finally, instead of sending the data to tape via the backup server (as shown in (4a) and (4b) in Figure 4-9), the backup software uses the SCSI *extended copy* command to send the data directly from disk to tape. This means, of course, that the data is being backed up on the raw-device level. Device-level backups are often referred to as *image-level* backups.

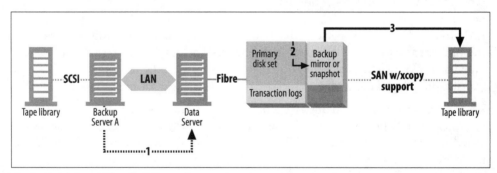

Figure 4-16. Server-free backup configuration

Server-Free Restores

When restoring data from a server-free backup system, you typically restore the data on the image level (file recoveries are rare but technically possible). *Image level* restores copy the entire image back from tape to disk. File level restores act just like nonserver-free restores, copying the file(s) you select from tape to disk. However, it's important to mention that performing server-free backups doesn't necessarily mean you are going to perform server-free restores. In fact, some server-free backup applications don't support server-free restores at all. The ones that do support server-free restores do so ŏnly for image-level restores. To see why this is the case, let's see how a server-free image-level restore works.

Image-level server-free restores

The server-free backup system in Figure 4-17 is the same one illustrated in Figure 4-16. Recall that we created a split mirror or snapshot, then used extended copy to back up that snapshot or mirror to tape. To reverse the process, you first have to create the snapshot to which you're going to restore. Since the entire snapshot is going to be overwritten, it really doesn't matter if it's an older snapshot or one that was just taken. Regardless, the snapshot or split mirror must be created, as shown in (1) in Figure 4-17. Next, the server-free backup application can use the *xcopy* command to restore the backed up data directly from tape to disk, as shown in (3).

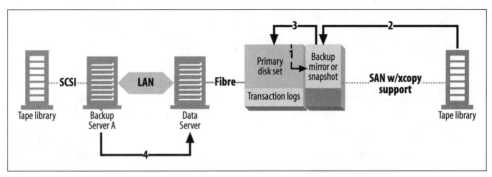

Figure 4-17. Server-free restores

The next step is important. Just as you need tŏ stop the application that was writing to the disk during backups, you need to do so during the restore. Otherwise, you'd really confuse things and corrupt the data. Also, depending on your operating system and filesystem type, you usually need to unmount the filesystem you're about to restore. (This is shown as (4) in Figure 4-17.) The reason for this is that the next step is going to completely overwrite the blocks underneath the filesystem. If you do this while the filesystem is mounted, the filesystem is immediately corrupted. Finally, you can restore the image from the backup mirror or snapshot to the primary disk set. Once this has been accomplished, mount the filesystem and resume the application. (If the application is a database, you will probably need to perform a transaction log restore first.)

 A fully functional server-free backup system automates all the previous steps when you select an image-level restore.

File-level server-free restores

As complicated as image-level restores may seem, file-level restores from server-free backups are even worse. In the top-left corner of Figure 4-18, you can see the original file-to-disk mapping shown in Figure 4-15. Below that, you can see that a snapshot or mirror is created of it, and that mirror is backed up to tape.

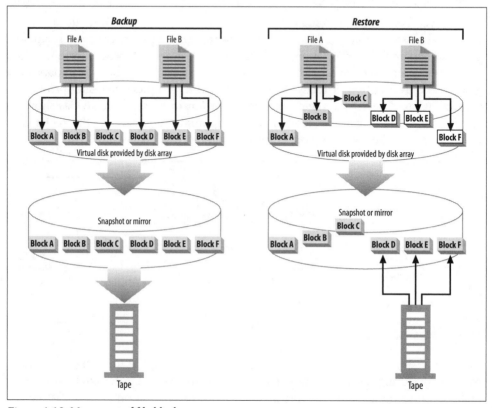

Figure 4-18. Movement of file blocks

Time passes; files are added, deleted, and modified. Due to the way disk technology works, you can see that File A and File B still use the same blocks, but the blocks are now in completely different places on the disk. Now assume that File B has been deleted, as represented by the white disk blocks.

To perform an image-level restore, you first need to create a snapshot or mirror to restore to. This, of course, duplicates the new block layout of the disk. If you then restore the blocks of data associated with File B, you can see you're restoring them to the wrong place. This overwrites the blocks of some other file, which corrupts that file.

Therefore, file-level restores from server-free backups need to be performed from the filesystem level, which is why file-level restores from server-free backups aren't server-free at all. When you request a file to be restored, the backup software knows that the file was backed up via an image-level server-free backup. It then consults its file-to-block map made during that backup and knows which blocks of data it needs to read from tape. Those blocks are then passed to the client software running on the client where the file needs to be. It then reassembles the blocks into a file it can pass to the filesystem. The filesystem then places the file's blocks in the appropriate site.

Advantages and Disadvantages

The advantages of server-free backups and restores are rather significant:

- Offloads backup traffic from LAN, CPU, and I/O channels of both clients and servers
- Neither backup client nor backup server's performance is impacted
- Safe, reliable online backup of active filesystems, although this can be accomplished in other ways
- High speed data transfer
- Full or incremental backup (not available with all server-free products)
- Image, directory, and file restore (not available with all server-free products)

Cost is the main disadvantage in server-free backups. Server-free backups usually require some change in your primary disk set; it definitely needs to be on a SAN. Depending on the backup vendor you choose, you then need to do one of three things. You can:

1. Put your primary disk set on an enterprise storage array capable of making split mirrors.
2. Use an enterprise volume manager that can make split mirrors that are visible to other hosts.
3. Use an enterprise volume manager that makes snapshots visible to other hosts.

Option 1 requires an enterprise storage array. Options 1 and 2 require additional disks, if you aren't already using split mirrors for backup. Option 3 requires additional software. However, some backup products include the software to do this when you purchase the server-free backup add-on to their product. This software, of course, also comes at a price. The data mover can also exist as intelligence on the disk array, a Fibre Channel router, or another dedicated appliance on the SAN.

The other disadvantage to server-free backups is that the process is rather complex. It requires much more design on the part of the backup software company, since it needs to do the file-to-block mapping. When something goes wrong, there are more pieces of software to troubleshoot.

LAN-Free, Client-Free, or Server-Free?

Which backup option is appropriate for your environment? The answer may be apparent if you ask yourself a few questions:

- If you're currently performing standard, LAN-based backups, is it negatively impacting the performance of any clients, or are any of the clients difficult to back up during the available window?

  The easiest way to solve this problem is to turn the affected backup clients into device servers and attach them to one or more tape libraries. The difficulty comes when deciding which tape libraries to connect them to. Suppose that you've only got one client with this problem. You don't necessarily want to buy a separate tape library just for one client. You can physically connect some of your first library's tape drives to the affected client and use library sharing* to share the library between this backup client (which is now a device server) and the main backup server. Unfortunately, you probably sized that tape library based on how many drives you needed for the main server, and you are now taking away some of its resources. When you are in this situation, you will almost always benefit from LAN-free backups by connecting the main server and device server(s) to a SAN and using drive sharing to dynamically allocate drives to the servers that need them.

- If you've already turned more than one of your clients into a device server that backs up its own data to locally attached tape drives, but aren't yet using drive sharing, would being able to dynamically share drives between multiple device servers be beneficial to you?

  This scenario assumes you already encountered this situation, and have already physically allocated certain tape drives to certain servers. Depending on the number of servers and tape drives involved, you'd probably benefit from a LAN-free backup configuration.

- You've already turned one or more of your clients into a device server—whether or not you're using drive sharing. The I/O load of backing up its own data to its own tape drives is certainly less than what normal LAN-based backups would generate, but it still creates a load. Is the load generated by LAN-free backups still greater than what you'd like?

If you've answered yes to the questions so far, you are a candidate for either client-free or server-free backups. The decision between the two is a bit more complex. Basically, you should get quotes for both systems, evaluate the cost of each in your environment, and then compare that cost to the benefits in Table 4-3.

---

* If your backup software supports library sharing.

Table 4-3. Comparison of LAN-free, client-free, and server-free backups

	LAN-free	Client-free	Server-free
Backup client CPU, memory, and I/O load of TCP/IP processing to transfer data across LAN	Significantly reduced (must still send metadata to backup server)	Significantly reduced (must still send metadata to backup server)	Significantly reduced (must still send metadata to backup server)
Backup server CPU, memory, and I/O load of TCP/IP processing to transfer data across LAN	Significantly reduced (must still receive metadata from backup client)	Significantly reduced (must still receive metadata from backup client)	Significantly reduced (must still receive metadata from backup client)
Backup client CPU, memory, and I/O load of moving the data from disk to tape	Same as LAN-based, since client is now responsible for moving split mirror or snapshot's data from disk to tape	No I/O load	No I/O load
Backup server CPU, memory, and I/O load of moving the data from disk to tape	Significantly reduced (must still handle I/O of index operations)	Same as LAN-based, because server is now responsible for moving split mirror or snapshot's data from disk to tape	Significantly reduced (must still handle I/O of index operations)
Must client be on SAN?	Yes (for drive sharing)	Yes	Yes
Must client's primary disk be on a SAN?	No	Yes	Yes and SAN must support *extended copy*
File-level recoveries	Yes	Yes	Probably not

	LAN-free	Client-free		Server-free	
		Snapshot	**Backup mirror**	**Snapshot**	**Backup mirror**
Additional disk	None	Cache disk only	Equivalent to usable disk on primary storage	Cache disk only	Equivalent to usable disk on primary storage
Additional software	Dynamic drive allocation	Snapshot control, backup control	Backup mirror control, backup control	Snapshot control, backup control with *xcopy* support	Backup mirror control, backup control with *xcopy* support
Additional server	No	Yes	Yes	No	No
Allows homegrown solutions	No	Yes	Yes	No	No

CHAPTER 5

NAS Architecture

The growth of the network attached storage (NAS) industry caught many people by surprise. It appeared to be nothing new—simply repackaged NFS. How popular could that be? Many people laughed when someone suggested that you could put database files on a filer. However, anyone who is following the NAS industry will tell you that no one is laughing now. Believe it or not, such configurations are now commonplace and are even supported by some database vendors! What has made NAS so popular? This chapter answers that question, along with a few others:

- What's wrong with good old NFS and SMB?
- How is NAS any different than NFS/CIFS?
- Is it true that some filers are faster than local disk?
- Which is better, NAS or SAN?

What's Wrong with Standard NFS and CIFS?

As mentioned in Chapter 1, before NAS there was NFS and SMB (now referred to as CIFS). Large data centers usually had one or more dedicated Unix (NFS) and Windows (SMB) file servers, each of which served hundreds of thousands of files to hundreds of users. Although we didn't know any better back then, there were a number of difficulties with such a configuration.

Usability

Many users needed to access files on both NFS and CIFS file servers. Some users even needed to access the same file with Unix-based applications and Windows-based applications. An example of such an application might be an engineering application that runs on Unix. Such an application might generate huge reports that could be stored as comma-separated (CSV) files. Such files are easily imported into Microsoft Excel, which can generate all sorts of reports and graphs. A user in this situation would probably use FTP to transfer the CSV file from the Unix system to their

Windows workstation. Some applications even require users to modify the file on the Windows workstation, and then send it to back to the Unix system via FTP. Since users quite often don't clean up after themselves, this practice usually results in many duplicate files on each machine. Over time, this results in a significant waste of resources.

Manageability

There are a number of manageability issues with traditional NFS and SMB/CIFS servers. Perhaps the most important issue is that you usually need a separate server for each protocol. The development of Samba for Unix (and other products like it) has helped, but there are still issues with cross-platform usage. As of this writing, it's somewhat difficult to read a drive shared by a Windows system on many Unix systems. (Although there is an FTP-like client for Samba, it's nowhere near as transparent as it needs to be.*) Although you can solve this problem by using Samba to provide CIFS services to Windows clients, it's commonplace for Windows administrators to resist using a Unix box to provide file sharing to the Windows community. (It's about as easy as talking a Unix administrator into using a Windows machine running NFS server software to provide NFS services to his Unix servers.)

The result is that CIFS data is usually served by a Windows machine, and NFS data is usually served by a Unix machine. Given the drastic differences between these two operating systems, each machine is usually managed by a different person—or even an entirely different group of people. This aggravates the duplicate file problem just discussed. Many environments have little or no communication between the Windows and Unix administrators. This means that only the user that creates the duplicate file will even know that the duplicate file exists! Thus any attempt to fix such a problem on a global level will be unsuccessful.

There are other manageability issues with traditional Unix and Windows file servers. Administrators must keep track of security alerts, patch alerts, and new releases to each operating system, and many of these updates require lengthy reboots of the servers. Keeping up to date with both operating systems can become quite a time-consuming process.

Performance

Traditional NFS and CIFS systems have serious performance inefficiencies, including, but not limited to:

- The design of the protocols themselves (although the design has improved in recent years)

---

* It's possible to transparently access Windows filesystems on Linux systems using Samba.

- The path that all I/O requests must take (the same as any protocol running on top of IP)
- The lack of RAM caching
- Inefficient filesystems that result in significant amounts of fragmentation

In large environments, these performance inefficiencies can create a number of problems. The first thing that happens is that users start to complain about poor performance when transferring large files. This, of course, leads to lost time as the administrators of the systems try to find the cause of the performance loss. Eventually, they will determine that the cause of the problem is an overloaded server. At some point, the only solution to this problem is the purchase of another server.

Availability

Historically, NFS and CIFS servers have not been the most available servers in the data center. Most environments spend their high availability budget elsewhere—usually on the database servers. Unfortunately, the downtime associated with the loss of a single disk on an NFS or CIFS server can result in days, or even weeks, of downtime. Although this lost time may not cost the company money directly, it results in significant reductions in productivity and morale. What's the point in working hard if your data is just going to get lost? These problems also cause people to want to save their data on their local hard drive, instead of the network drive. At some point, this will bite somebody when their local hard drive crashes, and they realize it isn't being backed up.

When a system is really important, many people suggest monitoring it proactively so that they can rapidly react to events which may impact system availability. However, proactive monitoring of traditional NFS and CIFS systems is also not always an easy thing to do, either.

Scalability

What happens when the most popular network-mounted drive on your NFS or CIFS server becomes full? You basically have two choices:

- Add space on the existing drive
- Add another network drive

If you have a newer volume manager (e.g., VxVM) and filesystem (e.g., VxFS or JFS), the first option (adding space on an existing drive) might not require downtime. Otherwise, growing a filesystem can be quite an operation. Even if you could get the system to recognize the disk drive without a reboot, the native volume managers of many Unix and Windows systems don't allow you to dynamically grow a RAID device or filesystem. If this is the case with your operating system, you need to embark on an incredibly time-consuming process that includes backing up the filesystem, reformatting the volume and filesystem with the additional drive, and restoring the original data to the new filesystem. Some feel that this is the proper thing to do even if you can dynamically grow the filesystem. It ensures that the RAID device will be laid out exactly as you wish, instead of how it ends up being laid out after adding a new device to an existing RAID group.

The second option (add another network drive) is more common. When */admin1* fills up, create */admin2*. When the *F:* drive fills up, create the *G:* drive. This is how things are normally done. Of course, this creates a great deal of confusion for both administrators and users. Instead of being able to remember that all files of a certain type are underneath a particular mount point, both users and administrators find themselves searching through multiple mount points to find the resources they need. This results in lost productivity and increased network traffic. Wouldn't it be nice if you had one place where all network mounted software was available or one mount point under which all (or at least a predictable range of) users could be found?

Enter Network Attached Storage

Over the last few years, NAS vendors have been creating systems that offer all the advantages of NFS and CIFS without any of the previously mentioned disadvantages. A few vendors have even gone above and beyond the call and have added functionality that would have never been dreamed of before the advent of NAS.

 This book uses the term *filer* as a generic term for all NAS servers. This term has not been trademarked and is already being used by several NAS vendors.

I am currently aware of almost 20 companies that I would consider original NAS equipment manufacturers. (That means 20 companies that are producing 20 unique filers.) There are dozens more that are rebranding these filers and selling them under their own name. With one or two exceptions, all the features discussed in the rest of this chapter are available with at least two of these vendors.

One of the biggest areas in which NAS has improved over traditional NFS and CIFS is performance. Not only are today's filers faster than traditional NFS and CIFS, some of them are even faster than equivalently priced local disk. These performance improvements are due to advancements in two areas. First, there have been some performance improvements in the actual NFS and CIFS protocols. Second, today's filers use brand-new architectures designed from the ground up with NFS and CIFS in mind.

NFS and CIFS Advances

Although NFS was originally developed by Sun, and CIFS was originally developed by IBM and further developed by Microsoft, many people outside these companies have helped to further the development of these two protocols. This is due to the nature of the open systems community; many vendors besides Sun and Microsoft stand to benefit from these protocols becoming well documented and fully accepted standards. Therefore, members of the Storage Networking Industry Association (SNIA) have helped to further these protocols.

Advances in NFS

Sun released NFS in 1985 and has made a number of improvements in its implementations since then. The first set of improvements did not require changes to the protocol itself. Then in 1995, changes were also made to the protocol, primarily enabling it to handle 64-bit file sizes. The following is a summary of some of the enhancements in NFSv3:

Close-to-open file consistency
> Early implementations of NFS did not envision a file that would be written on one system but read on another system. This was because in 1985, it was uncommon for a single user (or application) to access more than one computer at a time. Of course, as mentioned in the first chapter, 1985 also saw the introduction of windowing systems that allowed one user to access many computers at a time. Modern NFS clients make accessing a single file from multiple NFS clients safer by writing all modified data to the server in the *close* system call, and checking for cached data in the *open* system call.

Dynamic retry
> This feature allows clients to adjust their NFS retry values to reflect servers with varying speeds. If a client notices that a certain server is slow, it can increase the retry timeout values for that server to avoid unnecessary retries. The same is true for a fast server. A client with dynamic retry notices that the server is faster and changes the retry timeout values for that server, resulting in increased performance for fast servers.

Improved retry cache heuristics
> Most NFS server implementations have implemented the suggestions given by Chet Juszczak in a Usenix paper in 1989 ("Improving the Performance and Correctness of an NFS Server," *Usenix Conference Proceedings*, January 1989). These heuristics allow an NFS server to notice that a retry request is redundant and suppress the transmission of its reply.

Client-side disk caching
> It's a common misconception that NFS doesn't allow for client-side disk caching—that only memory caching is permitted. Many people believe that disk

caching is available only with AFS. Not only is this not true, disk caching of NFS data was introduced in Solaris 2.4, using the CacheFS feature. Modern filers take significant advantage of this feature.

Large block transfers

NFSv2 limited read and write operations to 8 KB. NFSv3 allows the server and client to negotiate the block size they will use, usually based on the amount of available bandwidth. Modern implementations are using block sizes as large as 48 KB.

Safe asynchronous writes

This new feature of NFSv3 allows the server to respond immediately to the *write* system call, instead of waiting until the data has been written to disk or NVRAM. The client can then use the *commit* system call to check back at a later time and determine if the file has indeed been written to disk. Although this doesn't increase the speed with which the data is written to disk, it does reduce the amount of time a client application must wait before moving on to another task.

The readdirplus operation

A lot of people did not realize that doing a single *ls –l* in an NFS mount with 1,000 files resulted in 1,001 NFS operations. This is because the *readdir* system call only included the names of the files in a directory; it did not include the sizes or attributes of the files. NFSv2 required a separate system call for each file in order to display this information. NFSv3 introduced the *readdirplus* system call that returns all of this data in a single NFS operation. (However, as will be discussed later, this system call has been replaced in NFSv4.)

NFS over TCP

Historically, NFS used UDP for almost all implementations. Recently, many vendors have introduced implementations of NFS that can run over TCP. This enhancement can significantly increase the reliability of NFS over highly congested networks, but it comes at a significant cost. Due to the overhead of TCP, it's the opinion of many vendors that NFS over TCP should be used only where it's necessary.

NFSv4 is on its way, bringing a new list of performance and integrity enhancements. However, since there are few NFSv4 implementations at this time, the following is a separate list of enhancements provided by this latest version of NFS:

Elimination of ancillary protocols

In NFSv2 and NFSv3, the *mount* obtained the initial filehandle, but file locking was managed by the Network Lock Manager protocol. NFSv4 is a single protocol using a single port, which (among other things) allows NFS to easily cross firewalls and the Internet. Locking is now fully integrated into the protocol.

A compound RPC procedure
> This allows clients to transmit several file operations in a single, compound request, significantly reducing the number of round trips required for a traditional file operation.

Stateful open and close operations
> These ensure the atomicity of share reservations and support exclusive creates. Additionally, the *open* operation lets the server delegate authority to a client, allowing much more aggressive client-side caching.

Other operation enhancements
> The *create* operation is now used only for certain special file objects such as directories, symbolic links, and device nodes. Otherwise, the *open* and *close* operations are used. File access rights are also checked as part of the *open* operation, instead of NFSv3's *lookup* and *access* procedures. The *lookup* operation has been greatly simplified and streamlined. NFSv4 is also built on a strong security model, using an extensible authentication architecture built on GSS-API. As of this writing, both Kerberos and LIPKEY are supported by this model. The *readdirplus* operation (introduced in NFSv3) has been dropped in favor of a rewritten and more streamlined *readdir* operation.

As you can see, there have been many enhancements in NFS over the years, resulting in it being a much more robust protocol than the one introduced in 1985.

CIFS Advances

Although CIFS is an acronym for "Common Internet File System," CIFS is more than a network-mountable filesystem. CIFS is also used indirectly by Microsoft as a transport protocol for other high-level Windows functions, including network printing, resource location services, remote management/administration, network authentication (secure establishment services), and remote procedure calls (RPCs). Having said that, this book concerns itself mainly with the network-mountable filesystem features that are provided by CIFS.

The filesystem features of CIFS are based on the Server Message Block (SMB) protocol, which has been around since 1984. It's a little more difficult to describe the advancements in CIFS since that time, however, since Microsoft has not published many of their advancements to CIFS. However, as a member of the Storage Networking Industry Association (SNIA), Microsoft recently participated in the authoring of the CIFS specification—joining forces with employees from IBM, EMC, Network Appliance, HP, and Veritas. You can read more about this specification at *http://www.snia.org/English/Work_Groups/NAS/CIFS*. Although Microsoft will probably continue to use CIFS in ways they don't publicly document (especially in the area of RPCs and network authentication), they appear to be cooperating with other vendors that are trying to provide SMB-based services using CIFS. The following list summarizes the features that are currently available in modern implementations of CIFS.

File access

CIFS supports all the standard file access system calls, including *open*, *close*, *read*, *write*, and *seek*.

File and record locking

CIFS supports file and record locking and also allows nonlocked access to files. A file locked by one application is protected from any other application, including applications that don't support locking. File locking in CIFS uses a concept called opportunistic locks, or oplocks. (The sidebar "Caching Versus Multiple User Access" has more information about locking.)

Safe caching

CIFS supports caching, including read-ahead and write-behind caching during what it calls *safe* conditions. Safe conditions include one client reading or writing to a file, and several clients reading the same file—but not writing to it. If more than one client is modifying a file simultaneously, safe caching is disabled, and all file operations are sent to the server. (The sidebar "Caching Versus Multiple User Access" provides more information about caching.)

Caching Versus Multiple User Access

Early implementations of SMB used absolutely no caching, and all requests for a file on a network drive would be synchronously forwarded to the file server. All file states were managed by the file server. This design allowed each SMB client to receive a current, highly coherent view of all files. However, demands for higher performance could be met only by introducing caching. How do you allow multiple clients read-write access to a file and still allow caching? The answer is called *opportunistic locks*, or *oplocks*.

Oplocks allow an application to receive an exclusive lock on a file. Once this lock is achieved, all multiclient operations can be suppressed, because the client that received the lock is the only one accessing the file. Prior to releasing its lock, a client must flush its changes to disk. Oplocks result in a significant decrease in network traffic for SMB mounts.

It's interesting to note that the original version of SMB was designed with multiple user access in mind—at the expense of performance. NFS seems to be designed in the reverse order, and subsequently, NFS file locking isn't as robust as that which is offered by CIFS and oplocks. (Locking has been greatly improved in NFSv4.)

File change notification

Applications can register with the CIFS server to be notified if and when the contents of a file change. This allows several servers to access the same file without having to constantly poll the server for changes.

Protocol version negotiation

There are several versions, or *dialects*, of CIFS implemented in the field. For example, even different versions of Windows use different dialects of CIFS. This feature allows a Windows 2000 server to "step down" in order to communicate properly with a Windows 95 server.

Extended attributes

This feature allows extended attributes about a file to be stored with that file. These attributes may include access control list information, the author of the file, or a description of the file's contents.

Distributed replicated virtual volumes

This allows the subtrees of a particular volume to actually be volumes on other servers. Clients negotiating a particular subtree are automatically and transparently directed to the appropriate server.

Server name resolution independence

Clients may use any name service they wish to resolve CIFS server names. This allows clients to use DNS in order to access CIFS filesystems on any CIFS server on the Internet.

Batched requests

Several requests can be batched into a single message, reducing latency caused by several round trips between client and server.

Unicode filenames

Historically, there were dozens of character-encoding schemes, including ASCII and EBCDIC. Each scheme mapped each character to a number, resulting in the same character being represented by multiple numbers. Unicode provides a unique number for every character, no matter what the platform, no matter what the program, no matter what the language. Many major software companies are adopting Unicode for its obvious advantages. (You can read more about Unicode at *http://www.unicode.org*.)

Sequential scanning

If this extended attribute (i.e., SEQUENTIAL_SCAN) is set on a file, it indicates that the file is to be accessed sequentially from beginning to end. This can create a significant performance increase for applications that read files this way.

Native TCP support

Although not mentioned in the specification, one significant performance enhancement in recent years has been allowing CIFS to run natively on top of

TCP/IP. Most early versions of CIFS/SMB ran over NetBIOS. Although Net-BIOS can now run on top of TCP/IP (sometimes referred to as NBT), NetBIOS is an inefficient protocol and has been essentially removed from current versions of Microsoft Windows products. As of this writing, Microsoft is the only vendor offering a commercial version of CIFS that offers native TCP support.*

System Architecture Advances

Although significant advancements have been made in the protocols themselves, many believe that the greatest performance enhancements have come from creating filers designed from the ground up to be dedicated entirely to serving network-mounted filesystems via NFS or CIFS. (Early filers did not support CIFS, but all major NAS vendors do today.)

 No single NAS vendor has implemented all the advances discussed here. In fact, there are vendors that have implemented none of these enhancements. Ask your NAS vendor what they have done to improve performance and reliability.

To understand the architectural improvements NAS vendors have made, we must first look at how traditional NFS and CIFS services are provided. Historically, such services were available only by using the appropriate software on a Unix or Windows server. Unix servers served NFS volumes, and Windows servers served CIFS volumes. One of the problems with this design is that a dedicated server was not required. This often meant that NFS and CIFS volumes were served by a machine that had many other tasks.

Even a dedicated NFS or CIFS server was required to do quite a bit of work to process a single NFS or CIFS request. A look at Figure 5-1 should help illustrate this. Each request is received on one of the server's network interface cards, or NICs, in the form of network packets. This request must then be processed by the appropriate network layer software, such as TCP/UDP and IP. Once the packets have been assembled into a coherent NFS or CIFS request, the request must then be passed to the CIFS or NFS drivers. These drivers then request the file from the filesystem, which then reads the file from the disk via the disk drivers. The disk drivers then pass the file back to the filesystem, which passes it to the NFS or CIFS drivers. These drivers then pass the data to the network layer for transmission across the network. The network layer then creates the necessary packets and sends the data across the network via the NIC.

---

* Samba, a free product, also offers native TCP support for CIFS (see *http://www.samba.org*).

Streamlining the Process

"Of course," you say. This is how things are done. In a sense, filers have to follow this same paradigm. However, there is one significant difference. Consider that modern Unix or Windows systems must be able to do more than serve NFS or CIFS files. Even a dedicated NFS server can still process email, name service requests, login requests, and dozens of other functions. Since NFS is only one of many functions the server is designed to perform, the instructions for processing NFS requests don't reside permanently in memory. This is true for each step illustrated in Figure 5-1. Each step is processed by the kernel—or more likely by an application called by the kernel. This means each step probably requires a CPU interrupt and main memory. Depending on the size and configuration of the server, the instructions for one step are paged out in order to make room for the instructions for the next step.

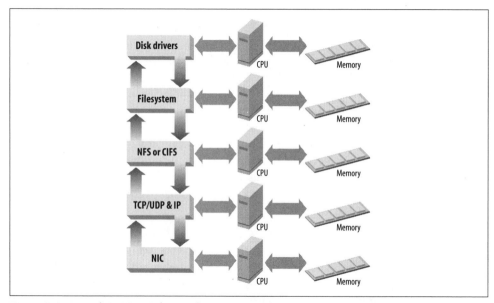

Figure 5-1. Typical NFS/CIFS data path

Can you imagine how much faster NFS and CIFS requests could be if their instructions resided permanently in memory? As wonderful as this idea sounds, it's simply not possible with the standard Unix or Windows system architecture. However, a system that does nothing but serve NFS and CIFS requests is a different matter.

The first thing to do is remove from the kernel and its accompanying software any instructions that aren't absolutely necessary for processing NFS or CIFS requests. (Sorry, Eric: *sendmail* has got to go.) When this is done well, the results are astounding. Imagine a kernel with NFS, CIFS, TCP, UDP, IP, filesystem, and device drivers compiled into it—and yet it still fits one or two floppies! Once this has been accomplished, anything is possible. A kernel of such small size can actually be implemented completely in hardware, possibly resulting in even more performance improvements.

The difference between a Unix or Windows server serving NFS or CIFS and a filer doing the same is roughly the equivalent of a router and a layer three switch. A router runs a software-based kernel that must process dozens of different protocols. A layer three switch, on the other hand, supports only two or three protocols and thus can implement them in hardware. No one would doubt that a layer three switch can route faster than a standard, software-based router. The same is true of any good filer.

It's important to note that not all filers have followed this method of creating micro-kernels and have chosen instead to use a general-purpose operating system, such as Linux or Windows. If nonessential services aren't removed but are disabled, it's still possible for systems based on a general-purpose operating system to experience performance improvements over simply running NFS or CIFS on a standard server.

Making It Even Better

Although significant advancements were made with the NFS and CIFS protocols, and the handling of these protocols has been streamlined, some NAS vendors felt that they could make things even better with a few other improvements. The following is a list of improvements made by some NAS vendors:

NVRAM cache

Assuming that a typical user opens a file, modifies it a few times, and saves it after each modification, significant performance improvements can also be implemented using RAM-based caching. Some NAS vendors made this even better using NVRAM (non-volatile RAM). NVRAM removes the objection to RAM caching, since data that resides in NVRAM will survive a reboot or crash.

SAN backend

Although NAS and SAN are competitors in one sense, that doesn't mean that NAS vendors can't take advantage of the advancements being made in the SAN industry. Most major NAS vendors use Fiber Channel backends. When you purchase one of these systems, you're also getting a system that was designed from the ground up with fast and reliable storage in mind.

One of the biggest complaints about SANs, a lack of interoperability, isn't a problem with filers. Since filers are meant to be simple to install, the SAN components that are used in a filer will have already been tested together with that filer. (If everyone bought SANs that way, interoperability concerns would be almost nonexistent.)

Advanced filesystems

Another area of advancement is that of the filesystem software that is being used on some filers. At least two major vendors have written filesystem software designed specifically for their particular architecture. This results in even more efficiency and integrity improvements over the traditional NFS/CIFS architecture.

High Availability and Scalability

Another area where modern filers have improved over the traditional NFS/CIFS model is in the area of availability. As mentioned earlier in this chapter, many companies choose to spend their high availability budgets on other servers, resulting in NFS and CIFS servers that are significantly less reliable than the other servers in the environment. Filers need to be reliable, and NAS vendors set out to make them so. Filers include availability features that aren't typically built into an off-the-shelf Unix or Windows system. This list doesn't mean to imply these features are available only on NAS; they are also available for Unix and Windows in third-party solutions. However, they are usually available in off-the-shelf NAS systems without using third-party software.

Preconfigured RAID

Although many people install third-party hardware or software RAID on their Unix and Windows servers, such software and hardware is often not included in base configurations. Filers, however, almost always come with built-in, pre-configured RAID arrays. The level of RAID depends on which vendor you purchase your filer from. (See Appendix B for definitions of the various levels of RAID.) However, most have implemented RAID so that you can easily and dynamically grow the size of your NFS and CIFS volumes without any of the hassles discussed earlier in this chapter. They also typically include hot-swappable disks and built-in hot spare drives.

NVRAM cache

Although NVRAM has already been mentioned as a performance improvement, it also significantly improves reliability and availability. Using NVRAM for cache allows all the performance gains of RAM-based caching without sacrificing the reliability features of disk-based caching.

Active/active failover

A traditional HA model includes an *active* server and a *standby* server. The active server is used during normal operations; the standby server isn't. Only during a failover situation does the standby server get used. This is an incredible waste of money and is the reason many people have not employed HA systems already.

Active/active failover, on the other hand, employs a different method. Each server in an active/active configuration shares the load of the services being provided by the cluster. A failover situation simply means that one or more servers in the cluster are no longer carrying their fair share of the load. This means that the other servers in the cluster will have to work harder. However, all servers are being used during normal operations. Active-active failover is available with some filers.

Preinstalled backup client (NDMP)

Both Unix and Windows systems include some type of software to perform backups, but such software was designed mainly for manual backups. Backing up terabyte-sized filers requires enterprise-class backup tools. On a typical Unix or Windows system, you need to purchase and install a third-party backup package in order to take advantage of such tools. Most filers, on the other hand, come preinstalled with support for the Network Data Management Protocol (NDMP). Although you'll need to purchase a commercial backup and recovery product to take advantage of this protocol, you don't need to install any software on the filer itself. (NDMP is covered extensively in Chapter 7.)

Snapshots/checkpoints

As with many of the features in this list, snapshots aren't a new concept. It's just that they are normally offered only via third-party software products. However, at least two NAS vendors now include them in their base product, although one of them calls them *checkpoints*.

When you create a snapshot, the software records the time the snapshot was taken. Once the snapshot is taken, the software gives you or your backup utility another name through which you may view the filesystem. For example, when a Network Appliance creates a snapshot of */home*, the snapshot can be viewed via */home/.snapshot/snapshot_name*. Creating the snapshot doesn't actually copy data from */home* to */home/.snapshot/snapshot_name*, but it appears as if that's exactly what happened. If you look inside */home/.snapshot/snapshot_name*, you'll see the entire filesystem as it looked when */home/.snapshot/snapshot_name* was created.

Creating the snapshot takes only a few seconds. (For more discussion on the concept of snapshots, see Chapter 4.)

Automatic host-to-host replication

This is slightly different from an HA system. Clusters in an HA system typically share the same set of disks via shared SCSI or a SAN. Host replication/mirroring actually copies the data to another host for disaster recovery purposes. Once the initial copy has been made, all changes on one host are automatically replicated to the secondary host. Since it's copying only the deltas, only a small amount of network bandwidth is required. If the primary host is disabled, the secondary host can take over. Host-to-host replication used to be available only with database products, and it's also available with third-party software you can buy for Unix or Windows systems. Now a few NAS vendors offer this feature as well, although it's typically an extra-priced option.

Most filers are also highly scalable. You can start with a base system with a standard RAID configuration and add to this configuration as your needs grow. The reason many filers are easier to scale than many Unix or Windows systems is that they are designed with that in mind. Such functionality is often available on a Unix or Windows system, but it will probably be provided by extra-cost, third-party software.

Low Total Cost of Ownership (TCO)

Another area where filers excel is in total cost of ownership. The savings come from three areas:

- Low individual component cost
- Single server for NFS, CIFS, and HTTP services, giving you one type of host to buy disks for
- Low maintenance cost

Low Individual Component Cost

As anyone who has purchased hardware for a Unix system knows, you often pay much more if the hardware is going to be installed into a Unix system, especially if the Unix platform vendor is the only source for a given part. Sometimes you are even paying more for the same card, simply because it will be installed in a Solaris server. Many, but not all, filers are built using standard off-the-shelf hardware. Of course, all parts are precertified before being used in any NAS configurations. Also, by buying less expensive disks, you can buy more disks, place them in a RAID array, and create a system that is significantly more reliable than any single disk would be.

Single Server for NFS, CIFS, and HTTP Services

No longer do you need to maintain a separate server for NFS, CIFS, and HTTP services. A single filer can serve NFS and CIFS data, and many of them can also serve static web data via HTTP. One major e-commerce vendor's images are all served from a single filer using this method. While their pages are created dynamically, the images are static and can thus be served from a filer. Another new concept supported by NAS is WebNFS. Using the *nfs://* nomenclature instead of *http://* tells the web server that it should access an NFS mount. Although this new feature has not yet been adopted by all web server software, it offers another option for using filers in a web environment. In addition to NFS, CIFS, and HTTP, some filers also make files available via the NCP, AFP, and FTP protocols.

Not only do you not need to maintain a separate server for each protocol, users that need to use both protocols can access their files from Windows and Unix-based workstations without having to move them back and forth. This removes the problem discussed earlier in this chapter that results in a single file being stored in multiple places.

Ease of Maintenance

Perhaps the greatest argument for filers is how easy they can be to install and maintain. The phrase, "It just works," is a common one among those who have had to manage filers. Once they are configured, they can also be extremely easy to maintain.

Multiprotocol Servers

One of the most important reasons filers are easier to maintain than their Unix/Windows counterparts is that filers support multiple protocols. A single filer can support all of the protocols in this list:

CIFS

The CIFS protocol allows the filer to share its files with any Windows or OS/2 client. It should be mentioned that these are complete CIFS implementations, offering all of the same functionality available with a Windows-based CIFS server.

NFS/WebNFS

Files on a filer can also be served via NFS. This allows Unix and Linux clients to mount these drives. Windows and Mac clients that are running NFS client software can also mount files that are served via NFS.

A recent addition to the NFS family is the concept of WebNFS. As you probably already know, a URL is composed of six parts, the first of which describes the protocol/data source. For example, a URL that begins with *http://* specifies that the web server should use the Hypertext Transfer Protocol, or *http*, to display the objects described after the *http://*. There are normally eight protocols that can be listed here, including *ftp://, gopher://, mailto://, news://, telnet://, WAIS://, http://, and file://*. Sun has proposed the addition of *nfs://*. Using *nfs://* in the protocol field of the URL notifies the web server that the object is stored on an NFS server. Some NAS vendors are listing support for this nomenclature.

HTTP

HTTP is an interesting recent addition to the list of protocols supported by filers. Although much of today's web content is dynamic, almost all dynamic pages contain reference to some static content—usually images. As mentioned earlier in this chapter, filers can now store and display this content.

Other protocols

Some filers also support other protocols, including NCP, AFP, and FTP. The Network Core Protocol (NCP) is used for sharing files between NetWare servers. The AppleTalk Filing Protocol (AFP) is used to share files between Macintosh workstations. The File Transfer Protocol (FTP) is the standard protocol for copying files between Unix systems. A web client can also access it with a URL starting with *ftp://*.

Not only do filers support all these protocols with one box, they usually support multiple protocols on one filesystem. This means that a single copy of a file could be accessed on a Unix client, a Windows client, and a web browser.

Simplified Management

As mentioned earlier, most filers use streamlined kernels, also referred to as *micro-kernels*, that contain only the lines of code necessary to provide NFS and CIFS services. Of course, there must also be support for maintaining the system. Many filers have also made such management easier than a typical Windows or Unix box.

As mentioned in Chapter 6, if you maintain a Unix NFS server, you probably need to log in using *telnet* or *ssh*, and issue the appropriate commands. Windows versions 2000 and XP include terminal services that can remotely access the console and manage your CIFS shares. Filers offer a number of options that are simpler than the traditional methods used to maintain NFS or CIFS servers:

Web browser
> Some filers can be maintained via a web browser. As long as you know the administrator password, you can maintain such filers via any web browser in your environment.

rsh
> A few NAS vendors support managing their filers via *rsh*. *rsh* is obviously an insecure way to manage filers, so hopefully it isn't your only option.

ssh
> Some vendors also include an *ssh* service that can be used instead of *rsh*.

telnet
> Of course, many NAS vendors also support maintaining their servers via *telnet*.

Secure GUI
> Some NAS vendors support a secure GUI that doesn't send its authentication information in clear text.

Simplified Physical Architecture

The physical architecture of most filers is also simplified and thus easier to manage. Most start with a short, rack-mountable base system that contains the CPU and memory components. Attached to that are rack-mountable disk arrays that are usually attached to the filers via Fibre Channel. Almost all are designed to be easily assembled, installed, and configured.

Ease of Use

Filers are also easier for the users that are accessing the files. The main reason for this is the fact that a single file can be accessed via NFS, CIFS, or HTTP. Users can create a file on a Unix system, open that file in their word processor or spreadsheet on their Windows system, and then send an email to their coworkers containing a URL that points back to the same exact file—without having to attach the file to email. Performing these tasks in a traditional NFS/CIFS environment requires much more work on the part of both the creator of the document and the receiver of the email message—not to mention the Unix, Windows, and network administrators.

Managing NAS

Once you have received your new filer, what do you need to know to make it into a production system? As the network architect or system administrator, you will, of course, need to have a clear understanding of the basics of daily management. This includes knowing what tasks are involved in NAS management, what you should expect to do on a regular basis, and how these tasks can be simplified.

This chapter covers:

- The different uses for NAS
- Installing NAS
- NAS configuration
- Data migration
- Maintenance: support, monitoring and tuning

The Different Uses for NAS

As mentioned in Chapter 5, NAS offers high performance, high reliability, high availability, and multiprotocol access. Although just about every environment can benefit from these features, there are a few applications and market segments in which NAS is especially beneficial.

Data Consolidation

Sharing the home directories of thousands of users using workgroup NT/Unix "storage" servers can result in excessive management work, both in setup as well as hardware and software maintenance. The same is true with project data and department storage areas that are distributed and managed by distributed IT groups. Consolidating all your distributed data into a smaller number of systems that share them directly to users is a much simpler alternative. This results in the following features:

Ease of setup

Setting up a filer is easy. Most filers are designed to plug in to the network and share data, unlike general-purpose hosts. You simply need to assign users to their home directories and share every home directory to users over CIFS or NFS. Some filers even provide features to configure automatically created shares. Sharing home directories from NAS is a much easier task than exporting and sharing home directories distributed across multiple servers on the network.

Additional features

Filers are best-of-breed devices and as such, offer additional features, such as high-availability setups, data protection (snapshots, mirroring), and highly reliable filesystems.

Internet Applications

Web, email and groupware applications are all in need of fast, reliable and scalable storage. These include large web applications such as e-learning, e-commerce, streaming media, and services hosting (also called xSPs). Filers can be deployed in a distributed fashion a lot quicker and with fewer local management needs. The advantages of using NAS for Internet applications can be seen mainly in the implementation of large storage capacities on a tight schedule:

Quick implementation

Internet projects are known to have demanding implementation schedules. Most filers can be installed in a matter of minutes and enable customers to shorten the implementation of the whole solution.

Quick learning curve

NAS basics aren't complex to learn and master. Most system administrators quickly become familiar with the configuration interfaces offered by filers.

Business Applications

Databases and other business applications, such as Oracle, MS-SQL, Sybase, Informix, SAP, JD Edwards, are all examples of software that can benefit from NAS. The advantages of using NAS with business applications can be seen in the following areas:

Scalability

Server upgrades are easier because storage is separated from the server. Similarly, database growth is easier because disks can be added on the fly to an online volume, with no need for a reboot or any extra steps.

Management

Some databases can require complex schemes of disk setup, which become unnecessary when the database is hosted on one or two optimized RAID volumes. Time allocated for performance tuning is freed for tuning the application logic itself instead of the storage system.

Availability

With instant snapshot capabilities, some filers offer a way to back up certain databases at any point in time and to restore corrupt databases in a matter of seconds. This facility doesn't require backup application plug-ins for the specific database, as the backup used is a simpler, application-neutral file-level backup. (Note that this facility requires that the database support backup of files by third-party software. Oracle and Informix, for example, currently include this support.)

 SAN systems also have many, if not all, of these features. For a comparison of SANs and NAS, please see Chapter 1.

Installing a Filer

Once you purchase a filer, you need to install it. Two initial steps in that process involve preparing your network for a filer and installing the operating system on the filer.

Network Setup

Traffic to and from a filer is restricted to network sharing protocols and a basic set of maintenance protocols, such as DNS, NIS, and WINS. A general-purpose server is open for other protocols and services, such as email, NetBIOS browsing elections, Active Directory replication, and LDAP server replication.

The high bandwidth needed for data traffic between compute servers and NAS filers is a factor when choosing the right network topology in NAS implementation. It's therefore quite common to have a dedicated storage LAN (also referred to as a *backend network*), which is used for traffic between the filers and compute servers. Also common is a dedicated client LAN (also referred to as a *frontend network*), used for traffic between filers and desktops. Benefits of such topologies include a more secure backend network and higher compute server throughput (since client traffic doesn't interrupt server traffic). The major drawback is the need to manage two separate networks.

Operating System Installation

Depending on the vendor and type of filer, you can do the installation of the operating system yourself. Some filers, however, come preconfigured, with the operating system already installed. In most systems, the operating system is installed with a set of floppies and a CD or a network installation that follows. Most NAS devices use proprietary operating systems, Linux-based operating systems, or versions of embedded Windows. Make sure you talk to your vendor about your particular system.

Proprietary operating systems

Some major NAS vendors offer operating systems that are written internally or licensed from operating system vendors such as VxWorks. These operating systems usually provide multithreaded kernels, with networking protocols and filesystem primitives built on top. Their special design allows improved internal data paths and kernel subsystems that are tuned for file service.

Proprietary operating systems are usually faster than traditional operating systems, which have to support a richer set of I/O device drivers. On the other hand, support for new I/O adapters and storage devices is slower than for general operating systems, because drivers have to be ported to the proprietary operating system from more common operating systems.

Auspex, EMC and Network Appliance all use proprietary operating systems (Net-BIOS, DART, and Data OnTAP, respectively).

Linux-based operating systems

Linux has gained a clear market share in the server market with its high performance, reliability, and low price. Linux is a general-purpose operating system. Nevertheless, since Linux source code is open to the public, it's easier for Linux-based NAS vendors to deliver new capabilities to their systems.

Major drawbacks of current Linux-based filers are the lack of mature reliable filesystems and multiprotocol support. Although both exist, in the form of ReiserFS and ext3 as new filesystems, and Samba and kernel NFS support, these options are less proven than their counterparts that run on proprietary operating systems.

RAIDZONE provides Linux-based filers.

Embedded Windows

Windows NT Embedded Version has been available for quite some time, and Microsoft recently announced the Windows 2000 Server Appliance Kit (SAK). Both are operating systems intended for special purpose systems. Windows 2000 SAK-based filers include many regular Windows 2000 services, such as Active Directory and Unix Services, so such filers can offer native support for CIFS protocol while still supporting NFS. Since Windows NT Embedded and Windows 2000 SAK are essentially just generic operating systems, the risks and costs of maintaining a general-purpose operating system are still in place.

Compaq NAS filers use the Windows 2000 SAK.

Configuring a Filer

Unlike a general-purpose compute machine with a local keyboard, monitor, and mouse, filer configuration is closer to a networking device. What are the interfaces used for configuring a filer? What are the configuration parameters available to a filer administrator?

Configuration Interfaces

There are a number of different interfaces you can use to configure and otherwise administer your filers.

Console

Most devices come with an RS-232 console port, so you can connect to your filer using any dumb terminal, such as Windows HyperTerminal.

If you administer multiple systems, you should consider a network terminal server—a device that provides access to multiple console ports over the network. A console is mostly limited to single connection, but using a terminal server, you can configure the console to be shared among multiple administrators. A network terminal server also provides remote connection to the consoles, so that you can dial in to it and operate your systems remotely.

Command-line interface (CLI)

Among Unix system administrators, the command line is still the most used and favored method of management. And while all NAS vendors provide some form of GUI, the GUI isn't always capable of the same functionality as the CLI. The CLI can be used in both console, *telnet*, *rsh*, and *ssh* sessions. (*telnet, rsh*, and *ssh* sessions may be limited to a single user or may allow multiple users.) Some vendors took the command line one step further and offer menu-based systems.

Remote shell: rsh

Some systems allow you to run certain commands through *rsh*. At a minimum, this requires configuring the *hosts.equiv* on the filer to allow other hosts access through *rsh*, but it might require extra settings as well. *rsh* isn't at all secure. For this reason, most security-conscious administrators require the use of *ssh*.

Secure shell: ssh

ssh offers a more secure way to administer a system via the command-line syntax: the transport is secure, but the user interface stays the same. However, not all NAS vendors support *ssh*.

HTTP

Web-based administration provides a graphical interface that is accessible through a web browser. Some vendors base their implementation on Java. Java offers more sophisticated graphical representations than plain HTML, but some have concerns about Java's stability and security.

Configuration Files and Scripting

As with most Unix vendors, many NAS vendors keep some or most of their configuration information in text files. Text files represent a simple method of configuration—for those who are familiar with text editors. However, this also presents the potential problem of multiple administrators trying to edit the same file, which can have disastrous results.

Common uses for text files are for quota configuration and user mapping (between CIFS and NFS). Any filer that uses Samba as its CIFS implementation is configured through *smb.conf*.

Unix system administrators find scripting capabilities a requirement for large-scale deployments. There are multiple reasons for creating in-house scripts, such as the ability to add more complex reports and alerts than those that come with the product. Scripting can use several mechanisms:

Parsing of command output through rsh/ssh
> Most vendors try to give commands a consistent look, so they can be parsed using shell scripts, Perl string manipulation, and so on.

SNMP get commands for scripting in-house monitoring or alerting features
> This facility might be useful for customers who prefer to build their own monitoring systems rather than buy off-the-shelf products.

Application programming interfaces (APIs)
> Some NAS vendors implement an internal configuration database, also called a registry.

Currently there is no consistent management API for filers. This is a shame, since it discourages third-party independent software vendors (ISVs) from developing value-added management features for NAS.

Configuration Security

Network configuration is susceptible to security breaches. (Out-of-band management of SAN equipment presents the same risks.) Since most filers are configured via the network, here is a list of different methods that can mitigate these risks:

Physical console protection
> The most secure option is to disable control of the filer via the network and allow such control only from the console and a direct serial cable.

Administration hosts

Assignment of specific list of hosts as administration hosts. This limits the exposure to unauthorized configuration.

HTTPS/SSL

Because HTTP connections are usually based on clear text login and password going over the wire, it isn't considered a secure mechanism. Some vendors supply an option to use HTTPS and SSL 2.0/3.0 to secure the connection between the management host and the managed NAS.

rsh

Similar to HTTP, *rsh* is considered as an insecure mechanism. A hostname/IP address check can verify the source of the commands being issued; however, this can be easily spoofed.

SNMP

SNMP was not originally designed with high security in mind, but there are some facilities you can use to provide a higher level of security. SNMP communities can prevent unauthorized SNMP managers (the SNMP-enabled host that manages the devices on the network) from viewing or changing SNMP objects. There are three SNMP operations:

get

SNMP *get* retrieves data from a managed device.

set

SNMP *set* sets values in the managed device. This can have security issues, since there is no authentication done on the sender.

trap

SNMP traps can alert the SNMP management station. Because traps can be used as triggers for other system events, they also convey a security risk.

Since most filers use SNMP mainly for monitoring purposes, SNMP *set* isn't widely implemented in filers.

Access control lists

Access control lists (ACLs) provide a way to reflect administration hierarchy. Access to different levels of administration tools (mostly portions of a GUI) and entities (such as volumes) can be granted to specific organizational roles. For example, different users can administer specific volumes.

Configuring the Storage

A filer's storage is configured in two ways. The first is disk space allocation, in which you decide how many physical disks are going to be assigned to each volume. (A volume, or virtual device, usually consists of several physical devices in a RAID group.) The second is user space allocation, in which you configure, via quotas, how much of a particular volume any individual user is allowed to use.

Disk space allocation

Planning and setup of disk space is a major concern when configuring NAS for the first time. The methods and mechanisms to configure drives and volumes differ greatly between the different products. What are the building blocks of disk space allocation?

Physical disk drives
> These are the actual drives that are configured into RAID groups or sliced up into smaller units, and so are often called *slices*.

Disk shelves
> Shelves are the containers of disk drives. Shelves consists of bays, or slots, used to populate power supplies, disk drives and fans. For most vendors, a disk must be in a specific slot, because each slot has its own physical address or SCSI logical unit number (LUN). The address is then matched against the RAID configuration database to find the disk's location in the RAID group. Some vendors include this detail within the disk, in what is called a *RAID label*. This helps with disk allocation and management, because the physical location of the disk is no longer relevant.

RAID group
> This is a group of physical disk drives, slices, or possibly a logical representation of them. Some NAS vendors perform RAID on multiple levels, striping together disks that have already been mirrored on a lower level. RAID groups affect reliability and performance. A RAID group can be configured in a few ways, also called *RAID levels*. RAID can also be implemented in hardware and software. Neither is automatically more efficient than the other. It's the vendor's implementation that makes a difference. Only benchmarks can really demonstrate how efficient a particular RAID implementation is in your environment. (See Appendix B for descriptions of the various levels of RAID.)

Volume: the logical storage unit
> A volume is built out of one or more RAID groups. A volume is therefore susceptible to RAID group failures. Usually one RAID group failure will cause the entire volume to fail, but this isn't the case if mirroring techniques are implemented in the RAID layer.

Filesystem: where data is stored
> Filesystem implementations differ significantly, but there are always some configuration parameters for the filesystem, such as the maximum number of inodes or performance optimizations.

User space allocation: quotas

You need to decide how much disk space will be allocated to users. Some vendors offer a way to assign default quotas to all users; others offer more granularity by setting quotas to groups and directories. Quotas can prevent situations in which one user fills up a volume used by thousands of users. With quotas, you can also monitor and report on disk usage.

There can be three types of quota identifiers:

User

This quota is based on the NFS/CIFS user identifier, whether it's the Unix UID or CIFS SID. This quota is calculated based on the number of blocks or inodes that the specific user owns at a given moment.

Group

This quota is based on the NFS/CIFS group identifier, whether it's the Unix GID or CIFS SID. This quota is calculated based on the number of blocks or inodes the specific group owns at a given moment. As of this writing, most filers don't support SID-based group quotas.

Directory

This quota limits a specific directory in a volume and is calculated based on the number of blocks or inodes included in the specific directory.

There can be two quota types:

Hard

Hard quotas put a hard limitation on the specific identifier. For example, if a user has a hard quota of 50 GB, he gets an error when he tries to write beyond the 50-GB limit; that is, he is prevented from exceeding his quota.

Soft

Soft quotas, as the name applies, are a relaxed form of hard quotas. Instead of limiting the user from writing any more data to the filesystem, there is some form of notification to the user or the administrator of being close to exceeding the quota. This helps the user community clean up their data before they are blocked from writing.

Configuring the Network Interfaces

The network is the basis of access to the filer and, as such, it's extremely important. Configuring your network correctly from the start ensures good performance in the future. Network configuration differs mainly by interface type. The following is a list of possible interfaces for a filer:

10-Mb Ethernet

Because 10-Mb Ethernet is limited to half-duplex communication with a network throughput of a maximum of 1 MB/s, it isn't recommended in modern NAS configurations.

100-Mb/Fast Ethernet

100-Mb Ethernet offers good performance for desktops and servers at a low price per port. 100-Mb Ethernet can be configured to be full duplex, and some implementations offer flow control as well. The theoretical maximum network throughput of 100-Mb Ethernet is approximately 12 MB/s. Typical issues involve duplex settings and the decision to use a hub or a switch.

Gigabit Ethernet

Gigabit Ethernet offers transfer rates of over 70 MB/s. (Although 1000 Mb divided by 8 should result in a throughput of 120 MB/s, most implementations aren't yet capable of anything near that.) Most Gigabit Ethernet NICs process frames faster then their 100-Mb Ethernet counterparts, so they provide less network latency, and faster response time to the user. Newer NICs also offload the TCP/IP processing from the host CPU, bringing total throughput closer to the theoretical maximum of 120 MB/s.

Hub versus switch

Hubs use a shared bus, which means that every port in the hub receives every frame that goes over the bus. This has major limitations, because Ethernet was implemented using the CSMA-CD algorithm—retransmitting based on collision detection. With a shared media, collisions always occur, increasing the retransmit ratio and the number of lost frames. As well, hubs are half-duplex by nature.

Layer 2 and 3 switches filter out unnecessary traffic based on the MAC address and IP address, respectively. Each switch port receives only the traffic targeted to its own assigned addresses, thus creating a virtual channel that is secure and separate from the other channels in the switch. As well, switches offer full-duplex capabilities.

Autonegotiation

100-Mb Ethernet and Gigabit Ethernet offer autonegotiation of speed and duplex settings, and a way to failover to lower settings, based on what is negotiated. In real life, however, this doesn't always work correctly. Duplex and speed settings should be the same on both sides, whether autonegotiation is used or not. Since there are a number of different implementations of autonegotiation, unexpected settings often result, which is why most vendors suggest you not use autonegotiation. Instead, they will tell you to manually set the duplex and speed settings at all points in your network.

Duplex issues

100-Mb Ethernet and Gigabit Ethernet NICs and switches can be configured for half- or full-duplex transmission. An easy way to find out if you are having issues with duplex mismatch is to check for a high error rate in interface statistics (mainly CRC errors). Again, both sides of the network must be set to use the same duplex setting.

Flow-control

This is a method of controlling the traffic between two peer-to-peer nodes. An interface that is receiving data packets and is almost out of receive buffers sends a "pause on" frame to its link partner. The link partner stops transmitting data packets until it receives a "pause off" frame or a timeout expires. Enabling flow control reduces the possibility that one interface will overrun the other (which causes dropped packets and retransmissions).

Some devices have one configuration option that enables the device to both send and receive flow control frames. Other devices have separate options for sending and receiving. When "send" (or "transmit") is enabled, it means that the device will send pause frames. When "receive" is enabled, it means that the device will respond to pause frames it receives.

Flow control doesn't eliminate problems when a high-speed interface transmits data to a lower speed interface (e.g., Gigabit Ethernet sending to 100-Mb Ethernet) and the transfer size is large. The difference in line speeds (accompanied by a large transfer size) causes too many packets to become queued on the switch's outbound 100-Mb Ethernet port, and the switch drops packets. The switch can't send "pause" frames to the Gigabit Ethernet interface, as that interface may also be sending to other interfaces and this would negatively affect their performance. Also, most 100-Mb Ethernet devices don't support flow control.

EtherChannel/Gigabit EtherChannel
EtherChannel is a Cisco proprietary standard for aggregating a few physical links into a combined virtual IP address. The virtual link offers protection against link failure and basic load balancing (in which traffic is distributed over the different links based on hashing of the last two bits of the source MAC address of the incoming Ethernet frame). The major obstacle to this is that the switch must support EtherChannel in order for it to work.

Port Aggregation: 802.3ad
Port Aggregation is an emerging standard for discovery and setup of network links to provide load sharing and balancing. Since it's a standard, it allows better vendor interoperability than EtherChannel. However, EtherChannel has been around longer.

Asynchronous transfer mode (ATM)
ATM is a switching technology that uses digital signals to transfer cells of 53 bytes each. Cells are asynchronously processed, then queued and multiplexed with the other cells over the wire. The common standards are the following:

OC-3
Offers a bit rate of 155.520 Mb/s

OC-12
Offers a bit rate of 622.080 Mb/s

ATM offers built-in high availability, because links can be automatically trunked.

Fiber Distributed Data Interface (FDDI)
Based on the token ring protocol, FDDI contains primary and backup token rings, each offering 100 Mb/s. Backup rings can also be used for data transfer.

The popularity of FDDI has significantly decreased due to the advent of Gigabit Ethernet. Some NAS vendors have even dropped support for it.

Virtual LAN (VLAN)

VLANs use 16 additional bits in an Ethernet frame to create a virtual network of nodes that may be across multiple switches. One reason for using a VLAN is to isolate traffic of a certain type. If there are ports on a given switch that aren't in a particular VLAN, they will not see that VLAN's traffic, even if they are in the same subnet. You can use a VLAN to isolate NFS and CIFS traffic from the rest of the network.

High availability

Obviously, with NAS-based storage, if your network is down, your storage is down. One of the best ways to increase the integrity of your NAS-based storage is to use a high availability network, using multiple paths and link aggregation software to provide trunking and failover.

Configuring the Network Protocols

Once your filer's network setup has been determined, the next setup questions to be answered are:

- How do I set up access to the NAS storage for my users?
- What protocols do I need to configure?
- What protocol configuration parameters should I expect?
- What other issues are related to multiprotocol access?

NFS

NFS configuration involves creating an export list that consists of paths to export, creating an access list specifying who can access what, and mounting clients to these exports using static mounts or automounter. The protocols and configuration issues you can expect in an NFS configuration are:

NFSv2

NFSv2 supports transfer sizes from 1 KB to 8 KB and uses only UDP as a transport protocol. It's designed to work optimally with much smaller average file sizes than are common today. NFSv2 doesn't support attribute caching, and it's less efficient than NFSv3 with reading directory contents. It will therefore probably be optimal only in special cases, such as mail directories, in which attributes are changing so fast, it's better not to cache them, and files that are small by nature. In short, use NFSv2 only if you've determined that NFSv3 isn't for you.

NFSv3

Most modern NFS implementations default to NFSv3. NFSv3 offers bigger transfer units and a more efficient operation mix. This means more I/O instead of attribute operations. Since most operations now include file attributes, this eliminates the need for extra operations from the client side. NFSv3 also lets you use TCP as a transport protocol (previous versions used only UDP). NFSv3 is covered in more detail in Chapter 5.

NFSv4

NFSv4, which was published as RFC-3010 in December 2000, offers many new and appealing new features. NFSv4 is a stateful protocol (with OPEN and CLOSE operations) that includes security enhancements, combines many operations into one stream using the new COMPOUND operation, offers extensive attribute set (including ACLs), and solves the historic issues of stale filehandles when replicating or migrating filesystems. It also offers integrated lease-based file locking,* client-side caching, and share reservations (similar to CIFS—Access read/write/both or Deny none/read/write/both) NFSv4 is covered in more detail in Chapter 5.

Automounter and NAS

Automounter is an extra service on top of NFS daemons and services that uses NIS maps to manage automatic mounts. Automounter removes the need for manual configuration of mount points in specific mount tables; this is handled by the automounter daemon. The need to consolidate mount-point administration, which served as basis for the automounter design, correlates to NAS well, because NAS has consolidated the storage that is being managed.

Automounter can also improve availability in home-directory environments, where lots of users are logging in and out from lots of workstations. Automounter automatically unmounts unused mounts, so that the number of active mounts is reduced to the necessary minimum required to service active users.

CIFS

CIFS shares can also be configured easily, and access can be restricted to certain users and hosts. Configuration issues you can expect to face when using CIFS are:

Vendor interoperability

CIFS is still a work in progress. Therefore, not all implementations are the same. There are issues with performance, mainly regarding different approaches towards the combination of TCP/IP and CIFS. There is no easy method (other than an actual benchmark) to estimate the interoperability and expected performance levels of a new CIFS filer. Other issues include the ability to be a domain controller and support for other protocols. Many vendors can't be a domain controller. Some vendors don't support the older SMB protocol flavors implemented by clients such as pure NetBIOS.

---

* Unlike previous NFS versions, in which the Network Lock Manager (NLM) was devised as a patch to solve the locking demand.

Opportunistic locks (oplocks)

Oplocks allow the client to lock a file in a way that allows the server to revoke the lock, i.e., oplocks enable safe client-side caching. Oplocks have a great effect on CIFS performance, because they enable the client to cache data in memory. Memory access times are much faster than network access times, so this caching results in lower response times of client to filer requests. Oplocks also create a reduced load on the filer, because they decrease the number of CIFS operations that must be sent to the filer. A typical session with oplocks enabled looks like the following:

a. Client A requests to open File A with an oplock.

b. Server acknowledges, and Client A can now aggressively cache File A's data and state, because no other client can open the file without being notified.

c. Client B requests to open File A.

d. Server revokes the oplock of Client A; Client A flushes cached data to server.

e. Client A acknowledges the revoking of oplock.

f. Server replies to Client B's open request.

There are four options when requesting oplocks from a server:

Exclusive oplock

Only the requesting client can open the file, and this client can perform file data read and write caching, metadata caching, and record lock caching. The server can revoke the oplock at any time, but the client will have time to flush its cache.

Batch oplock

A batch oplock is similar to an exclusive oplock, with the additional guarantee that the server will revoke the batch oplock prior to another client making changes to the file.

Level II oplock

This allows other clients to open the file as well, with the other clients indicated that the file is already opened. The client can therefore cache read data. The client is guaranteed that the server will revoke the Level II oplock prior to another client successfully writing to the file.

No oplock

Only the requesting client can open the file, and this client can perform file data read and write caching, metadata caching, and record lock caching. The server can revoke the oplock at any time, but the client will have time to flush its cache.

Oplocks can only be obtained for files. The "Locking" sidebar offers more insight on locking.

Locking

NAS enables multiprotocol access. Since you just saw that protocols take different approaches to locking, it's difficult to design a system that enables safe multiprotocol locking, lock releasing, and lock recovery without breaking any protocol semantics.

You should verify carefully how your vendor implements file locking, because an incomplete or incorrect implementation can lead to unexpected results or worse—data corruption.

Microsoft Distributed File System (DFS)

The DFS allows system and network administrators to permit users access to files that are distributed across the network. DFS makes files distributed across multiple servers appear as if they reside on a single mount point. This means users no longer need to know, or even care, which server their files are physically located on. Some NAS vendors have done some work to become DFS-aware, which provides for extra features within a Windows environment.

Samba

According to the Samba FAQ:

> Samba is a suite of programs that work together to allow clients to access to a server's filespace and printers via the SMB (Server Message Block) protocol. Initially written for Unix, Samba now also runs on Netware, OS/2, and VMS.

> In practice, this means you can redirect disks and printers to Unix disks and printers from the clients in LAN Manager, Windows for Workgroups 3.11, Windows NT, Windows 2000, Linux, and OS/2. There is also a generic Unix client program supplied as part of the suite that allows Unix users to use an FTP-like interface to access filespace and printers on any other SMB servers. This enables these operating systems to behave much like a LAN server or Windows NT server machine, only with added functionality and flexibility designed to make life easier for administrators.

Recent versions of Samba (2.2.x and above) can also serve as DFS servers and NT4 domain controllers. One of Samba's strength is its support of authentication protocols and configurations. Samba supports password files, NIS, LDAP, and forwarding to DCs. For more information, visit the web site *http://www.samba.org*.

Samba "The Next Generation" (Samba TNG)

Samba TNG is a new branch of Samba that offers more complete support for serving as domain controller than Samba 2.2.x does. Due to a few new ideas and different internal architectures, the Samba code line was branched into Samba and Samba TNG. For more information, visit the web site *http://www.samba-tng.org*.

HTTP

NAS can serve static HTML pages over the Web. Configuring HTTP access to the filer consists mainly of setting up the document directory and access policies (from which users can request web pages). Since most filers can act only as a static file web server, you might need to configure a forwarding URL, so that the filer can forward the requests for nonstatic pages to a fully capable web server to process.

FTP

Some filers can be configured to offer their files via FTP as well. FTP access is usually configured for each user, including a separate root directory. This often means maintaining a separate password file. In some multiprotocol devices, FTP requests can be configured to authenticate through NT authentication as well.

Emerging protocols

DAFS and iSCSI are two emerging technologies on the market that will soon be used for NAS data transfer. They are covered in Appendix A.

Language support

Multilingual support in a multiprotocol environment is a complex business with obvious market needs. The current situation isn't ideal. Not only do different protocols take different approaches towards language support, there isn't even one common standard on the market.

Here's a list of the character sets used in various versions of DOS and Windows:

OEM
> OEM is the old DOS model. Generally, these are single-byte characters with a number of "code pages" to select which glyph is represented by a particular byte value.

ANSI
> ANSI is a more up-to-date single-byte model used in 32-bit platforms (Windows 95/98/ME and NT). While similar in principle to the OEM, the ANSI code pages include more useful characters and fewer symbols.

Multibyte
> Multibyte character sets are used for East Asian languages.

Windows 9x, NT, 2000, and XP use Unicode. However, Win9x's implementation is a simple conversion from the current ANSI set to Unicode. It doesn't have a complete implementation. It can't display a unique glyph for values it doesn't understand and can't preserve the character's encoding.

The redirector and Explorer in NT, 2000, and XP are fully Unicode-compliant. In principle, any Unicode character can be displayed (but not always with a unique glyph), and the numeric representation of the encoding is always preserved.

NFSv4 adds support for the universal character set 4 (UCS-4). UCS is another character standard that was developed at the same time as Unicode, and it uses a four-octet value to represent characters. After constraining the most significant bit to zero for internal data-processing reasons, the remaining 31 bits allow for over two thousand million values. The four octets are named Group (G), Plane (P), Row (R), and Cell (C). The entire space is then a 4D structure consisting of:

- 128 groups, each specified by a value for G
- 256 planes in each group, each plane specified by a value for P
- 256 rows in each plane, each row specified by a value for R
- 256 cells in each row, each cell specified by a value for C

If the values of G and P are 00, this represents a plane referred to as the basic multilingual plane, or BMP. The ISO and the Unicode Consortium cooperated during the development of both codes to ensure that the BMP coincides with the Unicode code table. Characters within the BMP (i.e., characters with values of G=00 and P=00) correspond to the same character in Unicode. Unicode also includes some guidelines for usage that aren't in UCS.

Configuring Authentication/Directory Services

There can be numerous options to authenticate users in a multiprotocol filer, including local password files to NIS, NT domains, Active Directory, and LDAP.

Local password databases

A simple replacement for the more sophisticated directory services, local password files can be used to authenticate users. The most common format of this file is the Unix */etc/passwd* format. Some vendors can keep the local password in proprietary databases.

Network Information Service (NIS)

NIS is a client server-based service. An NIS domain consists of an NIS master, one or more NIS slaves, and NIS clients. The NIS slaves serve as a backup for the master and distribution of NIS data to subnets other than the master's subnet. A typical Unix NIS server holds data such as *hosts*, *passwd* and *group* tables.

To configure NIS on a filer, you need the NIS domain name and the NIS server list. Some implementations let you configure NIS cache behavior as well. The typical default behavior uses a broadcast message to find available NIS slaves in the subnet, but explicitly configuring a list of servers makes NIS more secure.

Some implementations let you configure NIS cache behavior, if applicable. *passwd* and *group* NIS tables are used quite often for UID/GID-to-username matching and file-access authentication. Caching the most accessed keys is therefore a way to improve NFS/CIFS file-attribute operations response time.

Microsoft

Microsoft has supported the sharing of computer resources over the network for a long time, starting with peer-to-peer networking, followed by the concept of a workgroup, then domain, and finally, complete directory services. Here are some of the issues you will face when using Microsoft's various authentication and directory schemes:

Workgroup mode
> Small sites may not need the functionality of domains and ACLs and can configure CIFS for workgroup membership. Shares can be accessed using share passwords and/or user authentication, but ACLs can't be set on files. Some implementations allow only plaintext password authentication in workgroup mode. Implementations based on Samba can also be configured to use encrypted passwords in workgroup mode using the *smbpasswd* file.

Plaintext Passwords

Windows clients can send their passwords in either plaintext or encrypted format. With the introduction of Windows NT4 Service Pack 3, Microsoft changed the default behavior of all its client operating systems to disable the use of plaintext passwords. If your CIFS implementation requires you to use plaintext passwords (usually required for workgroup mode), you can merge Samba's PlainPassword registry files into your PC's registry. PlainPassword files can be found in the Samba source tree, in the *docs* directory.

NT4 domain mode
> Configuring NAS into an NT4 domain requires a working domain with at least one live primary domain controller (PDC). If the NAS box and PDC aren't on the same subnet, the Windows Internet Naming Service (WINS) is needed to help the filer find the domain controller. Usually, the filer serves as a member server in the domain. Domain emulators such as Samba and HP-UX Advanced Server/9000 might have different configuration requirements. (One notable difference is the ability of the filer itself to serve as a domain controller).

Windows 2000 Active Directory (AD)
> While many vendors claim to have "full compatibility" with Windows 2000 and Active Directory (AD), some can serve only as NT4 member servers, and thus

AD can't be changed from mixed-mode to native-mode. AD offers many new features that are beyond the scope of this chapter, but for first-time configurations, the most obvious change is the use of DNS as a service locator instead of WINS. This requires entering correct DNS entries for the domain controllers and the filer prior to the NAS installation.

User mapping

Filers configured to support multiprotocol users need some mechanism to translate between the different security architectures of CIFS and NFS. NFS inherited the Unix permission scheme, with its UID/GID and permissions octets for owner, group, and world. CIFS behaves much differently, with access control entries (ACE) granting or denying specific permissions to specific users or groups, each described by a security identifier (SID). Thus a mechanism is needed to translate the Unix UID/GID to an appropriate CIFS SID and vice versa.

The common method for achieving this involves using the only common field—the username. A mechanism that runs on the filer itself (for example, a daemon or script) can map between the different usernames and their underlying UID/GID and SIDs. An organization that has a consistent naming convention for usernames across all platforms will enjoy a smoother and simpler operation.

Applications

The following section describes some applications your new NAS server would work well with.

Home Directories

Home directory configurations depend on the number of users needed. You can have multiple volumes and multiple exports and shares for users. Your aim is to give users a simple way to access their home directories from everywhere in the network. NAS filers have a way of simplifying this for both NFS and CIFS.

NFS automounter
> NFS automounter can be used to map an export path on the filer to something other than the actual mount path. For example, a directory on the filer called *nas:/home/curtis* can be mapped in automounter maps to */u/curtis* or */users/curtis*. Even if in the future the account called *curtis* is moved to directory called *nas:/home2/curtis2*, the change needs only to be done in the automounter map. The change is transparent and doesn't affect the user's scripts or any other reference to his home directory; */u/curtis* is still accessible.

CIFS special sharing features
Some filers have special features for this need. The system can automatically forward your mapping to *server**username* to any parent directory that contains a directory named *username*. When the user tries to map a drive to his home directory, he is automatically routed to the correct place. An enhancement to this feature provides the ability to combine it with user mapping, so that it routes correctly even if the username isn't the same between Unix and Windows.

Email

Some vendors supply configuration documents describing how to configure their devices so they can store data from specific applications, such as email. If you wish to do this, consider the following factors:

Average file size
Some email applications, such as Netscape Mail, keep each mail message in a separate file. Some, such as *sendmail*, keep all of a single user's messages in a single file. Still others, such as Microsoft Exchange, keep all mail in one database file. How your email application stores email affects the average file size. This, in turn, affects performance, filesystem configuration, and the backup strategy.

Heavy read environment
Most email applications create a lot of read activity because data is read mostly from the server. Most filesystems record the access time (called, in Unix, *atime*) of files. Doing that in a heavy read system can be costly, as the update of access time requires a write. This can affect performance-tuning efforts, because some filesystems give you the option not to update access time.

Caching issues
As described previously, there are many implementations of email software. Caching of mail files, especially client-side caching, might be a good performance practice—or a data corruption disaster. Consult with your vendor when configuring your NAS caching with email software.

Databases

Configuring NAS for a database requires delicate planning and a closer look at small details. Care must be taken with the location of database files and transaction logs, as well as the setup and testing of your backup and recovery system. You must also ensure that your database vendor supports NAS-based datafiles.

Data Migration

Now that your filer is configured, you're ready to start copying data into it. If your data is currently stored elsewhere, you need to migrate it to the filer.

Migration from Distributed Local Storage to NAS

Consolidation of local disks distributed on different hosts and, optionally, on different platforms (and thus different filesystems—UFS, VxFS, JFS, and NTFS, to name a few) is a common goal for NAS implementers. There are a number of ways to migrate data to filers, and a few caveats to keep in mind while migrating the data, such as permissions and soft links.

Migration methods and tools

Here are some tools and techniques that can help with migrating from local storage to NAS:

Using a local tape

> You can back up the data using a local tape drive and a backup application that is available on both the source and the filer. The biggest problem with this method is finding a common backup and recovery application.

Migration to remote tape device

> Using the remote tape *(rmt)* facility Unix-based NAS vendors provide, you can actually use a remote tape for the migration. Since there's extra work that needs to be done to encode the data stream and send it to the remote host handling *rmt*, this process is usually slower than using a local tape device. *rmt* also doesn't support Windows clients.

Copying data using the network

> Since a large data set migration can cause network overload and interrupt regular network traffic, you might prefer do the migration during offline hours or on a different network, assigned only for the migration.

Piped dump and restore

> If you migrate data from Unix, you can eliminate the tape drive during data migration by directing the output of *dump* to *restore*, as shown here:
>
> ```
> rsh source "dump 0f - /vol/vol0" | rsh destination "restore rf -"
> ```

tar

> *tar* (for tape archive) is a common copying tool. Since the native *tar* utility that comes with modern Unix versions often doesn't handle soft links, use GNU *tar* *(gtar)* instead. GNU *tar* is also available for Windows platforms.
>
> A typical migration command line with *tar* is:
>
> ```
> tar cf - . | ( cd /target; tar xf - )
> ```

cp and xcopy

> Some of the easiest methods to use are Unix's *cp* or Windows' *xcopy*. Since the NAS filer appears as a network drive, you can simply copy the data over to it. Remember to do this at an appropriate time.

When using the *cp* command, make sure you issue the *–d* option along with the *–r* option. The *–d* option tells *cp* not to follow symbolic links when copying. The *–r* option causes a recursive copy.

Migration issues

When migrating data to NAS, you must make sure to preserve permissions and soft links and take full advantage of the filer's performance, (that is, as much as you can within the limits of your network).

Migrating permissions
Care must be taken when migrating permissions; not all tools can transfer this kind of information (also called *metadata*, or data that describes data). Make sure the method you use to transfer the data preserves permissions, including any access control lists.

Migrating soft links (symbolic links)
Soft links also aren't trivial to migrate. CIFS doesn't translate symbolic links, so copying Unix data that contains symbolic links to a CIFS volume causes the symbolic links to be copied as regular text files. Some Unix tools follow symbolic links, and thus copy the target of the links instead of the links themselves. Some backup applications have options for following symbolic links or backing them up as soft links. Soft links also raise another issue. What if a user's home directory contains a soft link to a file that is now migrated to NAS? It might be that the path to the new location is different than it was, and this soft link will become stale after the migration. In any case, you should verify that the migrated data is accessible as expected, just like the source.

Performance
Since migration consists of copying data, it would probably help to migrate data in parallel and use incremental copies. Parallelism raises the total migration throughput, and copying incrementally saves down time.

Migration Between Filers

In the current environment of acquisitions and reorganizations, redistribution of data between directories, volumes and physical devices is a common requirement for many companies. In addition to the tools mentioned earlier, there are additional, proprietary tools just for doing migration of data between filers:[*]

NDMPcopy
NDMPcopy is an extension of the NDMP specification. NDMPcopy uses the NDMP protocol for transferring data between two NDMP data servers. The

---

[*] This list of tools is far from comprehensive, and it isn't meant as an endorsement of Network Appliance or EMC.

servers can be on the same physical host as well as on separate hosts. The advantage of this approach is that the data flows between the two servers using a dedicated network connection. Apart from full copies, this also supports incremental copies up to level 2. The smallest unit of transfer is a directory. NDMPcopy is supported on Network Appliance filers for local and interfiler copying and on Auspex filers (called TurboCopy), for internode copying only.

Figure 6-1 shows NDMPcopy's data flow.

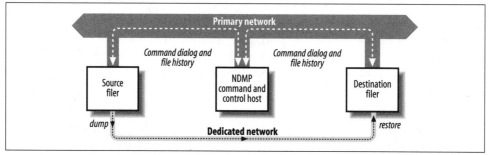

Figure 6-1. NDMPcopy data flow

Network Appliance SnapMirror

SnapMirror is a mirroring technology that can also be used for data migration between filers. Recent versions make it possible to migrate the NFS filehandles that are used on the source export to the target and thus maintain the transparency of the migration. Recent versions also offer better granularity, allowing migration of top-level directories in addition to volumes.

EMC Celerra data movers: unmount/mount volumes

Moving volumes between data movers that sit on the same Celerra box can be done simply by unmounting them on one data mover, then mounting them again on another. If pre-setup was done so that every volume has its own IP address, migration can occur transparently for the NFS user.

EMC Celerra TimeFinder/FS

TimeFinder, EMC's mirroring product, was extended for NAS usage with the name of TimeFinder/FS. TimeFinder/FS migrates complete volumes from one Symmetrix storage system to another. Celerra volumes can be mirrored to a remote Symmetrix storage system; the mirror can then be split, and the second volume mounted and shared using the remote Celerra system.

Maintenance

This section describes some tasks and issues a filer administrator faces in the day-to-day management of a filer. They include the following:

- System failures
- Performance monitoring and analysis
- Network and storage management
- Performance tuning
- User support

Hardware Failure

All hardware is prone to failure. Be prepared with a plan of action for each specific part, whether it's a disk, fan, power supply, CPU, or motherboard. Most vendors supply field replaceable units (FRUs) for parts that are likely to break in the field. Here are parts most prone to failure:

Disk

Whether your system is configured to use RAID 1, 1+0, 4, 5 or any other special combination, single-disk failures are usually repaired by regenerating the content of the failed disk onto a hot spare disk. This can take a few hours, so make sure to include hot spares in your system and replace any failed disks within a reasonable amount of time.

Power supply

Some systems have different power supplies for the filer head and the storage shelves. If redundant power cabling is in use, a power supply failure won't cause the whole system to go down.

Fan

There are many different kinds of fans in a filer: CPU fans, system head fans, storage shelf fans, and chassis fans. Not all fan failures are critical, but some might be. Check with your vendor as to how fan failures are handled by the system.

Memory

Whether it's main (RAM), cache (also called L2 cache) or NV-RAM, memory consists of memory modules, such as SIMMs or DIMMs that are small integrated circuit boards with memory chips on them. In some designs, memory comes on proprietary boards.

Motherboard/chassis

These parts are mentioned together because few systems are designed to allow you to replace one without the other. This can be critical, as replacing a chassis might take a long time. Also, in some designs, a chassis failure may cause a complete system malfunction.

CPU

If your system doesn't offer more than one CPU, a CPU failure results in a system failure. Care must be taken with CPU replacements and, in general, it's best to let an experienced hardware technician do this. If your system supports more than one CPU, consult your vendor as to how to handle the failure of a single CPU.

Cards

SCSI cards, Fibre Channel HBAs, and NICs all fall under this category. Some designs allow for card redundancy, such as using EtherChannel to avoid having a single NIC failure take down a network link, and using multiple channels from adapters to storage systems to protect against a single link failure. Other cards can't be redundant by nature, e.g., parallel SCSI cards.

Hardware Upgrades

Some systems allow you to upgrade single components, such as disk drives and CPUs, while others require you to upgrade the entire machine at once. Check with your vendor about which parts are upgradeable and which aren't. (Disk shelves for example, can usually hold newer drives but only up to a certain size).

Onsite Spares

Some vendors sell you lower-priced parts to use as quick onsite spares. Some of the more common parts for this purpose are spare disks, which are usually kept inside the system itself as hot spares. Companies with strict mean time to recovery (MTTR) requirements require complete spare systems onsite (which are sometimes also used as part of a test environment as well). Such spare systems should be thoroughly tested so that they can be put into production quickly when required.

Software Failure

There are a few different reasons your software may fail. Here are the most common:

System bugs

NAS is designed and programmed by humans, which means it's prone to bugs. A bug can cause unexpected results for operations, generic unexpected behaviors (or under certain conditions or loads), and feature malfunction. Fixes might be supplied by software upgrades as well as *patches*, which are small pieces of software that need to be applied to the original software.

System panics

If the NAS operating system code encounters an illegal condition (e.g., a C function for reading a disk block is called with an illegal disk block number), it deliberately causes itself to crash and reboot. In most systems this step also dumps all memory contents into a file, often called a *core* file, which can then be sent to the vendor's support center for further analysis.

System hangs

With most filers, system hang-ups are rare. This is due to a mechanism called *watchdog*, which provides a coordinated check between the operating system and the hardware. The operating system increments a special counter in memory every few milliseconds, and a hardware mechanism checks periodically to ensure that the counter is indeed refreshed. If the counter isn't refreshed, it's a sign that the operating system kernel has hung; the hardware then resets itself, and the system reboots.

Software Upgrade

Depending on the vendor, a software upgrade can involve anything from a simple five-minute procedure to a few hours of work. There are minor software upgrades and also major upgrades, which include such things as filesystem changes or whole new feature sets. There are some administrators who prefer not to upgrade their systems if everything is working fine, but usually it's smarter to follow the vendor's recommendations (which are based on the vendor's knowledge of features and stability of the code). Be sure to check with your vendor for their recommendations.

Monitoring, Analyzing, and Reporting

It's highly recommended to record baseline performance statistics for later use. Many customers assume that if everything is fine on day 1, it will be fine forever. Murphy's Law usually says otherwise. A baseline is useful for identifying true good performance, so that your assessment isn't based on merely a subjective feeling. Performance tuning itself are discussed later in this section.

Monitoring: Built-in Tools

Many filers offer tools for monitoring operational status and performance and error counters for the CPU, memory, network, and filesystem. Here are some common counters:

CPU utilization

This is the amount of time the CPUs are busy with handling incoming client requests and outgoing replies, filesystem handling, monitoring data capture and management, and possibly RAID system activity.

Network interface statistics

These are counters that show the amount of traffic that has been received and transmitted, as well as possible interface errors such as NIC buffer overflows, frame CRC errors, and Ethernet collisions.

Filesystem and disk utilization

These record generic filesystem traffic and also specific storage device read/write activity and are mainly used to decide whether a system is disk-bound or not. Specific volumes or disks that are overutilized can be identified.

Network Management Tools: Vendor-Supplied

Some vendors supply their own proprietary management software, such as EMC's ControlCenter and Network Appliance's DataFabric Manager. These are designed to fill the gap between local management tools and complex implementation of full-blown network management frameworks and offer features more tailored to the specific devices that they are meant to support.[*]

EMC Control Center Symmetrix Manager

This is part of the EMC Control Center management suite and manages the Symmetrix storage (the back-end of Celerra filer). Its capabilities include:

- Access to internal configuration and operational status, with physical and logical views
- Status and performance of channel and disk directors
- Monitoring performance data captured continuously from the system

Network Appliance DataFabric Manager (DFM)

This enables remote, centralized management of NetApp data storage infrastructures consisting of NetCache appliances and filers. DFM comes with a web-based GUI and a command-line interface. It offers the following features:

- Automated discovery and appliance configuration
- Customizable reporting on volume, disks, CPU, and environmental status and utilization
- NFS, CIFS, and HTTP operations and network utilization
- Support for group- and volume-level resource control

Network Management Tools: Generic

Most NAS vendors don't offer built-in tools for storing and conveniently displaying long-term statistics. Instead, external tools are available for extracting information from the system and storing it in an external database, which can then be used for analysis and alerting purposes. In addition to the tools discussed next, there are also network traffic monitoring tools that inform you as to how the filer is using (or abusing) the network, including *NetMon, Ethereal, tcpdump,* and *snoop*.

---

[*] Again, this list isn't comprehensive. Other vendors also provide such tools, and this isn't meant as an endorsement of these products.

SNMP

The Simple Network Management Protocol is a standard protocol that gathers device counters and status. Most NAS vendors support the MIB-II version of SNMP, and some vendors offer what is called Extended MIB (Management Information Base). Extended MIB can offer more granular monitoring on specific NAS features.

SNMP managers

Any device that supports SNMP generic MIBs or comes with its own custom MIB file can be monitored using an SNMP manager application. These applications let you walk through the SNMP object trees and peek into values. They also help you keep track of values, manage alerts based on specific values or changes in values, and create graphs and reports.

Commercial network management applications

There are a few major network management applications and frameworks currently available. Examples of such products include CA UniCenter TNG, HP OpenView, IBM Tivoli TME, BMC Patrol. Details on these can be found in the relevant vendors' web sites. Some vendors offer special plug-ins for the major network management frameworks, which enable customers to benefit from the framework's drill-down graphical interface and monitoring and alerting tools to nail down specific filer's problems.

MRTG

The Multi Router Traffic Grapher (MRTG) monitors the traffic load on network links, but can be changed to handle any SNMP capable device. MRTG generates HTML pages containing GIF images that provide a live visual representation of this traffic. For more information on MRTG, visit the web site *http://people.ee. ethz.ch/~oetiker/webtools/mrtg/*.

Cricket

Cricket is another SNMP monitoring tool. For more information on Cricket, visit the web site *http://cricket.sourceforge.net*.

Storage Resource Management (SRM)

Organizations are known to grow storage in extraordinary rates. A new type of product was recently introduced that answers the demand for managing storage in a smarter way. Here's a list of how some of these products work:

Data collection

Scanning processes collect information on computers, groups, users, disks, file-systems, directories and files. This information is stored in a management database for later analysis. Since this database can become huge in a large environment, there must be some pruning and filtering, so that only critical data is captured, and that data is cleaned after some grace period.

Disk usage analysis
> The space on disks and filesystems is given thresholds, and alerts can be sent to administrators to prevent filesystems from becoming 100% full.

Disk space reclamation
> Some products can identify unnecessary or stale data and proactively clean it.

Quota monitoring and enforcement
> It's also necessary to enforce limitations based on file ownership and directories. Such policies must balance the space that is reasonably required by users without restricting additional storage to provide high availability, and performance and continuity of application servers, file and print servers, and database servers.

Filing policies
> You need to set and enforce policies about which file types can reside on corporate data servers. Allowing MP3 files, graphics, games, cartoons, and movies wastes precious disk space, compromises the integrity of data storage devices, and slows backup and recovery cycles. Blocking unwanted file types keeps data storage devices free and clean from Internet clutter.

Capacity planning and trend analysis
> There are two major demands for capacity planning—future growth planning and justification for recent storage costs. Capacity planning helps to answer such questions as: "When will my storage become full?", "Who is consuming all my disk space?", and "What is the rate users are filling up disk space?"

Enabling self-cleanup
> You can enable users to clean files on their own by notifying them on their own usage patterns, allocated space, and providing the tools for self-cleanup in the form of storage usage reports containing active links to problem file areas, such as outdated files, duplicated files, largest files and questionable file types. Users can then use the reports for cleaning their own files, by viewing, moving or deleting any or all files meeting certain policy-generated criteria such as age, size, type, or number of duplicates.

Performance Tuning

Arguably the most daunting task for system administrators, performance tuning is a combined process of measuring performance, identifying bottlenecks, and system tuning.

Measuring Performance

The first step to improving performance is measuring it. There are two things to look at when measuring performance of a networked system such as NAS:

Clean network

It's said that you should check your weight in the morning, before you even eat breakfast. That is what is called a clean measurement—without *background noise*. Any performance measurement should be taken when the network is relatively clean of irrelevant traffic and when the filer is idle. This is, of course, not always possible.

Baseline measurement

Before going into production, a thorough performance testing and documentation should take place. Everything should be tested, including raw I/O transfer rates and application performance details, such as average run time of SQL statements on a database located on your NAS.

The results can then serve as a baseline for future measurements. This is especially helpful to see if the performance of your NAS server is declining over time.

Measurement Tools

The following tools measure network performance:

NetBench (Ziff Davis)
    http://www.zdnet.com/zdbop/Netbench/nb_faq.html

IOmeter (Intel)
    http://developer.intel.com/design/servers/devtools/iometer/

CIFSBench (Network Appliance)
    http://www.netapp.com/technology/freeware/cifsbench.htm

Benchmark Factory (Quest)
    http://www.quest.com/benchmark_factory/index.asp

Postmark
    http://www.netapp.com/tech_library/3022.html

NAS Backup and Recovery

At one time there were few backup and recovery options for NAS filers. If you were willing to manually swap tapes, you backed them up with locally attached tape drives and the *dump* command. If you wanted to integrate your NAS backups into your enterprise backup system, you backed them up via NFS or CIFS. These two options were relatively simple, but they left a lot to be desired. Thankfully, today's landscape looks much different.

This chapter concentrates on the entire spectrum of data protection services available for filers today. Not all the features discussed here are available from all NAS vendors. In fact, some features are available on only one or two platforms. Since this market is so dynamic, This chapter will cover only general features; please contact vendors for specifics.

Snapshots and Mirroring

This section concentrates on two options you can use as a first line of defense against logical corruption and physical disk failure. Snapshots can give you multiple points in time to which you can recover instantly without a lot of overhead. Mirroring helps provide a standby system in case the primary system fails.

Snapshots

NAS-based snapshots are essentially the same as the snapshots discussed in Chapter 4. Here is a review of that discussion:

- Snapshots are a virtual copy of a filesystem. They require neither the space nor the I/O overhead of the backup mirrors discussed in the client-free section of Chapter 4.

- As long as the snapshot exists, it provides a view of the snapped filesystem as it existed at the time the snapshot was taken.

- Snapshots take only seconds to create.
- Snapshots are normally read-only copies.

In the SAN world, snapshots are created at the time of backups and give the backup system a static view of the filesystem. NAS snapshots, on the other hand, can be created many times a day, and each filesystem may have many different snapshots available at any one time. For example, a filer's snapshots can be configured as follows:

- Take a snapshot hourly during the day and keep 10 previous versions
- Take a snapshot daily and keep 10 previous versions
- Take a snapshot weekly and keep 7 previous versions
- Take a snapshot monthly and keep 4 previous versions

This results in 31 snapshots being online at any one time, and all 31 snapshots contain a view of what the filesystem looked like at the time that snapshot was taken. Even an end user can know where these snapshots reside and use them to recover her own files.

Figure 7-1 attempts to illustrate what the end user sees if there are multiple snapshots of her *D:* drive, which happens to be a network drive mounted from *filer*.

In the top left of the figure, you can see that the *D:* drive contains the *Important Documents* directory and a directory called *~snapshot*. A peek inside the *Important Documents* directory shows three important files. If you open up another Windows Explorer window and look at the *~snapshot* directory, you see that inside that directory resides some snapshots, called *hourly.0*, *nightly.0*, etc. If you open *D:\~snapshot\ hourly.0*, it contains the *Important Documents* directory. If you also open up *D:\ ~snapshot\nightly.0\Important Documents*, you'll see that those same three important documents are available via the snapshot. Therefore, the user accessing this desktop can use any one of the following files:

- The active files listed in *D:\Important Documents*
- A snapshot of those files made one or more hours ago by accessing the same folder name inside the *~snapshot/hourly.number* directory.
- A snapshot of those files made one or more days ago by accessing the same folder name inside the *~snapshot/nightly.number* directory.

Major recoveries from snapshots can be accomplished in one of two ways:

- The administrator can shut down the application using the original volume and then use standard copy utilities to copy the data from the snapshot back to the original volume. Sophisticated administrators could even write something using a find command that would figure out which files have changed and copy only those changed files.
- The filer can be told that the active filesystem is no longer the "original" filesystem. Instead, it's pointed to the snapshot that is now mounted read-write. This

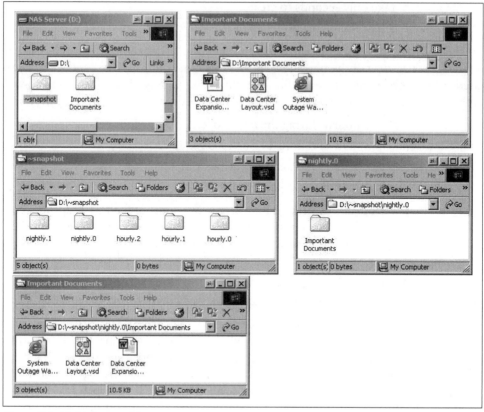

Figure 7-1. Multiple snapshots

allows for an instantaneous recovery from a snapshot. As of this writing, only one vendor offers this functionality.

 Snapshots are virtual copies of the filesystem that rely on the disks from the original filesystem's volume. Therefore, if you lose the primary volume's disks, your snapshots will disappear too.

Server-to-Server Mirroring

Server-to-server mirroring for filers is similar to traditional filesystem replication that has been available as a third-party application for both Unix and NT. The administrator chooses a source and a destination volume, and the source volume is automatically and continually replicated to the destination volume. Without getting into implementation details, suffice it to say that this helps protect against the loss of a disk on the primary system.

One application of this technology is to create a super filer that is used as a backup and recovery engine. For example, suppose you have five 1-TB filers you need to back up on a regular basis. Later in this chapter I'll describe the somewhat costly options that allow you to share tape drives between servers, to get this backup. However, what if you could get all the data into one place, and back it up from there?

Figure 7-2 shows one option. You can buy one large "super" filer that has enough capacity to mirror a number of smaller filers. You then mirror each smaller filer to a volume on the super filer across a WAN or LAN connection. A common practice is to put this super filer in a different location, thus providing an instant recovery path in case of fire.

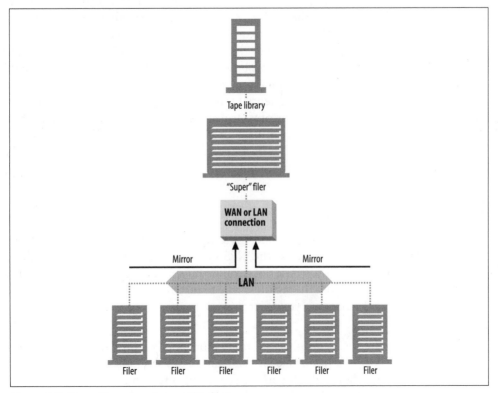

Figure 7-2. Super filer mirroring smaller filers

Note that by mirroring all of the smaller filers' data to the super filer, you no longer need to worry about backing up the data locally on the smaller filers. You can now back up this data around the clock via the super filer with no impact to the production filers.

They Work Together

If the production filers use snapshots, you actually have two levels of protection before you would ever need to use your tape backups. The first level are the snapshots, which protect you against logical corruption—perhaps the most common cause of restores. The second level is the mirror, which provides a real-time copy of your data in an alternate location.

Native Utilities

The first option for backing up some filers is to use the native utilities provided with the operating system that they are running on. Many filers are running on some type of Unix or Linux and thus have the *dump* and *restore* commands available. The Windows 2000–based servers have the *NTBACKUP* command available. The functionality available with this method of backup varies widely between different NAS vendors, but, in general, you lose most of the functionality provided by today's commercial software products. There will probably be no automated tape management, and there will be no database that tracks what filesystems were backed up to which tape. You might be able to use a sequential tape stacker to provide some amount of tape automation and save the output of your dumps to text files you can search, but if you are used to today's commercial backup products (or AMANDA from *http://www.amanda.org*), you will probably be rather disappointed with this option. It's really not a valid option for all but the smallest environments.

NFS/CIFS

NAS boxes were designed to do NFS and CIFS, right? Why not just use NFS or CIFS to mount to the backup server, treat the NFS/CIFS mount just like any other disk, and back it up to tape that way? A lot of people will say there's nothing wrong with doing it this way. It's certainly the simplest way to do things. Here are a few pieces of advice if you plan on backing up your filer this way:

Ask your NAS vendor the best way to do it
> Your NAS vendor has heard this question before and has probably tested a number of ways to back up their filer. If there are issues with backing up their filers via NFS or CIFS, they will tell you. They may also tell you that mixed volumes that serve both NFS and CIFS should be backed up via CIFS. (Details on why this is often true are provided in the next section.)

Make the network mount to the backup server
> One of the most common mistakes people make when backing up via NFS or CIFS is to mount the drive to a normal backup client and back the drives up from that client. The problem with this is that the data travels across the network twice. If possible, mount the NFS or CIFS drives directly to the backup server—via a dedicated connection if possible. This will cut your network traffic in half.

Can I Get Rid of My Backup System?

Some feel that snapshots and server-to-server mirroring can be used instead of a standard tape or optical-based backup and recovery system. I don't share this opinion for a few reasons:

Snapshots protect you only from logical filesystem corruption

Since snapshots (as defined in this book and in the NAS industry) are only a virtual copy of the filesystem, they rely on the physical volume the original filesystem resides on. If a single disk that is a part of that volume fails, the RAID software can handle this software. However, if multiple disks fail, the volume fails, taking the snapshot with it. Therefore, snapshots protect you only from logical corruption; they don't protect you against the loss of multiple disks.

Server-to-server mirroring often protects you only from physical disk failure

Mirroring allows you to mirror the original filesystem and/or its snapshots to another volume, possibly on another system. This protects against physical disk failure, but it may not protect against logical corruption. Depending on how the mirroring is implemented, a logical corruption on the original disk may be promulgated to the mirror. There are systems that mirror both the original filesystem and the snapshot; these can protect you against both physical and logical corruption.

Neither system protects you from human error

An offline backup has one feature no online backup can provide. You can make the backup, then test that backup by doing some sort of restore, and then place that backup on a shelf. You know that when you come back to that shelf next month or next year, that backup will be just as good as it was when you made it. It will work even if your entire backup system is destroyed by an upgrade of your backup software. If your backup database becomes corrupt, you've still got that uncorrupted backup on the shelf you can go back to. No matter what you do to the backup system, that tape's still good. This isn't the case with an online backup. Every time you upgrade your mirroring or snapshot software, you take the risk of corrupting your production data and its backup. This same risk exists every time you issue maintenance commands on either the production or mirror system. In my opinion, the only real way to protect against it is to make offline copies to tape or optical disk.

I think that snapshots and server-to-server mirroring provide a fine first line of defense against logical corruption and physical disk failures. In fact, using snapshots and server-to-server mirroring as your first line of defense makes the creation of tape- and optical-based backups much easier. You can back up snapshots and mirrors around the clock! Recoveries from snapshots and server-to-server mirroring facilities are much easier and faster than their tape- and optical-based counterparts. However, I still feel that they aren't a complete replacement for a good tape or optical-based backup and recovery system.

Issues with NFS/CIFS Backups of Filers

Backing up your filers via an NFS or CIFS mount is often a better option than backing them up via their native utilities. Backing them up this way allows you to treat them as any other filesystem and to use whatever backup product you see fit. If these servers are designed to serve NFS and CIFS data, what could be wrong?

Reduced performance

Probably the biggest disadvantage to backing up your filers via an NFS or CIFS mount is that the filer can't distinguish between file requests for the backup process and file requests for users or other applications. *dump*, *NTBACKUP*, and NDMP backups are often prioritized much lower than file serving requests—for good reason. You should give priority to the reason you bought the filer in the first place.

However, when you are backing the data up via NFS or CIFS, the backup application appears the same as any other application. It then receives the same priority as your Oracle database trying to update its datafile. Backup operations are also likely to constantly fill up cache, completely removing all caching services from normal file requests.

Unicode names

Filers must now support the new Unicode naming conventions supported by Windows platforms. The problem comes when you have a shared access filesystem that is served via NFS and CIFS. Since the current version of NFS doesn't handle all variations of Unicode names, it's possible (although unlikely) that you can create a file with a Unicode name that is completely legal in the CIFS world, but completely illegal in the NFS world. An NFS-friendly name can be created by the filer, but it will not be the same name as the original file. This is the first reason why backing up shared access filesystems via NFS is a *really* bad idea.

CIFS ACLs

The next problem is Windows access control lists. Although it's pretty easy to translate Unix owner, group, and other permissions into the Windows world, it's completely impossible to translate Windows ACLs into Unix permissions. Therefore, if you back up a shared access filesystem via an NFS mount, you will lose all ACL information.

Windows alternate data streams

Another problem is NTFS *alternate data streams*. In NTFS, a file consists of multiple streams of data. One holds the security information (ACLs, etc.), and another holds the actual data of the file. Another application of this would be a stream that holds the formatting of the data and one that holds the text to be formatted. Each file can actually have a number of streams holding various types of information. This data is completely hidden from the average user. If you're interested in this, and you'd like to create a hidden stream inside a file, simply enter this command:

```
C:\ notepad visible.txt:hidden.txt
```

This creates a file called *visible.txt* with a hidden stream called *hidden.txt*. You can also put data into this stream by entering this command:

```
C:\ type textfile > visible.txt:hidden.txt
```

This copies the contents of *textfile* into the *hidden.txt* stream inside *visible.txt*. If you know the name of a hidden stream, you can read the contents of it with the following command:

```
C:\ more < visible.txt:hidden.txt > newfile.txt
```

This creates a file *newfile.txt* that contains the data in the *hidden.txt* stream that's hidden in the file *visible.txt*.

 If you're as curious about this as I was when I first heard about this, there is a free tool called LADS (List Alternate Data Streams) that's available for download at *http://www.heysoft.de*. This tool shows if you have any files with alternate data streams.

Needless to say, this data doesn't convert to NFS well. In fact, it doesn't even translate to a FAT filesystem. If you copy an alternate data stream file to a FAT filesystem and back to an NTFS filesystem, the alternate data streams are deleted. This is the final reason why backing up a shared access filesystem via NFS is often a really bad idea.

Push Agent Software

Large environments normally back up Unix, Windows, and other machines by installing client-side software that communicates with a backup server during backup and recovery sessions. This software does the job of pushing the files from the backup client to the backup server. (This is why such software is often referred to as a *push agent*.) However, many filers run on a micro-kernel operating system that doesn't have room for such third-party software, which means this option isn't normally available to filers. Therefore, these filers require the use of the other backup and recovery options discussed in this chapter, each of which comes with the same disadvantage; you are forced to treat NAS data differently from other data.

However, there are some filers that are based on a general-purpose operating system, instead of the usual micro-kernel operating system. (These filers usually use either a standard Linux distribution or the Windows Server Appliance Kit.) While their competitors may argue that a general-purpose operating system is inappropriate for filers, one advantage that filers based on a general-purpose operating system have is that they can use the same push agent software other Unix and NT systems use. This means you can back up these filers just as you would other servers in your environment.

There have been a few attempts to write customized client software that would work with the microkernel-based filers. The only attempts I'm aware of are those that are created to run inside a Java Virtual Machine provided by the NAS vendor. Perhaps in the future, this will be a valid option; however, all current attempts at such customized software have not gained acceptance.

NDMP

As mentioned earlier, those filers that use a standard operating system can easily be backed up with standard backup client software. For those filers that use an operating system based on a micro-kernel, NDMP is usually the best backup and recovery option. One reason for its popularity is that NDMP backups can easily be integrated into your commercial backup and recovery system and therefore can be completely automated. Before taking a closer look at NDMP, though, let's study how it got here.

The History of NDMP

As discussed previously in this chapter, there was a time when the only way to integrate filer backups into your commercial backup and recovery system was to create an NFS or CIFS mount to your backup server and back up that mount. Since filers were designed to serve files via NFS and CIFS, this seemed like a relatively good option. However, there were performance and integrity issues with this method (as mentioned earlier in this chapter), and there was a negative response to the idea in general, "You want me to back up via NFS? Are you kidding?"

In 1996, Network Appliance and PDC Software* joined to create the network data management protocol (NDMP). Although it may seem that NDMP was developed for filers, the companies actually had a much loftier goal in mind.

They intended to define a mechanism that would allow for common administrative control of backup tape devices and data movement between active filesystems and the backup devices. Key design goals included operating-system independence, multisystem interoperability, use of standard protocols, and functionality equivalent to non-NDMP applications.

Most backup software companies port their client software (i.e., *push agent*) to each platform they wish to back up. This, of course, requires a lot of effort on the part of the backup software vendor, especially when you consider that each operating

---

* PDC became Intelliguard, and was later purchased by Legato Systems.

system vendor releases new versions of each OS from time to time. This method also creates a special challenge when trying to support the backup of filers running a microkernel. Such filers don't allow the installation of third-party software on their system. (They do this for many reasons, one of which is to simplify the support model for their filers.)

In 1996, Network Appliance and PDC asked a simple question. There is a standard protocol for file transfer (FTP), a standard protocol for mail (SMTP), and even one for monitoring (SNMP). What if there was a standard protocol for backup and recovery? Vendors that supported the protocol within their operating system could then be backed up by any backup software product that supported the protocol. NDMP was born.

The idea caught on, and as of this writing there are over 25 NDMP-compliant products on the market. There is an NDMP working group within SNIA and the IETF. NDMP history is illustrated in Figure 7-3.

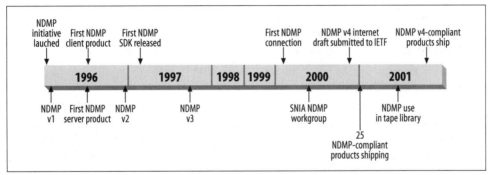

Figure 7-3. The history of NDMP (courtesy of NDMP.org)

What Is NDMP?

The following section contains direct quotes from the NDMP specification that were used with permission. They have been edited for brevity and to fit contextually within this chapter.

The Network Data Management Protocol (NDMP) defines a mechanism and protocol for controlling backup and recovery between primary and secondary storage. The purpose of NDMP is to allow a network backup application to control the backup and recovery of an NDMP-compliant server without installing third-party software on the server.

The control and data transfer components of the backup/recovery are separated. The separation allows complete interoperability at a network level. The filesystem vendors need only be concerned with maintaining compatibility with one well-defined protocol. The backup vendors can place their primary focus on the central backup administration software.

Definition of Terms

An understanding of NDMP begins with the following terms:

Data Management Application (DMA)
> The DMA controls the NDMP session. This is normally the commercial backup software application.

NDMP Host
> The host computer system that executes the NDMP server application. Data is backed up from the NDMP host to either a local tape drive or to a backup device on a remote NDMP host.

NDMP Service
> The daemon or server on the NDMP host that is controlled using the NDMP protocol. There are three types of NDMP Services: Data Service, Tape Service, and SCSI Service. Prior to defining what these services are, we must define a few other terms.

Primary Storage System
> A storage system that stores live or "in production" data on an active filesystem. This includes dedicated storage appliances such as filers and application servers. A Primary Storage System hosts an NDMP data service.

Secondary Storage System
> A storage system used for archiving or data protection. Examples are application servers or filers with direct attached tape drives, libraries or robots, or dedicated network attached archiving/data protection appliances. A Secondary Storage System hosts an NDMP tape service and often a SCSI service.

Data Connection
> The connection between the two NDMP servers that carry the unidirectional backup/recovery data stream. The data connection in NDMP is either an interprocess communication mechanism (for local operations) or a TCP/IP connection (for three-way operations).

Control Connection
> A TCP/IP connection that carries bidirectional XDR-encoded NDMP control messages between the DMA and the NDMP Server.

Data Service
> A NDMP Service that transfers data between primary storage and the Data Connection. Data services provide an abstracted interface to the filesystem or primary storage of the NDMP server. A data service is the source of data during backup operations and the destination during recovery operations. Examples of data services are filers and general compute platforms with direct or SAN attached storage.

Tape Service

A NDMP service that transfers data between secondary storage and the Data Connection and allows the DMA to manipulate and access secondary storage. Tape services provide an abstracted interface to tape devices or other types of secondary storage attached to the NDMP server. A tape library may implement its own NDMP server and associated tape service or may be connected through an external NDMP server. A tape service is the source of data during recovery operations and the data destination during backup operations. The tape service also provides a mechanism for tape positioning and I/O on behalf of the DMA. Examples of hardware controlled by tape services are individual tape drives, tape libraries, or servers with one or more writeable CDROM drives.

SCSI Service

A NDMP Service that passes low-level SCSI commands to a SCSI device typically used by the DMA to manipulate a SCSI or Fibre Channel attached media changer.

NDMP Server

An instance of one or more distinct NDMP services controlled by a single NDMP control connection. Thus a data/tape/SCSI server is an NDMP server providing data, tape, and SCSI services.

NDMP configurations

In the simplest configuration, a DMA backs up the data from the NDMP server to a locally attached tape subsystem. The NDMP control connection exists across the network boundary while the NDMP data connection between the data and tape services exists within the NDMP server implementation. This is often referred to as *filer to self*, and is illustrated in Figure 7-4.

You can also use NDMP to simultaneously back up to multiple backup devices physically attached to the NDMP server. In this configuration, there are two instances of the NDMP data and tape services on the NDMP server. The NDMP control connection exists across the network boundary while the NDMP data connections between the data and tape services exist within the NDMP server implementation. This is also called *filer to self*, and is illustrated in Figure 7-5.

NDMP can back up data to a tape library that's physically attached to the NDMP server. In this configuration, there's a separate instance of the NDMP server to control the robotics within the tape library. This configuration is illustrated in Figure 7-6.

It's possible to back up an NDMP server that supports NDMP but doesn't have a locally attached backup device by sending the data through a raw TCP/IP connection to another NDMP server. In this case the NDMP data service exists on one server and the NDMP tape service on a separate server. Both the NDMP control connections (to server 1 and server 2) and the NDMP data connection (between server 1

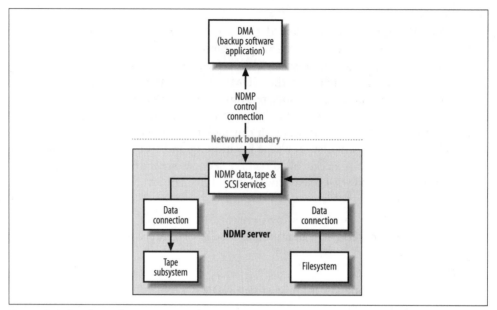

Figure 7-4. Simple configuration

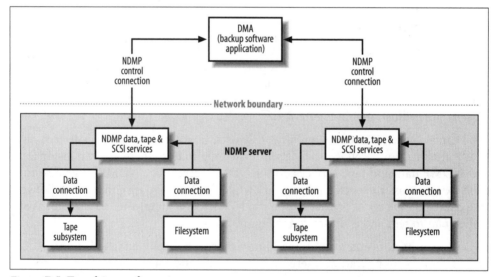

Figure 7-5. Two-drive configuration

and server 2) exist across the network boundary. Depending on which server is providing which service, this may be referred to as *filer to filer*, *filer to server*, or *server to filer*, and it's illustrated in Figure 7-7. In addition, there's a new configuration I refer to as *filer to library*.

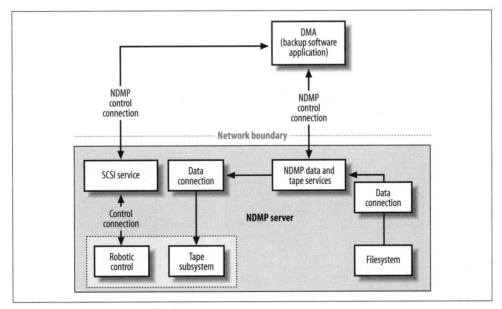

Figure 7-6. Tape library configuration

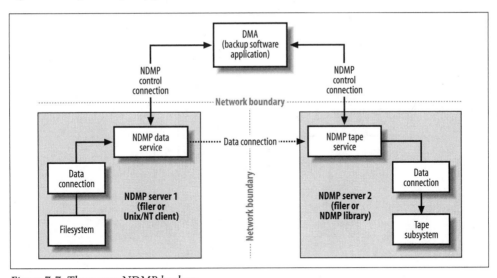

Figure 7-7. Three-way NDMP backup

Filer to self

If the data service and tape service are both running within a single filer, this is referred to as filer to self. Even if you have multiple filers sharing a tape library via a SAN, this is referred to as filer to self.

Filer to filer

If the data service is on one filer, and the tape service is on another filer, this is referred to as filer to filer.

Filer to library

A variation on filer to filer is when the tape service is running on an NDMP-compatible tape library. Each tape drive within such a tape library has a small computer running the NDMP tape service. Since the tape drives appear as a filer to the DMA, this might be referred to as filer to filer. However, I'd like to use the term *filer to library*.

Filer to server

If the data service is on one filer, and the tape service is running on a nonfiler server controlled by the DMA, this is referred to as *filer to server*. For example, if a filer was being backed up via NDMP to a Unix or NT backup server running a commercial backup product, it's called *filer to server*.

Server to filer

If the DMA-routed backup data coming for a non-NDMP backup client is routed to an NDMP tape server, it's referred to as server to filer. This configuration is extremely rare.

All these incarnations are illustrated in Figure 7-8.

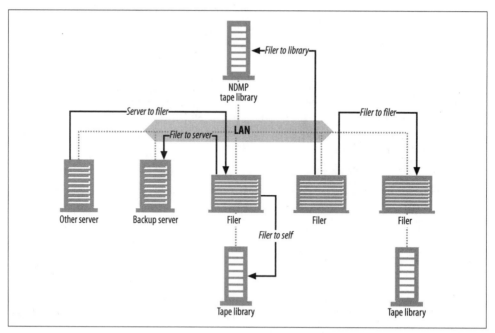

Figure 7-8. NDMP incarnations

NDMP backups aren't portable

It's important to understand that NDMP sends a stream of backup data to the DMA, along with data that explains what's in the stream. The DMA doesn't need to understand the backup stream; it only needs to understand the metadata that is passed via the NDMP protocol. What format is the stream in? That's a good question.

NDMP allows the operating-system vendor (i.e., the filer vendor) to determine the format of the backup stream that is sent to the backup software. This means the vendor can use *dump*, *tar*, *cpio*, *MTF*, or any backup format they choose. As of this writing, most vendors use some type of portable format. In most cases, you can take an NDMP backup tape, manually manipulate it with *mt*, and be able to read the backup on the tape with the native utility that was used to write it. The reason you must manipulate it with *mt* is that the DMA places its own label on the tape, and often encapsulates the NDMP stream within its own header information. Therefore, you must get past the tape label and other headers before you can use a native utility to read the tape.

There are several problems with this situation. The first problem is that manually reading the tape removes all features you hoped to obtain when you moved to NDMP, especially automation and file indexing. You need to know what's on each tape to read them manually. (I don't know about you, but I don't relish going back to the days when I had to manually read *dump* tapes every day.) You will also need to manually manipulate the tape to move past the DMA's tape label, and any other metadata surrounding the NDMP image. This metadata serves an important role, but it does create extra steps when reading the tape manually.

The second problem is that none of the NAS vendors that support CIFS uses a truly native utility. They have created their own version that supports all the Windows-specific information stored in a CIFS filesystem. None of this data is restored if you read the tape manually using the standard version of that native utility.

The third problem is that NAS vendors are under no obligation to use a portable format or to use it in such a way that the tape can still be read with native utilities. In fact, while NDMP tapes may be readable with manual manipulation on a Unix system, they will probably be completely unreadable on another NAS vendor's system. If you've been in the industry for a while, you may remember the days when we backed up SunOS, Solaris, HP-UX, Irix, and AIX systems all to the same tape. We used *dump*, *tar*, or *cpio*, and each system could read the other systems' native format (with a few exceptions). HP-UX had its own backup format, but you didn't use it if you wanted a portable backup. The state of NDMP today is that there is no standard format between NAS vendors, meaning that one NAS vendor can't read another NAS vendor's NDMP backups—at all. This means you can't easily move from one NAS vendor to another, as you can in the Unix and Windows worlds. You will be required to keep at least one working NAS server from each NAS vendor you have used to perform NDMP restores from that vendor's backups.

The NDMP working group has discussed the idea of a standard backup format, but it's considered out of scope. NAS vendors tell you that one of the reasons this is the case is that they don't feel the market pressure to do so. I am hoping that this will change. If you are as concerned about these issues as I am, let your NAS vendor know. We need a standard backup format that is readable across all products and NAS vendors that use it! This would allow the DMAs to also understand the format, allowing you to restore your NAS data even without a filer.

Versions

The SNIA working group is now completing work on NDMP v4 and is beginning work on NDMP v5. These section summarizes differences between the versions:

- NDMP v1 supported only local operations, i.e., filer to self. Specifically the tape subsystem needed to be directly attached to the data server via SCSI or FC. Although still supported by some systems, NDMP v1 is no longer active.

- NDMP v2 added support for three-way configurations and direct access restore (DAR). The NDMP data server (filesystem) and NDMP tape server (mover, SCSI, and tape Interfaces) can exist on separate systems and communicates via a TCP connection. However establishment of the TCP connection is unidirectional. The NDMP tape server always listens for a data connection initiated by the data server. There is no way for the data server to listen for a connection. NDMP v2 is currently the most actively used version.

- NDMP v3 adds support for bidirectional three-way configurations—configuration, log, and file history interface improvements—and standard support for NDMP-based data migration (NDMPcopy). The bidirectional three-way configuration (adding explicit connect and listen support to the data interface) allows NDMP data migration. One data server listens while the other connects, then one performs a backup while the other restores from the same stream. The configuration interface provides additional information about the NDMP server, the supported data connection types (IPC, TCP, etc.), the filesystem, and tape/SCSI devices attached to the NDMP server. Due to the prominence of NDMP v2, vendors that support only v3 have experienced compatibility issues.

- NDMP v4 adds support for protocol extensions, which allows vendors to implement value-add functionality without requiring a protocol revision or adversely impacting the existing installed base of NDMP products. It also significantly improves the precision of the protocol definition and removes ambiguity that existed in earlier specifications, especially in the areas of expected behavior and error handling. V4 also adds a mechanism for recovering file history information from a backup stream without changing the active filesystem and supports establishment of TCP data connections over a different subnet than that used for the NDMP control connection. The latter allows the use of high speed private networks for three-way configurations. It's expected that by 2002, all major vendors will support NDMP v4.

Using NDMP

In order to back up your NAS via NDMP, you need an NDMP-compatible backup software package to act as the data management application (DMA). If a significant portion of your backups are performed via NDMP, you will definitely want to evaluate a number of products. There are several features that figure prominently during such an evaluation.

Robotic support

The first important feature to consider is their level of robotic support. Some vendors can't support using tape services on filers. They require all NDMP backups to be filer to server, where the backups of each filer are sent across the network to an NDMP-capable backup server. Other vendors support using filer-based tape services, but they don't support robotic control via the filer. Such vendors require a configuration like the one on the left in Figure 7-9. Drives are directly connected to each filer via SCSI, but all robotic control is via the backup server. This configuration can also be used if you decide to use a non-NDMP scheme for controlling the robotics.

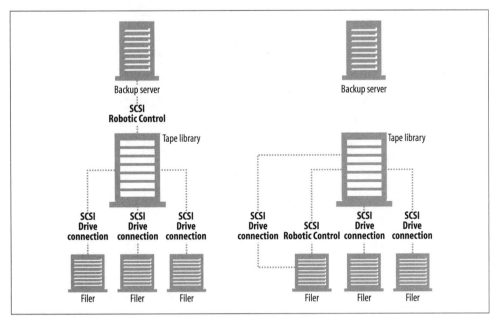

Figure 7-9. SCSI-based NDMP robotic support

The next level of robotic support allows connecting the tape drives and robotic control directly to the filers, as depicted at the right side of Figure 7-9. This configuration doesn't require the filers or robot to be anywhere near any type of backup server, so it may have advantages in certain environments. It also doesn't require a dedicated SCSI HBA on the backup server, as the configuration at the left side of Figure 7-9 does.

Both configurations have one major disadvantage, however. The tape drives connected to each filer are completely dedicated to NDMP-based backups. As discussed in Chapter 4, this requires you to purchase a much larger library than would be necessary if you were sharing these tape drives.

The solution for NAS backups is the same as for non-NAS servers. Attach the tape library and filers to a SAN, and share the library using LAN-free backup software. Like parallel SCSI-based robotic support, there are two levels of LAN-free backup support for filers.

The first level is depicted at the left of Figure 7-10, where the tape drives in the tape library can be shared only between filers. This means that the tape drives that are connected in this way can be used only by the filers, and not by any other host that may be connected to the SAN. While this is better than the way drives are dedicated to each server with parallel SCSI, it certainly has its disadvantages.

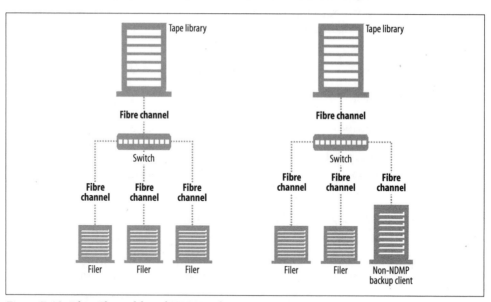

Figure 7-10. Fibre Channel-based NDMP robotic support

The next level of LAN-free backup support for NDMP is depicted at the right of Figure 7-10. Such a configuration treats the NAS filers the same as any other LAN-free backup client and allows you to dynamically share tape drives between filers and nonfilers. Obviously, this configuration is the most flexible.

Filer to library support

As discussed several times already, users want a dynamically shared tape library resource that can be used 24×7 instead of being shackled to a specific server. SANs provide a solution to this problem, but it's by no means the only solution.

As described in Chapter 1, several tape library vendors have started shipping NDMP-enabled, Ethernet-connected products. When added to a LAN, they can be thought of as any other network resource such as printers and filers. Fast (100 Mb/s) and Gigabit Ethernet (1000 Mb/s) are now increasing deployed around the world with the 10-GB standard currently evolving. This provides the bandwidth backbone for backup solutions such as this to become realistic

Such libraries are simple to install and configure. As shown in Figure 7-11, you simply add the relevant cabling to your existing Ethernet infrastructure and then configure IP addresses for each NDMP tape server within the library. Each NDMP tape server may control one tape drive, a subset of tape drives or all tape drives. (Figure 7-11 shows a single Gigabit Ethernet connection from the library to the switch. I believe this will be the way all of them will be configured soon, but early implementations use multiple 100-Mb connections instead of a single Gigabit Ethernet connection.)

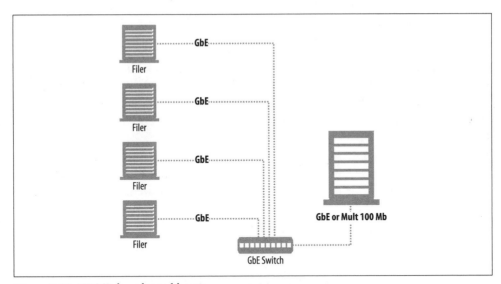

Figure 7-11. NDMP-based tape library

The NDMP server provides dynamic tape-drive sharing as part of the protocol so once the tape library is configured and connected to the LAN, there is no extra software to be purchased to provide this service. (That is, except for the NDMP agent for your backup software, which you hopefully have purchased already.) Simply configure the new NDMP tape servers into your backup application software, and you are ready to back up.

New tape drives can be used in NDMP libraries irrespective of whether servers backing up to it have local tape device driver support. This occurs because NDMP backups write to a trusted network end point that happens to be the NDMP tape server. However, to work correctly, the NDMP tape server needs to have local tape device driver support for all its devices. In fact servers with absolutely no tape device driver support can use NDMP tape libraries.

In general, the performance of these libraries is equivalent per data stream to that observed on Fibre Channel SANs. That is, backups are often limited by tape bandwidth, not network bandwidth. However, the CPU usage per MB transferred is currently higher than equivalent SAN deployments.

The final issue with such libraries is the reason they are included in this section. Since NDMP implementations vary in quality, you can't simply purchase an NDMP agent and automatically assume that you can back up and recover to and from any NDMP-capable device. Backup software vendors therefore certify whether or not a particular NDMP implementation is supported or not. If an NDMP library sounds like it might fit your needs, make sure your backup software supports it.

Filer to server support

Not everyone wants to back up their filers via a filer or NDMP-compatible tape library. Some would like to simplify matters by simply backing up all their filers to their Unix or NT backup server. This would be known as a filer to server backup. Unfortunately, some backup software products don't support such backups.

Direct access restore support

If you have large filers, you may find this feature important. In order to understand what direct access restore is, you must first understand how NDMP restores work without it. Have you ever recovered a single file from a *tar* archive via the command line? You do so with the following command:

```
$ tar xvf device-name filename-to-be-recovered
```

What happens if the file is at the end of the *tar* archive? *tar* reads blindly through the archive, looking for *filename-to-be-recovered*. What you see is a long pause, followed by the display of the filename. What happens if the file is at the beginning of the *tar* archive? *tar* again reads blindly through the archive, looking for the file. It displays the filename as soon as it finds it, but it continues looking through the archive until it reaches the end. You see the filename displayed, followed by a long pause. Only after the long pause is your command-line prompt returned. Although you've probably never noticed, unless you hit Ctrl-C after you see the filename displayed, the recovery time is unaffected by the position of the file within the archive. Whether it's at the beginning or the end of the file, *tar* always reads through the entire archive looking for the pattern you selected.

NDMP without direct access support works the same way. If you have a terabyte-sized volume, and you need one file from that volume, your backup software blindly reads through the entire terabyte of data for every single restore. Direct access restore mitigates this problem by allowing the DMA to load only the tape the file is on and to move directly to the location of the file on that tape. The difference this makes with large restores can't be overstated. If you have large backups and need to selectively recover individual files, you will definitely want a DMA that supports direct access restore. However, keep in mind that additional backup information referred to as file history must be passed from the data server to the DMA to enable DAR. Enabling file history results in additional DMA processing and network traffic.

What About LAN-Free, Client-Free, and Server-Free Backup?

Earlier in this book, we discussed three kinds of backup that can be performed with SANS:

- LAN-free
- Client-free
- Server-free

Whether or not NAS systems can perform the above types of backups depends on whether or not you look at the NAS system as storage or as additional clients of the backup and recovery system.

One way to think of NAS filers is to consider them no different than an enterprise array sharing disk to its clients. Filers provide storage to their clients, and the only difference between a filer and a disk array is the protocol the filer uses to share its storage with its clients. Another way to think of NAS filers is to acknowledge that they are actually servers—merely specialized servers. They aren't just disk arrays; they are clients of the backup and recovery system.

LAN-free backup occurs when multiple backup clients share a tape library and are backing up their data locally via Fibre Channel. If you think of the NAS systems as storage, LAN-free backup doesn't really apply, because they are merely disk drives. If you think of them as backup system clients, however, LAN-free backups do apply, as discussed previously in this chapter and illustrated in Figure 7-10.

Client-free backups occur when the data is viewed via another source and then transferred to tape using that source, instead of sending the data through the backup client. Therefore, client-free backup can occur with NAS only if you consider them as storage. First, you create a snapshot, if it's possible to do so. Then you back up that data to tape without ever going through the client that is using the data. You do this by creating an NFS or CIFS mount to the backup server and backing that up. This is the equivalent of mounting a split mirror on a SAN.

If you think of the NAS as clients of the backup and recovery system, then client-free backups are rare. In order for this to happen, the NAS vendor needs to allow you to access the disks behind their filer (often referred to as a *filer head*). You then establish and split an additional mirror of the disks behind the filer head, and mount this mirror to a backup server via the SAN. Usually the only NAS vendors to allow this are those that started as SAN vendors and have put a NAS head in front of their storage array. Since the storage array can create additional mirrors, they can perform client-free backups. Also, by employing server-to-server mirroring of a targeted volume (or snapshot) as shown back in Figure 7-2, you can move the backup-to-tape burden from the source filer and perform a LAN-free backup on the destination filer, overall providing the same benefits as client-free backups on a SAN.

Server-free backups occur when the data moves directly from online storage (disk) to offline storage (tape) without going through any server's CPU. In order for this to happen with NAS, you can consider them only as storage. Then, when you are performing NDMP backups that move the data directly from their storage to tape without going through anyone else's CPU, it's like they're performing server-free backups.

However, if you consider a NAS filer as just another client of the backup and recovery system, server-free backups are even more rare than client-free backups. Again, the backup and recovery system needs access to their SAN-attached disks and uses the extended copy command to move data directly from their disks to tape without going through any CPU. As with client-free backups, usually the only NAS vendors that allow this are those that started as SAN vendors and have put a NAS head in front of their storage array. Since the storage array can use extended copy, it can perform client-free backups.

Therefore, LAN-free, client-free, and server-free backups of filers are all in the eye of the beholder.

Database Backup and Recovery

Prior to the advent of NAS or SAN, all enterprise-class databases, and even most workgroup-class databases were backed up the same way. The database vendor created a backup and recovery API (e.g., Oracle's RMAN), and any backup and recovery software vendors that wanted to back up their database simply wrote to that API. When the backup and recovery software wanted to back up a database, it called the

API, the database sent it one or more streams of data, and these streams were written to tape.[*]

This method is illustrated in the following eight steps are also shown in Figure 7-12.

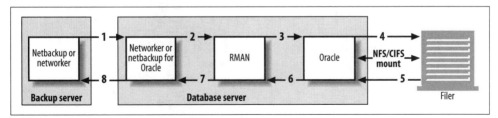

Figure 7-12. Standard database backup method

1. Backup software (e.g., NetWorker, NetBackup) asks its backup agent to back up a database

2. Backup software's agent (e.g., NetWorker Module for Oracle, NetBackup for Oracle) tells database backup API it needs to back up database.

3. Database backup agent (e.g., Oracle's RMAN) tells the database it's going to be backed up.

4. Database (Oracle) requests data to be backed up from storage.

5. Storage passes data to be backed up to database.

6. Database passes data to be backed up to API.

7. API passes data to be backed up to backup agent.

8. Backup agent passes data to be backed up to backup software, which backs it up to tape or disk.

The only problem with this method is that it uses a completely different data path than most backup and recovery options discussed in this chapter. The data paths of the various options discussed in this chapter are shown in Figure 7-13.

Unfortunately, almost all database backup APIs assume that the data will be passed through the database, which retrieves it from storage just as it does during normal operations. As you can see from Figure 7-13, the only data path that involves the database server in any way is the NFS/CIFS option. This means that, in most cases, you will be forced to use NFS or CIFS as your backup method, because it's the only way to pass the data through the database. This is true even if the filer uses a general-purpose operating system and standard push-agent software. As you can see in Figure 7-13, the path for push-agent software doesn't go through the database server,

---

[*] This section uses Legato NetWorker and Veritas NetBackup. There are dozens of other products that perform similar backups of databases. NetWorker and NetBackup were chosen only because many people are familiar with them. This isn't an endorsement of these products.

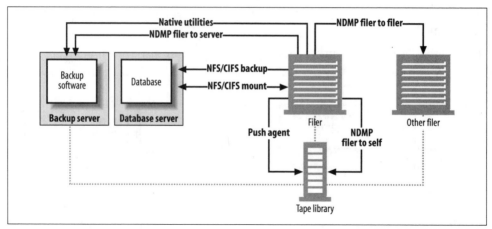

Figure 7-13. NAS backup option data paths

and the database server is where the database and database backup API software resides. Therefore, a filer based on a general-purpose operating system will be of no help in this situation.

If you want to back up your filer via snapshots, native backup utilities, NDMP, or anything other than the NFS/CIFS method, you can't (in most cases) use standard database backup API software. In some cases, such as Oracle, this means you need to write your own script to shut down the database or put it in backup mode prior to performing your NAS backup. In other cases, such as SQL Server, you can't perform point-in-time recovery of your database if you don't use the database backup API. In a few cases, such as Network Appliance's backup agent for Exchange, you can use the database backup API but will need to buy a customized backup solution from your NAS vendor.

I don't want to seem like I'm being hard on NAS. The issues discussed here are no different than those discussed in Chapter 4 with client- and server-free backups. Because backups that use NDMP, a filer-based push agent, or snapshots behave like the client- and server-free backups discussed in Chapter 4, your database must support third-party backup in order for you to back up filer-based data files using these methods. And, if you want to perform client- or server-free backups of these data files on your filers, you're probably going to need a custom solution, and there's a good chance you'll need to write it yourself.

Benefits Summary

Table 7-1 summarizes the benefits of the various backup and recovery options for NAS filers.

Table 7-1. NAS backup and recovery options summary

	Native utilities	NFS/CIFS	Client software	NDMP: filer to self	NDMP: filer to filer	NDMP: filer To NDMP library	NDMP: filer to backup server
Impact on file serving	Medium	High	Medium	Low	Creates medium load on two filers	Medium	Medium
Load on backup server	Very low	High	Medium	Very low	Very low	Very low	Medium
Speed of restore	No direct access	Quick; no different than a standard restore, except for NFS/CIFS load on LAN and filer	Quick; no different than a standard restore	Quick (with DAR)	Quick (with DAR)	Quick (with DAR)	Quick (with DAR)
Cost	Time required to create scripts	No additional cost	Additional instance of client version of backup software	Must purchase NDMP agent	Must purchase NDMP agent	Must purchase NDMP agent and library	Must purchase NDMP agent
Availability	Most filers	Any filer	Filer must use full operating system	Filer and DMA must support NDMP	Filer and DMA must support NDMP	Filer and DMA must support NDMP	Filer and DMA must support NDMP
Portability of backups	Portable to any client that can read native utility	Portable to any client of backup and recovery system	Portable to any client of backup and recovery system	Limited	Limited	Limited	Limited
Can use database backup APIs	No	Yes	No	Rarely (some custom solutions available)	Rarely (some custom solutions available)	Rarely (some custom solutions available)	Rarely (some custom solutions available)

Table 7-1. NAS backup and recovery options summary (continued)

	Native utilities	NFS/CIFS	Client software	NDMP: filer to self	NDMP: filer to filer	NDMP: filer To NDMP library	NDMP: filer to backup server
Miscellaneous	Must perform own tape manage-ment	Backups and restores take same precedence as user requests for data; NFS backup will lose CIFS info					

Disruptive Technologies

Today, one of the biggest decisions facing IT professionals and application designers is what kind of storage to use. Administrators choose between using a SAN for block-level I/O or using NAS for file-level I/O. Once that decision is made, your environment is locked into that storage resource for the life of the application or server.

One of the most revolutionary advances in computing is the separation of storage from the host processor. So why is it that the CPU is still running at about the same usage? In the world of SAN, we have increased throughput by bringing data through a much quicker medium. However, we have added the overhead of Logical Volume Managers and enterprise class filesystems. In the case of NAS, technology has moved the filesystem and volume management to an appliance; however connectivity is through the LAN. One type of I/O is replaced with another. An admin has now removed the CPU overhead of filesystem and volume management and replaced it with TCP/IP.

The innovations on the horizon will help remove these obstacles and bring to fruition the promises of SAN and NAS—allowing for emancipating storage from the CPU.

- The Direct Access File System (DAFS) is a type of network filesystem that requires a direct protocol for transport. It allows for direct memory-to-memory connection between host and storage, which allows for file-level I/O with direct attached performance.

- Virtual Interface (VI) is a direct access transport (DAT) that allow for memory to transport translation and transport back to memory translation. VI is an embedded technology designed into the interface both on the host and the storage, allowing for multimode clustering.

- InfiniBand is a technology designed to replace the current I/O subsystems in the market today. It allows memory-to-memory communication between hosts and enables more efficient communication between the CPU and I/O subsystem. InfiniBand is also a big advancement in the world of host clustering.

- iSCSI allows for block-level I/O across IP—thus the name iSCSI. Those that understand networks can now manage huge storage networks. With the help of a router, a block device can be formatted on the opposite side of the world. Networks are a bit congested today, and the addition of storage traffic to the same network can make things a little slow. So, most likely there will be a separation of traditional IP and iSCSI traffic, thus making a LAN and a type of IP SAN. Hardware-accelerated NICs will also reduce CPU overhead and increase network performance.

DAFS: Direct Access File System

The first revision of the DAFS spec has been released, and DAFS products should be shipping soon. DAFS is a new network filesystem based on the NFS v4 spec that isn't tied to any one transport. DAFS is designed for low-latency, high throughput data transfer and makes good use of direct memory-to-memory network technologies.

DAFS is an extension of what the market has been tending towards—the ability to make storage a resource. The consequence of treating storage as a network-wide resource is that storage doesn't have to be managed at every server. This trend started with the first NFS filers, which allowed for a managed pool of virtual storage that was separate from the host processor. This pool centralized the management of the storage and made replacing and expanding host processors much easier, but the CPU overhead of using a network filesystem and local filesystem in an NFS or CIFS world was no better or worse than using a local filesystem. It was obvious that a more efficient form of data sharing was needed, and DAFS was born. The ability to share gigabytes of storage between multiple servers allows for centralized management and limited stress on the host CPU—with the throughput of local disk.

DAFS attempts to accomplish this goal by using direct access transport (DAT). DAT describes the functionality and concepts necessary to support the DAFS protocol, rather than a specific interface. DAT must first provide remote direct memory access (RDMA), which is the ability to move information between a local memory buffer and a remote memory buffer. The second important function of DAFS is to allow application software to directly access the NIC or channel adapter hardware—bypassing the operating system. This direct access allows applications to access the hardware without intervention from the operating system and initiate I/O, which greatly reduces operating system overhead. Direct access also allows the application to manage packet fragmentation and reassembly, reliable data delivery, multiplexing and demultiplexing data from different connections and checksum computations. All of these are normally taken care of by transports such as TCP, but using RDMA allows for the separation of bulk data and control information. This separation allows the application to specify the location of the destination memory a packet belongs, thus increasing control over packet ordering.

DAFS should be able to support many systems accessing the same pool of data simultaneously, even systems running different operating systems, which would, of course, allow file sharing between NT and Unix platforms. To accomplish this, the DAFS protocol has included in its spec high-speed consistent locking, which allows lock caching through delegation.

As shown in Figure A-1, DAFS also may be deployed in many different ways:

Application interface
> The application can be updated so that it understands the I/O necessary to use DAFS.

OS level library
> The OS can be taught to see DAFS as a client-level driver the OS can understand.

Kernel level driver
> The DAFS driver can be moved out of the user space and into the kernel space, allowing for integration into the OS.

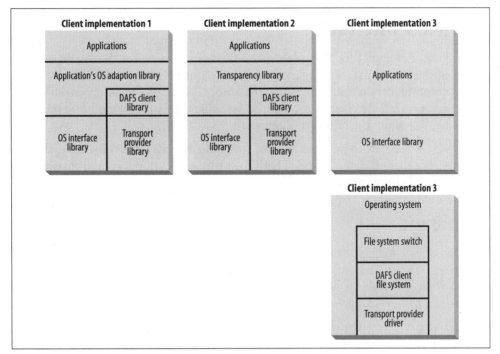

Figure A-1. DAFS implementation options

There is definitely debate among DAFS vendors about which would be more efficient: a kernel level driver or one that resides at the user level. One vendor feels that user-level drivers would be more efficient because you can bypass the operating system with VI and a user-space DAFS library. Another vendor feels that integration into the kernel is key to an efficient DAFS protocol. Only time will tell who is right. (Perhaps they both are.)

Some may ask, "What will I need to do DAFS in my data center?" That is a difficult question to answer. There are different implementations being worked on at this time. Most are filer-based, much like the NAS filers of today, and there will be a new generation of NAS filers in the near future. In some cases, new NICs will be needed. In others, you could use existing SAN hardware to achieve DAFS over Fibre Channel. In another form you may be able to use your current network interfaces and do DAFS over TCP. You wouldn't obtain much of a performance improvement, but you'd reduce the number of protocols you need to manage. Obviously, how you will implement DAFS depends on the implementation you choose.

Originally the DAFS protocol was written with VI in mind. As the spec neared completion, that idea was replaced with DAT, which included VI, InfiniBand, and WARP—all of which allow for memory-to-memory mapping. In essence, DAFS is transport-independent.

VI: Virtual Interface

VI has been developed for use in clustered servers, allowing for quick and efficient communication and data sharing in an enterprise cluster. VI allows for fast server-to-server communication (and memory-to-memory communication in most cases), allowing for a scalable cluster. All this can be achieved with commodity servers and hardware, so long as the NICs are VI-enabled.

VI allows off-the-shelf systems to be used to build enterprise class clusters that allow memory sharing and data sharing. This allows you to develop a robust cluster without the robust cluster price tag.

InfiniBand

InfiniBand is a marriage of two technologies: Future I/O developed by Compaq, IBM, and Hewlett Packard, and Next Generation I/O developed by Intel, Microsoft, and Sun Microsystems. It was designed as a specification for dataflow between processors and I/O devices.

InfiniBand is a bus architecture designed to replace the outdated PCI architecture that is widely used in microcomputing systems. InfiniBand allows for 2.5 GB/s of throughput and supports up to 64,000 devices. Like VI, InfiniBand is useful for clustering commodity systems, allowing for memory-to-memory communication and efficient clustering.

InfiniBand seems more like a network than a normal I/O subsystem in a computer system. It uses the 128-bit addressing in Internet Protocol Version 6 (Ipv6), allowing for an incredible amount of device expansion.

iSCSI

The iSCSI protocol is the mapping of SCSI procedure calls on top of TCP. It allows for access to block devices across a typical, Ethernet/IP-based LAN. Although this technology is available today, implementing it will almost certainly require a NIC and switch upgrade to support it.

iSCSI is in direct competition with Fibre Channel over which it has some major benefits. Probably the most important difference is the ability to route the storage to anywhere around the world. Though the latency may be high, this allows for native methods of replication, and connectivity to data from anywhere you can connect to the Internet. This is possible with Fibre Channel only after a few protocol conversions and specialized hardware. Even though the iSCSI hardware will be specialized, it will also be integrated into normal network technology in the future.

As with most technologies, iSCSI will take some time to become a standard. A data center manager may need to add new blades to his switches and new NICs to his servers to take advantage of iSCSI in the beginning. Even if new blades or switches aren't required, they might be a good idea to help isolate storage IP traffic from other IP traffic. This means that you will probably still need to manage two separate networks in order to have IP communication and a storage network.

An important related technology are hardware-accelerated NICs that remove the TCP/IP processing from the host's CPU and perform it on the card. They are essential to allowing iSCI to compete with Fibre Channel. Hardware-accelerated NICs are now available and should become more prevalent with time.

RAID Levels

Table B-1 contains a brief description of each RAID level. A more detailed description of each level follows.

Table B-1. RAID definitions

Level	Description
RAID	A disk array in which part of the physical storage capacity stores redundant information about user data stored on the remainder of the storage capacity. The redundant information enables regeneration of user data in the event that one of the array's member disks or the access data path to it fails.
Level 0	Disk striping without data protection. (Since the "R" in RAID means redundant, this isn't technically RAID.)
Level 1	Mirroring. All data is replicated on a number of separate disks.
Level 2	Data is protected by Hamming code. Uses extra drives to detect 2-bit errors and correct 1-bit errors on the fly. Interleaves by bit or block.
Level 3	Each virtual disk block is distributed across all array members but one, with parity check information stored on a separate disk.
Level 4	Data blocks are distributed as with disk striping. Parity check is stored in one disk.
Level 5	Data blocks are distributed as with disk striping. Parity check data is distributed across all members of the array.
Level 6	Like RAID 5 but with additional independently computed check data.

RAID 0

The RAID hierarchy begins with RAID 0—or the striping of several physical disks into one larger virtual disk. RAID 0 can then be combined with RAID 1 in two ways, referred to as RAID 0+1 or RAID 1+0, depending on how you combine them. The performance of RAID 10 and RAID 01 are almost identical, but they have different levels of data integrity. (As discussed later, RAID 10 does have a performance advantage during rebuilding operations.)

RAID 1

As shown in Table B-1, RAID 1 mirrors two sets of disks. Although all RAID 1 data needs to be written to two disks, there are several algorithms that do this. The first is *synchronous*, in which a write request is acknowledged back only after both drives complete the write. *Asynchronous* writes occur when write commands are sent sequentially to the drives without waiting for acknowledgement. *Semisynchronous* writes limit sequential writing to a specific number of operations. Since both disks have an identical copy of the data, read requests can come from either disk. Therefore, both disks in a RAID 1 pair can share the load created by read requests. This is why a RAID 1 pair can actually perform faster reads than a single disk.

RAID 0+1

RAID 01 (or RAID 0+1) is a mirrored pair (RAID 1) made from two stripe sets (RAID 0), hence the name RAID 0+1, because it's created by first creating two RAID 0 sets and mirroring them together using RAID 1. If you lose a drive on one side of a RAID 01 array, then lose another drive on the other side of that array before the first side is recovered, you will suffer complete data loss. It's also important to note that all drives in the surviving mirror are involved in rebuilding the entire damaged stripe set, even if only a single drive is damaged. Performance during recovery is severely degraded unless the RAID subsystem allows adjusting the priority of recovery. However, shifting the priority toward production will lengthen recovery time and increase the risk of the kind of catastrophic data loss mentioned earlier.

RAID 1+0 (RAID 10)

RAID 10 (or RAID 1+0) is a stripe consisting of n mirrored pairs. Only the loss of both drives in the same mirrored pair can result in any data loss, and the loss of that particular drive is $1/n$ as likely as the loss of some drive on the opposite mirror in RAID 0+1. Recovery involves only the replacement drive and its mirror so the rest of the array performs at 100% capacity during recovery. Also, since only the single drive needs recovery, bandwidth requirements during recovery are lower and recovery takes less time, reducing the risk of catastrophic data loss.

RAID 2

RAID 2 is a parity layout that uses a Hamming code* to detect errors and determine which part is in error by computing parity for distinct overlapping sets of disk blocks. (RAID 2 isn't used in practice; the redundant computations of a Hamming code aren't required because disk controllers can detect the failure of a single disk.)

RAID 3

RAID 3 can accelerate applications that are single-stream bandwidth-oriented. All I/O operations will access all disks since each logical block is distributed across the

---

* A Hamming code is a basic mathematical error correction code (ECC).

disks that comprise the array. The heads of all disks move in unison to service each I/O request. RAID 3 is effective for very large file transfers, but it isn't a good choice for a database server, since databases tend to read and write smaller blocks.

RAID 4 and RAID 5

RAID 4 and RAID 5 compute parity on an interleave or stripe unit (an application-specific or filesystem-specific block), which is a data region that is accessed contiguously. Use of an interleave unit allows applications to be optimized to overlap read access by reading data off a single drive while other users access a different drive in the RAID. These types of parity striping can require write operations to be combined with read and write operations for disks other than those actually being written, in order to update parity correctly. RAID 4 stores parity on a single disk in the array, while RAID 5 removes a possible bottleneck on the parity drive by rotating parity across all drives in the set.

Some implementations have solved RAID 4's bottleneck issue by writing precalculated stripes in a combined write across all disks in a RAID 4 parity group. This substantially decreases the load on the parity disk while freeing the disks more for read activity. The major benefit of RAID 4 is the ability to add disks to a RAID group without the need to recalculate parity information (as RAID 5 requires).

Although there are many different ways to implement the striping in RAID 5, the main decision is regarding the stripe size. In general, the stripe size should ideally match the average filesystem inode size that will be stored in the RAID group. (An inode is the atomic unit of a filesystem, usually ranging from 512 B to 32 KB.)

RAID 2 isn't commercially implemented, and RAID 3 is likely to perform significantly better in a controller-based implementation. RAID levels 4 and 5 are more amenable to host-based software implementation. RAID 5, which balances the actual data and parity across columns, is likely to have fewer performance bottlenecks than RAID 4, which requires access of the dedicated parity disk for all read-modify-write accesses.

It's possible that corruption could occur in a RAID 4 or RAID 5 volume. If the system fails while writes are outstanding to more than one disk on a given stripe (for example, multiple data blocks and corresponding parity), a subsequent disk failure would make incorrect data visible without any indication that such data is incorrect. This is because it's impossible to compute and check parity in the corruption of more than one disk block. For increased reliability, parity RAID should be combined with a separate log, to cache full-stripe I/O and guarantee resistance to multiple failures. However, this log requires that additional writes be performed. If generally addressable nonvolatile memory (NVRAM) or a nonvolatile solid state disk (SSD) is available, it should be used for log storage. If neither possibility exists, try to put the log on a separate controller and disk from those used for the RAID array.

The most appropriate RAID configuration for a specific filesystem or database tablespace must be determined based on data-access patterns and cost-versus-performance tradeoffs. RAID 0 offers no increased reliability. It can, however, supply performance acceleration at no increased storage cost. RAID 1 provides the highest performance for redundant storage, because it doesn't require read-modify-write cycles to update data, and because multiple copies of data may be used to accelerate read-intensive applications. Unfortunately, RAID 1 requires at least double the disk capacity of RAID 0. Also, since more than two copies of the data can exist (if the mirror was constructed with more than two sets of disks), RAID 1 arrays may be constructed to endure loss of multiple disks without interruption. Parity RAID allows redundancy with less total storage cost. The read-modify-write it requires, however, reduces total throughput in any small write operations (read-only or extremely read-intensive applications are fine). The loss of a single disk causes read performance to be degraded while the system reads all other disks in the array and recomputes the missing data. Additionally, it doesn't support losing multiple disks, and RAID can't be made redundant.

Index

We'd like to hear your suggestions for improving our indexes. Send email to *index@oreilly.com*.

R

RAID (redundant array of independent disks), 46, 139, 194–197
  configuration, choosing, 197
  controller-based, 47
  RAID 0, 194
  RAID 0+1 (RAID 01), 195
  RAID 1, 194
  RAID 1+0 (RAID 10), 195
  RAID 2, 195
  RAID 3, 195
  RAID 4 and RAID 5, 196
  software-based, 48
readdirplus, 119
redo logs, 93
redundant array of independent disks (see RAID)
release command, 73
remote shell (rsh), 136
reserve command, 73
resolution conflict messages, 73
restores
  client-free backups, from, 100–104
  file-level server-free, 110
  image-level server-free, 109
  SAN, 76
  server-free backups, from, 108
  snapshots, from, 104
rmt (remote tape), 152
routers and bridges, 36
RS-232 console ports, 136
rsh (remote shell), 136
  security of, 138

S

Samba, 11, 115, 146
  PlainPassword registry files, 149
SANs (storage area networks), ix, 5, 34
  addressing devices, 44
  advantages and disadvantages, 17
  backup and recovery, 66–112
  characteristics, 9
  components, 32–39, 66
    cables, 38
    disk systems, 37
    HBAs (host bus adapters), 32
    hubs, 36
    hubs switches, 36
    routers and bridges, 36
    servers, 32

    software, 38
    switches, 35
  eliminating single points of failure, 52
  fabric switches, 43
  iSCSI-based, future developments, 67
  LAN, contrasted with, 34
  NAS, contrasted with, 13–18
  SCSI, development from, 1
  security, 35
  uses for, 40–42
  zoning, 39
SASI (Shugart Associates System Interface), 1
SCSI service, 173
SCSI (Small Computer Systems Interface), 1, 34
  extended copy command, 68
  limitations, ix
  LUN (logical unit number), 139
  parallel SCSI, 2
  reserve and release commands, 73
  SASI, origins in, 1
  SCSI Parallel Interface (SPI), 3
  SCSI-2, 1
    reserve and release commands, 73
  SCSI-3, 3
  serial SCSI, 5, 22
secondary storage system, 172
secondary volume (S-VOL), 90
secure shell (ssh), 136
security
  filers, configuring, 137
  SNMP, 138
  user mapping, CIFS and NFS, 150
server-centric zone-naming, 51
server-free backups, 63, 68, 105–111
  advantages and disadvantages, 111
  backup mirror, static data copy, 107
  comparison to other methods, 112
  essential requirements, 106
  filesystem, mapping disk to, 107
  NAS systems, 183
  restores, 108
    file-level, 110
    image-level, 109
  xcopy, need for SAN support of, 108
shadow volume, 95
Shugart Associates System Interface (SASI), 1
S_ID (native address identifier), 25
silvering the mirror, 90
single-mode fiber, 23
slices, 139
slicing, 46

About the Author

W. Curtis Preston is president of The Storage Group, an integrator specializing in designing, implementing, and auditing storage systems for data centers of all sizes. He has specialized in designing storage systems for over nine years and has designed such systems for several Fortune 500 companies. He is the founder of *StorageMountain.com* (formerly known as *BackupCentral.com*), the first third-party web site dedicated to the entire storage community. *StorageMountain.com* helps thousands of visitors every day find the storage products they are looking for. Curtis is also the author of O'Reilly's *Unix Backup & Recovery*.

Curtis lives in San Diego, California, with his beautiful wife and daughters: Celynn, Nina, and Marissa.

Colophon

Our look is the result of reader comments, our own experimentation, and feedback from distribution channels. Distinctive covers complement our distinctive approach to technical topics, breathing personality and life into potentially dry subjects.

The animals on the cover of *Using SANs and NAS* are a hyrax (top) and a pika (bottom). The pika is of order *Lagomorpha*, the rabbit family, while the hyrax, order *Hyracoidea*, is an ungulate and has whales and elephants in its tree. Their nonrelationship is much like SANs and NAS: they look a lot a like, and many people confuse them, but they're actually two completely different animals.

The northern pika (*Ochotona alpina*) is a small short-legged creature with rounded ears, no visible tail, sharp curved claws and a grayish patch on the neck. It lives in Siberia, Mongolia, northeast China, and Japan. Grass and plant stems form its diet, and it gathers extra food in late summer and piles it to use in winter. The pika spends considerable time sunning itself on a favorite lookout rock, against which its salt-and-pepper coat is difficult to distinguish. The pika is alert and has excellent hearing and vision, which helps protect it from predators. They emit a sharp, high-pitched whistle to alert other pikas when predators are detected.

The rock hyrax (*Procavia capensis*) as per its name, lives on rocky hillsides and is an agile climber. It's a small, solidly built animal with a stump tail, short ears and legs, and gray-brown to black in coloring. Found in Africa and the Middle East, the hyrax is a social animal and lives in colonies of 50 or more. It feeds mostly on leaves, grass, and small plants but will climb to feed on fruit. The feet have flattened nails, resembling hooves, and a central moist cup that works as an adhesive pad when it climbs. Vocalization is an important method for transferring information for some hyraxes. Their loud and piercing calls are generally made after dark when hyraxes forage.

Mary Anne Weeks Mayo was the production editor and copyeditor for *Using SANs and NAS*. Leanne Soylemez, Claire Cloutier, Sarah Sherman, and Jane Ellin provided quality control. Edie Shapiro provided production assistance. John Bickelhaupt wrote the index.

Ellie Volckhausen designed the cover of this book, based on a series design by Edie Freedman. The cover image is an original engraving from the 19th century. Emma Colby produced the cover layout with QuarkXPress 4.1 using Adobe's ITC Garamond font.

Melanie Wang designed the interior layout, based on a series design by David Futato. Mihaela Maier converted the files from Microsoft Word to FrameMaker 5.5.6 using tools created by Mike Sierra. The text font is Linotype Birka; the heading font is Adobe Myriad Condensed; and the code font is LucasFont's TheSans Mono Condensed. The illustrations that appear in the book were produced by Robert Romano and Jessamyn Read using Macromedia FreeHand 9 and Adobe Photoshop 6. The tip and warning icons were drawn by Christopher Bing. This colophon was compiled by Mary Anne Weeks Mayo.